VIETNAM

VIETNAM

Nation in Revolution

William J. Duiker

Westview Press / Boulder, Colorado

Westview Profiles/Nations of Contemporary Asia

Jacket photo: The mausoleum of Ho Chi Minh in the heart of Hanoi (photo courtesy of *Vietnam* pictorial).

Published in 1983 in the United States of America by
Westview Press, Inc.
5500 Central Avenue
Boulder, Colorado 80301
Frederick A. Praeger, President and Publisher

Library of Congress Cataloging in Publication Data
Duiker, William J., 1932–
  Vietnam : nation in revolution.
  (Westview profiles. Nations of contemporary Asia)
  Bibliography: p.
  Includes index.
  1.Vietnam—History. I. Title. II. Series.
DS556.5.D84 1983   959.7   82-21946
ISBN 0-86531-336-9

Printed and bound in the United States of America

To Mary

Contents

List of Illustrations x
Acknowledgments xi

1   **Land and People**.. 1

    The Geographical Setting 1
    The Peoples of Vietnam 2
    Conclusion 11
    Notes 12

2   **Precolonial Vietnam** 13

    Prehistory 13
    The Origins of Vietnamese Civilization 14
    The Chinese Conquest....................................... 15
    Independence Restored 16
    March to the South 19
    The Coming of the West 20
    The Tay Son Rebellion 22
    The Nguyen Dynasty.. 23
    The French Conquest....................................... 23
    Conclusion 27

3   **The Roots of Revolution** 28

    The Nature of French Colonialism........................... 28
    Sources of Nationalism and Communism 33
    The Coming of World War II 37
    The August Revolution 39
    The First Indochina War Begins 43

Vietnam Enters the Cold War 43
Negotiations at Geneva 45

4   A Nation Divided 49

The Diem Regime 50
The Second Indochina War Begins 53
Tet 62
The Invasion of Cambodia 65
From Paris to Saigon 68

5   Politics and Government 71

The Dynamics of Vietnamese Political Tradition 72
The Impact of the West 74
The Republic of Vietnam 77
The Marxist Alternative 81
The Role of the Party 84
The Mass Associations 87
The Armed Forces 88
Unification 90
Conclusion 95
Notes 96

6   The Economy 97

The Effects of Colonialism 98
The Economy of South Vietnam 100
Building Socialism in the North 101
Collectivization in the Countryside 103
The National Economy Since 1975 106
The Second Five-Year Plan (1976–1980) 108
The Crisis on the Economic Front 110
Transformation to Socialism in the South 111
Conclusion 115

7   Culture and Society 116

Philosophy and Religion 118
Education in Confucian Vietnam 120
The Creative Arts 121
Wind from the West 124
Culture and Ideology 127
The Evolution of Vietnamese Culture in
    Contemporary Marxist Perspective 135
Notes 137

8   Foreign Relations 139

Perspectives During the War of Liberation 140
March to the West 142
Relations with China 146

Annotated Bibliography 156
List of Abbreviations 162
Index 165

Illustrations

The Socialist Republic of Vietnam (map)........................ xii

The Linh Mu pagoda 17

The Imperial Palace at Hue..................................... 24

The River of Perfume 26

Ho Chi Minh as president of the D.R.V........................... 41

Tanks rumbling through downtown Saigon, February 1965.......... 59

Civilian and military leaders in Saigon, 1965...................... 60

Saigon, the "pearl of the Orient" 63

North Vietnamese tanks before the Independence Palace
in Saigon, April 30, 1975....................................... 69

The mausoleum of Ho Chi Minh, Hanoi......................... 82

Ho Chi Minh at the Third National Congress of the VWP.......... 86

Workers clearing the ground in a New Economic Area............. 107

Children acting in a play at a nursery school in Hanoi 121

Life on a canal between Saigon and Cholon 128

Acknowledgments

I would like to thank Wilbur S. Garrett, editor of the *National Geographic Magazine*, for permission to use photographs from a 1965 story in the magazine entitled "Saigon: Eye of the Storm." The editors of *Vietnam* pictorial were kind enough to grant me permission to reproduce several photographs from recent issues of their journal. Finally, I would like to express my gratitude to the Institute for the Arts and Humanistic Studies and to the College Fund for Research of the College of Liberal Arts at The Pennsylvania State University for providing financial assistance in support of this study.

William J. Duiker

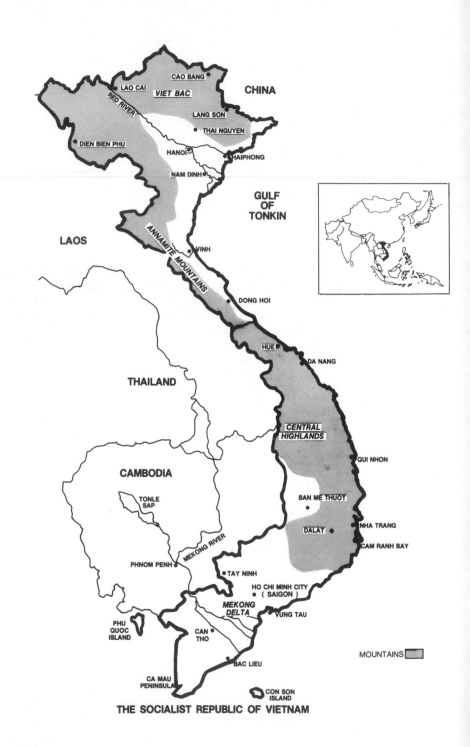

THE SOCIALIST REPUBLIC OF VIETNAM

1

Land and People

THE GEOGRAPHICAL SETTING

Vietnam lies along the eastern edge of the peninsula of mainland Southeast Asia. Shaped like an enormous letter *S*, the country extends from the border of China in the north to the tip of the Ca Mau Peninsula in the south, a total distance of slightly more than 1,000 miles (1,600 kilometers). Bordered on the east by the South China Sea, it is separated from its neighbors on the west for much of its length by mountains that extend from the Chinese border in the north to the extensive plateau of the Central Highlands. South of Saigon the country flattens out into the vast marshy delta of the Mekong River, which flows into the South China Sea after a journey from the mountains of Tibet nearly three thousand miles away. At the southern tip lie the dense mangrove swamps of the Ca Mau Peninsula. Of a total land area of 127,259 square miles (329,556 square kilometers), only about 16 percent is under cultivation. The remainder consists of mountains or dense forests.

Vietnam is often described metaphorically as two baskets of rice separated by a bamboo pole. In the north lies the crowded triangle of the Red River delta, the ancestral homeland of the Vietnamese people; in the south, the flat, waterlogged delta of the Mekong River, one of the great river systems of the world. These two rich alluvial plains, separated from each other by several hundred miles, provide the major source of food for the population. Here live more than two-thirds of all Vietnamese, now numbering more than 50 million. The vast majority are rice farmers, living in villages and hamlets scattered like mushrooms over the flat green plains. Linking these two deltas is the narrow waist of Central Vietnam. In some areas, a flat coastal plain separates the mountains on the western horizon from the South China Sea. In others, the mountains thrust directly up from the surf, as at the Pass of the Clouds, just north of Da Nang, where the border is less than 30 miles (48 kilometers) from the sea. Along this central coast, farmers struggle to eke a living out of the sandy soil. Conditions here, however, are not as favorable as in the deltas to the

1

north and south. The coast is frequently buffeted by typhoons, and much of the land is sandy and subject to periodic invasion by salt water.

The other prominent feature of Vietnam is the chain of mountains that stretches from the Chinese border to a point less than 100 miles (160 kilometers) north of the Mekong River. The most extensive range is located to the north and west of the Red River delta and extends southward from the southern Chinese provinces into northern Vietnam and Laos. These mountains are rugged and heavily forested and frequently reach a height of more than 9,000 feet (2,800 meters). Further to the south lies the Annamite chain (in Vietnamese, Truong Son, or Central Mountains), which stretches nearly 800 miles (1,300 kilometers) from the Vietnamese panhandle, just south of the Red River delta, to a point about 50 miles (80 kilometers) north of the city of Saigon. For most of its length, the Annamite cordillera forms the border between Vietnam and its neighbors to the west, Laos and Cambodia. At its southern extremity, it broadens into a high plateau known as the Central Highlands (Tay Nguyen), an area of more than 20,000 square miles (51,500 square kilometers) lying between the Cambodian border and the South China Sea.

For the most part, the mountainous regions are thinly populated and are inhabited mainly by non-Vietnamese tribal groups who live by hunting and fishing or by primitive agricultural techniques. Historically, the Vietnamese people, living in the deltas or along the central coast, considered the mountains dangerous, disease-ridden, and inhabited by barbarians; for centuries the mountains formed an almost impregnable barrier between the Vietnamese along the coast and their Southeast Asian neighbors to the west. In recent years, however, Vietnamese governments have attempted to encourage settlement by lowlanders in the higher regions to promote the cultivation of cash crops and reduce population density in the more crowded provinces.

The climate of Vietnam ranges from the tropical to the subtropical. In the Red River delta, temperatures vary from 41°F (5°C) in winter to more than 100°F (38°C) in summer. In the flat, steaming plains of the south, the temperature varies little, ranging from 79°F to 85°F (26°C to 30°C), and seasons are marked only by the division of the year into the dry season and the monsoon season, with the latter beginning in May and lasting until early fall. In general, there is plentiful rainfall over most of the country, permitting the cultivation of wet rice in all lowland areas. The mountainous regions have traditionally been relatively unproductive; favorable topography and a temperate climate in the Central Highlands permit the growing of cash crops like coffee, tea, vegetables, and in the lower regions, rubber.

THE PEOPLES OF VIETNAM

Mainland Southeast Asia is one of the ethnically and culturally most heterogeneous regions on earth. Several of the major families of man can be found within its borders. Most of the world's great religious and philosophical systems, including Buddhism, Confucianism, Hinduism, Islam, and Christianity, have been practiced there. It has been estimated that there are more different languages and dialects spoken in mainland Southeast Asia than in any other area of comparable size on the face of the earth.

This diversity is a product of geography and history. Chains of mountain ranges thrusting like giant fingers southward from China divide the peninsula into a series of isolated river valleys, from the Salween and the Irrawady in the west to the Red River and the Mekong in the east. Tribal groups migrating into the area from China or, some scholars maintain, from the Indonesian archipelago competed for control of the fertile lowlands, driving weaker peoples into the heavily forested and malaria-ridden mountains in between.

These topographical features have affected the dynamics of mainland Southeast Asian history and produced two distinct forms of human habitation. Constrained by their environment, the hill peoples have lived for centuries in isolated and frequently primitive conditions. Living on the slopes of mountains where water is scarce and erosion leaches the soil of precious nutrients, they turned in order to survive to a seminomadic existence marked by food gathering or slash-and-burn (swidden) agricultural techniques. Population was stagnant, cultural development was limited (few cultures, for example, possessed written languages), and political organization was usually primitive, often consisting of no more than a kin group organized in the form of a mountain village. By contrast, the lowland peoples typically represented the most dynamic force in premodern Southeast Asia. Plentiful water and an ever-fertile soil, enriched by the constant flow of rich nutrients in the sediment carried down from the mountains, made the river valleys attractive regions for the growth of human civilizations. Wet rice is one of the most productive grain crops known to man. It is nutritious and can be used as a staple food in a limited diet. Under proper conditions, it produces more food per unit area than almost any other grain crop. At the same time, cultivation of wet rice presents serious challenges to societies for which it has become a staple commodity. First, it requires an extensive expenditure of human labor and thus places constant upward pressure on the level of population growth. Second, it requires a relatively equitable distribution of water and thus the development of a system of canals and dikes to ensure the rational distribution of water throughout the region. The effects of these conditions on wet-rice societies are well known: Societies based on the control of water to assure an abundant harvest tend to expand to the limit of the irrigable land and tend to develop an administrative bureaucracy above the village level in order to control the distribution of water.

The Vietnamese

The population of Vietnam is a reasonably accurate reflection in microcosm of the population mix in the region as a whole. According to one estimate, there are as many as sixty different ethnic groups within the country. As throughout the region in general, these various ethnic groups can be classified broadly into lowland valley or hill-farm peoples. By far the most dominant, in terms of numbers and cultural achievement, are the ethnic Vietnamese. Comprising more than 85 percent of the entire population of the country, they are a lowland people who today inhabit both major river delta areas and much of the coastal plain. Throughout history, the vast majority of ethnic Vietnamese have been rice farmers. Relatively few would venture into the mountains, not only because of the insalubrious climate in upper regions but because of fear of hostile tribesmen. As a result, the distinction between lowland Vietnamese and upland peoples in neighboring mountains has been a fairly clear one throughout history, with the Vietnamese viewing the hill dwellers as barbarians and the latter fearing the intrusion of the Vietnamese on their ancestral lands.

The ethnic origins of the Vietnamese people have been the subject of dispute among scholars. In their physiographic makeup, they appear to represent an amalgam of at least two of the major ethnic groups that inhabited East and Southeast Asia in the Neolithic era. Some scholars speculate that they may be a mixture of aboriginal Australoid peoples with Mongoloid and Indonesian peoples who migrated into the region from neighboring areas. Linguistics is of little assistance in solving this mystery. Although the Vietnamese spoken language is tonal, and thus similar to those of the Sino-Tibetan language family spoken by most of the peoples in China, it possesses many similarities in syntax and vocabulary to non-Chinese languages spoken elsewhere in Southeast Asia. Some specialists classify it as a branch of the Sino-Tibetan language family; others identify it as a member of the Mon-Khmer family or even as a distinct language group.

The Overseas Chinese

The Vietnamese are not the only ethnic group inhabiting the lowland areas of contemporary Vietnam. The ethnic Chinese are the most numerous of the other groups. Unlike most of the present-day inhabitants of Southeast Asia, the Chinese are relatively recent arrivals. Most arrived as part of a continuing migration of Chinese into Southeast Asia during the seventeenth and eighteenth centuries. Some came in pursuit of commerce; others were Ming loyalists who sought refuge from the Manchu conquest of China in the mid-seventeenth century. In Vietnam, as elsewhere in Southeast Asia, most Chinese were urban dwellers and played a dominant role in commerce and manufacturing. In South Vietnam, the ethnic Chinese achieved prominence in foreign trade or in some handicrafts and often performed the role of middlemen in the rice trade. In the North, most were involved in commerce in Hanoi and Haiphong, but some were fishermen, dockworkers, or coal miners, and a few were engaged in rice farming. Like its counterparts elsewhere in Southeast Asia, the Chinese community was not homogeneous.

Most Chinese came from the coastal provinces of Fukien and Kwangtung or from the island of Hainan, areas that had a long history of trade with Southeast Asia. By the middle of the present century, the Chinese population of Vietnam numbered approximately 1.5 million.

During the precolonial period, the ethnic Chinese were permitted to retain their separate existence within the larger body of Vietnamese civilization. Under Vietnamese rule, most Chinese lived in separate communities called "congregations" (*bang*) and did not have the duties and privileges of their Vietnamese counterparts. This policy was continued under French colonial rule and even, to a degree, under the independent governments that emerged in the North and South after the Geneva Conference in 1954. The Saigon government of President Ngo Dinh Diem attempted with only limited success to assimilate the Chinese in South Vietnam into the larger society by prohibiting noncitizens from entering into commercial or manufacturing activities. The Communist regime in the North was more tolerant of Chinese distinctiveness. Although its ultimate objective was to assimilate the Chinese into Vietnamese society, it temporarily permitted members of the local Chinese community, numbering about 200,000, to retain Chinese nationality if they so chose. According to an agreement reached with the People's Republic of China (P.R.C.) in 1955, the process of integration was to be gradual and voluntary. In the meantime, those who elected to remain Chinese citizens were permitted to retain a certain degree of autonomy, including exemption from the draft and separate Chinese schools, and a small private commercial sector dominated by ethnic Chinese was tolerated. This cautious treatment undoubtedly reflected the need of the Communist government in Hanoi to obtain support for government policies from the local Chinese community and from the Chinese government in Peking.

With the end of the war in 1975 and the unification of the South and North, the situation rapidly changed. Although in the immediate aftermath of the fall of Saigon, the new revolutionary leadership in the South permitted private businesses to stay in operation, a number of wealthy merchants, most of whom were Chinese, were criticized for their disruptive economic activities and had their property confiscated. Reportedly, a few were publicly executed. Thousands of petty merchants and artisans within the Chinese community in Cholon were pressured to settle in the New Economic Areas that were being built with government funds in the countryside. In 1978, the regime issued regulations calling for the abolition of large-scale private commerce throughout the country. Official sources denied that the policy had racial motivations, but the clear consequence of the new policy was to deprive the majority of ethnic Chinese of their livelihood, and many were convinced that the regime was preparing to crack down on Chinese nationals in order to integrate them forcibly into Vietnamese society. In desperation, many sought to flee abroad, either on foot to South China or by sea to other countries in

Southeast Asia. An accurate count of the numbers who fled is not available, but observers have estimated that two-thirds of the more than 500,000 refugees who have left Vietnam in recent years have been ethnic Chinese. For those who stayed in Vietnam, the future is uncertain.

The Cham and Khmer

Two of the remaining major ethnic minority groups in Vietnam, the Cham and Khmer, can be classified as lowland peoples. Both represent the remnants of former kingdoms overrun by the Vietnamese in the course of their historic expansion south from their original homeland in the Red River delta. The Cham, a people of Malay extraction, trace their history to the kingdom of Champa, which flourished along the central coast of Vietnam from the early Christian era until its final destruction at the hand of the Vietnamese in the eighteenth century. Today there are slightly more than 50,000 people of Cham extraction living in Vietnam. Cham communities can be found throughout lowland areas of South and Central Vietnam, but most are located along the central coast near the port cities of Nha Trang and Phan Pang. Many are fishermen, and some are engaged in farming.

Like the Cham, the Khmer in Vietnam are the remnants of an empire that fell victim to Vietnamese southward expansion. During much of the traditional period, the Mekong Delta was under Cambodian rule, and the lower delta, then consisting primarily of swampy marshland, was only sparsely inhabited. In the seventeenth century the Vietnamese seized the area from its Cambodian rulers and absorbed it into Vietnam. The descendants of those Khmer who remained live today in settlements scattered throughout the lower provinces of the delta. Most are rice farmers like their Vietnamese neighbors, but they have retained their own customs and language and are Theravada rather than Mahayana Buddhists. Today there are more than half a million ethnic Khmer living in Vietnam, virtually all in the provinces south of Saigon.

Mountain Peoples

The vast majority of non-Vietnamese ethnic groups living in Vietnam today can be classified as hill peoples. Some, like the Thai, the Nung, the Meo, and the Yao, are Sinitic peoples who gradually migrated from the southern Chinese provinces during the last several centuries and settled in the mountain highlands adjacent to the Red River delta. Others, like the Rhadé and the Jarai peoples in southern Vietnam, are Malay peoples, probably the descendants of Malayo-Polynesian settlers who migrated into Southeast Asia in the third and second millenia B.C. and were forced by more aggressive later arrivals to move from the lowlands into the mountainous Central Highlands.

The most numerous are the Tho (Tay), a Sino-Tibetan people who today inhabit the mountains north of the Red River delta, an area frequently called the Viet Bac (northern Vietnam). They are closely related to the Nung, a mountain people numbering slightly more than 300,000, who have settled near the Chinese border. Most are rice or swidden farmers. Other major groups are the Muong, a mountain people closely related to the Vietnamese, who inhabit the mountains adjacent to Hoa Binh, and several tribal groups who live in the isolated mountains of the far northwest, like the Thai (nearly 500,000), the Meo (about 220,000), and the Yao (called Man by the Vietnamese and numbering about 200,000). In the South, the mountain peoples live in the Central Highlands. The largest numerically are the Rhadé and the Jarai, numbering more than 100,000 each. Residing in the higher elevations of the Central Highlands, the Rhadé and Jarai are related to the Cham. For the most part they live by the methods of slash-and-burn agriculture.

Traditionally, the relationship between highlanders and lowlanders in Vietnam has been an ambivalent one. Although trade and alliances against outside aggression have been characteristic of the relationship since the formation of the original Vietnamese state before the Chinese conquest, the mountain peoples were usually suspicious of the Vietnamese and frequently resisted their occasional encroachments on tribal territories. A few, like the Muong and the Tho, who are themselves closely related ethnically and linguistically to the Vietnamese, absorbed some measure of Vietnamese influence. Those living further in the mountains, like the Thai and the Nung in the North and the Malay peoples in the Central Highlands, maintained their separate cultural and religious traditions and had few historical contacts with the lowland population.

Under colonial rule, this tradition of autonomy was retained. Although the French extended their rule into the highlands, such areas were administered separately from the remainder of Vietnam. Most tribal groups kept their cultural and linguistic autonomy and were permitted to retain their traditional leadership at the local level. After independence in 1954, this system was abandoned in the South, where the new government in Saigon, in an effort to achieve centralized control over the entire country, abolished the autonomous structure set up by the French and attempted to make the tribal areas an integral part of the new republic. Lands traditionally viewed as under tribal rule were seized by the government and transformed into Rural Development Centers for the settlement of refugees from the Communist regime in the North. Native Vietnamese administrators were posted to the area and unrest was summarily quelled. By the late 1950s, tribal discontent had led to rebellion and the formation of a new multitribal alliance to press for autonomy, the Front Unifié pour la Lutte des Races Opprimées (FULRO). In the mid-1960s, under pressure from the United States, the Saigon government began to devote increased attention to the tribal areas in order to reduce the likelihood that minority peoples would side with the Communists in the civil war then raging in the Central Highlands.

By contrast, after 1954 the new regime in Hanoi dealt with the minority problem along the lines of the classical pattern established by Lenin in Soviet Russia. Cultural autonomy was combined with political control and a policy of gradually integrating the minority areas into North Vietnamese society. Separate autonomous zones were established in the Viet Bac and the Northwest. In these areas, tribal cultural traditions were retained, schooling was given in the local language, and administrators (often trained at a new minority institute in Hanoi) were selected from among the local population. Separate seats were assigned to minority representatives in the national legislature. In recognition of the primitive state of social and political development in tribal areas and the sensitivity of minority peoples to domination by arrogant lowlanders, the central government did not compel the tribal areas to advance quickly along the road to socialism but permitted them to adopt a slower pace. At the same time, the regime adopted a program to persuade mountain peoples gradually to abandon their tribal way of life, to adopt settled farming, and to exchange traditional feudal practices for a modern socialist outlook.

For the Communists, control of the Central Highlands was an essential component of their strategy to establish liberated areas from which to advance gradually into lowland areas and eventual power in the cities. The party leadership in Hanoi adopted a moderate program calling for cultural and administrative autonomy in the expectation that this would assist local revolutionary leaders in the South to mobilize the tribal population in support of the revolution and to transform the Central Highlands into a key liberated base area against the Saigon regime.

With victory in the South in 1975, the Communist regime in Hanoi began to implement its minority policy in the mountainous areas of the Central Highlands. But there are signs that the regime's efforts to integrate mountain minority peoples gradually but inexorably into the mainstream have run into difficulties. Reports from Vietnam indicate that dissident activity against the government has been on the rise in the Central Highlands and that FULRO has been revived. Significantly, signs of tribal discontent have begun to emerge in the North as well. Official reports from Hanoi accuse China of attempting to subvert the loyalty of the mountain peoples near the Sino-Vietnamese border, and there is evidence that antigovernment activities are on the rise. Reports in the media suggest that the government has begun to devote increasing attention to security problems in the area. In tacit admission of official concern over the loyalty of tribal peoples north and northwest of the Red River delta, two of the leading party veterans of minority extraction, Chu Van Tan and Le Quang Ba, were reportedly relieved of their posts in 1978 and placed under house arrest.

The Catholics

Not all minorities in Vietnam are identifiable by their racial or linguistic distinctiveness. As in most Southeast Asian societies, some of the most prominent minority groups are a product of religious preference rather than ethnic origin. The largest and undoubtedly the most influential are the Catholics. The conversion of Vietnamese to Roman Catholicism began in the seventeenth century, when French missionaries organized by the Société des Missions Etrangères became active in the area. At first, such proselyting was tolerated by the Vietnamese monarchy, and by the end of the century, according to some estimates, more than 200,000 Vietnamese had been converted to Christianity. In time, however, the Vietnamese monarchy came to view the spread of Christianity as a threat to the regime and its Confucian institutions, and the practice and propagation of Christianity were declared illegal. Missionaries were expelled, and a few who persisted were executed. Christianity survived, however, and after French rule was imposed in the late nineteenth century the number of Catholics rapidly expanded, particularly in the South. At the granting of independence in 1954, there were approximately 2 million Catholics in the country. With the division of Vietnam into two zones at Geneva, many Catholics in the North, fearful of persecution under the new Communist regime, fled to the South. By some estimates, of the 900,000 who left the North in the months following the conference, nearly two-thirds were Catholic.

Catholicism prospered under the new Saigon regime in the South. The first president, Ngo Dinh Diem, was himself a Catholic, and he viewed the Christian community as a primary bulwark of his regime against the Communist threat to South Vietnam. Catholics were given prominent positions in the government and in the armed forces. Many played a major role in commerce, the professions, and in cultural life. Catholic refugees from the North were settled in the suburbs of Saigon and in new Rural Development Centers in the Central Highlands to provide the basis of support for the anticommunist government.

In the long run, Diem's effort to build a strong constituency among Vietnamese Christians in the South backfired. The country's Buddhist majority grew increasingly restive at the government's apparent favoritism toward the Catholic population, and in the early 1960s lay and religious Buddhist groups increasingly voiced their discontent at alleged Catholic domination of the country. That discontent ultimately led to the collapse of the Diem regime and the rise to power of the military.

In the North, the new Communist regime, anxious to win the allegiance of those Catholics who had not departed for the South, as well as to avoid alienating Catholic opinion in the South and throughout the world, adopted a moderate position with regard to the church and its followers in the Democratic Republic of Vietnam (D.R.V.). The local Catholics were permitted to practice their religion, and relations with the Vatican were retained. Church activities were restricted, however, and some Catholics who attempted to emigrate were reportedly persecuted. In 1956, villagers in a heavily Catholic district along the central coast rioted against government policies and had to be subdued by North Vietnamese troops. In general, however, there was little evidence of open discontent over official policies among the Catholic community in the North, and spokesmen for the regime maintained that Catholic communities had been successfully integrated into the new socialist Vietnam and were as loyal to the regime's goals as their non-Christian compatriots. Foreign visitors to Catholic areas were assured that Catholics had willingly joined collective organizations and that many were even loyal members of the Vietnamese Workers' party (VWP).

How have the Catholics in the South fared since the unification of Vietnam in 1976? Undoubtedly many of the more anticommunist members of the Catholic community fled in the days immediately prior to the fall of Saigon. Of those who remained in the South, many reported later that because of their Catholic background, they were viewed with suspicion and were harassed by the new revolutionary authorities. According to one source, who later fled the country, "My family fled from the north in 1954 because they were Catholics. After 1975, freedom of religion was very restricted, although we attend church. Certain church activities, such as the youth organization, were not allowed. The Communists also started to use movies and other propaganda with an anti-religious theme."[1]

It seems likely that the party viewed the southern Catholics with a certain degree of suspicion and had some reservations about their willingness to assimilate into a new socialist Vietnam. Many were of middle-class origin and highly Westernized and had fled communism once before, in 1954. The regime therefore probably watched Catholics closely and attempted to restrict their activities, while permitting churches to continue in existence. There were periodic press reports that Catholic priests had been arrested and charged with carrying on activities against the state. Given the tense relations between the regime and the Catholic community, it is not surprising that a high percentage of refugees who fled Vietnam after 1978 were Catholics.

The Sects

Two other religious minorities, the Cao Dai and the Hoa Hao religious sects, have played a significant role in the history of modern Vietnam. Both emerged in South Vietnam during the interval between the two world wars. The Cao Dai movement appeared in 1925 among urban intellectuals in Saigon but soon took root in rural districts to the west and south and eventually established its headquarters in Tay Ninh Province. The religion (the name Cao Dai itself means "high tower") was based on an amalgam of Buddhist, Christian, Confucian, and Taoist beliefs. Although the movement had originated for religious and social reasons, it eventually took on a more political orientation in opposition to French rule in Vietnam. During World War II, it supported the Japanese in the conviction that the occupation authorities would grant Vietnam independence from French rule. After the war, its anticolonial orientation continued, and for a while

Cao Dai leaders were tempted to join the Communists against the French, but clashes between the two movements soon erupted in the Mekong Delta, and in late 1946 its leaders agreed to an alliance with the French against the forces of social revolution.

The Hoa Hao sect was founded in 1919 by the so-called mad bonze, Huynh Phu So. So, a mystic from Hoa Hao village in Rach Gia Province, founded the movement as a type of reformed Buddhism, with emphasis on simplicity and social justice. It prospered in rural areas in the south-ernmost provinces of the delta and along the Gulf of Thailand. As with the Cao Dai, its followers soon came to number more than a million, and after a brief period of flirtation with the Communists, its leadership turned to the French after clashes with Communist forces operating in the vicinity led to growing hostility and the assassination of Huynh Phu So, allegedly by order of the party leadership. After independence, the leadership and the bulk of the membership of the two sects continued to oppose the Communists, although a few dissident members joined the revolutionary movement when revolutionary war resumed in the late 1950s. At the same time, relations with Saigon were never close, particularly during the Diem era, because of the government's persistent efforts to bring sect areas under central rule. Like the Cao Dai, the Hoa Hao was a regional organization with parochial concerns rather than a full-fledged nationalist movement, and the political influence of the groups in South Vietnam has been limited and sporadic. Perhaps the primary importance was their resistance during the war to domination both by the Communists and by the Saigon government and their attempt, with varying degrees of success, to preserve a maximum of autonomy in areas under their control.

Like the Catholics and the overseas Chinese, the sects were un-doubtedly viewed with some suspicion by the new revolutionary regime that took power in the South in 1975. Sect areas had persistently resisted attempts to encroach on districts under their influence, by either the Saigon government or the liberation army forces, and resented efforts by any regime to integrate them into a centralized state. Hanoi was aware of such attitudes and attempted to minimize problems by handling the sects with delicacy. When the collectivization of agriculture got under way in the late 1970s, for example, sect areas, where the percentage of prosperous private farmers was higher than elsewhere in the South, were given special consideration, and the process of forming collectives was slower and emphasized voluntary means. Nevertheless, hostility to the new regime was high in areas controlled by the Hoa Hao, and eventually its priesthood was disbanded. Resistance was lighter among the Cao Dai, whose "Holy See" is still permitted to operate.

CONCLUSION

From the above discussion, it is clear that Vietnam is a relatively homogeneous society from an ethnic point of view, with about 85 percent of the total population belonging to the dominant Vietnamese culture. Nevertheless, the existence of several religious minorities, along with the ethnic minorities, has created difficulties for any government determined to create a centralized, highly integrated society. For the Saigon government, this was a serious problem that impeded its efforts to unify the South Vietnamese people against the Communist-led insurgency movement. In the years since reunification, it has been a source of continuing difficulties for the party leadership in Hanoi.

One further aspect of this problem merits brief mention here. Although a sense of common national identity is strong among all ethnic Vietnamese, history, politics, and geography have promoted the emergence of regional attitudes even within the majority culture. Vietnamese tend to recognize three separate regional groupings, each with its distinctive character: northerners, southerners, and central Vietnamese. Best-known, of course, because of recent Vietnamese history, are the distinctly different attitudes of northerners and southerners toward politics, social organization, and behavioral patterns. The peoples of the North are viewed as hardworking, serious, community-oriented, formal in their habits, and conservative in their resistance to change. Southerners are often described as easygoing, informal, rebellious, and individualistic. Centrists are often traditionalist and conservative in their outlook and tend to oppose both the Westernized bourgeois culture to the south and the social radicalism represented by Communist rule to the north. Some of these contrasts are undoubtedly a consequence of climate and geography. Where the North is densely populated, short of arable land, and relatively traditional in its social patterns, the South is considered a "frontier area," with excess land, a higher level of social mobility, and a more informal attitude toward social relationships. Not only was the recent civil war a product of such attitudes, but it also tended to accentuate them. Today the Communist regime is attempting, with considerable difficulty, to reduce such differences and create a more homogeneous population by assimilating the easy-going southerners into the highly regimented system already in existence in the North.

NOTES

1. Quoted in Bruce Grant, *The Boat People: An "Age" Investigation* (Harmondsworth: Penguin, 1979), p. 102.

2

Precolonial Vietnam

PREHISTORY

The origins of the Vietnamese people are shrouded in mystery. It has sometimes been asserted that their ancestral homeland was not in the Red River delta, where they first appear in history, but elsewhere, probably in South China. At present, there is little evidence to confirm this view. Archeological evidence indicates that human habitation in the area of the delta and the adjacent mountains extends back at least several hundred thousand years to the early Paleolithic era. Recent finds by Vietnamese archeologists at Mount Do in Thanh Hoa Province have confirmed that early men lived in the area at roughly the same time as the famous earliest examples of Peking Man and Java Man, about 500,000 years ago.

Unfortunately, there is little to link such scattered evidence to present-day inhabitants. The first clear signs of the probable ancestors of the modern-day Vietnamese and their neighbors in the adjacent mountains recently appeared as the result of archeological finds in the Hoa Binh and Lang Son provinces, suggesting the emergence of Mesolithic and Neolithic cultures in the vicinity of the delta at least 8,000 to 10,000 years ago. Available evidence suggests that the earlier stages were characterized by hunting and food gathering; the later stages show signs of the cultivation of agriculture and the domestication of animals—an indication that the inhabitants of the area had mastered primitive agricultural techniques as early as 9,000 years ago. If this is the case, the Vietnamese were among the first peoples to practice settled agriculture.

By 1300 B.C., the Stone Age civilization had clearly passed into the Bronze Age. Concrete evidence for this transformation appeared with the discovery of finely crafted bronze drums at an archeological site at Dong Son in Thanh Hoa Province. Bronze work of this type has been found in neighboring areas in Southeast Asia and in China, and some archeologists have speculated that the technique of bronze working was imported into Vietnam from the north. Others, noting the sophistication of the workmanship, have speculated that the technique may have been first mastered by the inhabitants at Dong Son and later spread throughout the region.

Whatever the case, other evidence at the site confirms that, by the end of the second millenium B.C., the inhabitants in the vicinity of the Red River delta had created an advanced civilization based on foreign trade and the cultivation of wet rice.

THE ORIGINS OF VIETNAMESE CIVILIZATION

Were the inhabitants of these Neolithic and Bronze Age sites ancestors of the present-day Vietnamese? At this point, evidence is too scanty to permit firm conclusions, although some experts suggest that the peoples who inhabited these Neolithic sites probably belonged to the Australoid-Negroid group, early inhabitants who may later have combined with Mongoloid elements from South China to form the ancestors of many of the current peoples of mainland Southeast Asia, including the Vietnamese. What seems clear is that sometime during the last millenium of the pre-Christian era the ancestors of the present-day Vietnamese had emerged as a significant force in the lowland and upland regions in the vicinity of the Red River delta. This was a period of rapid change throughout the area. During the previous several centuries, Chinese civilization had been gradually expanding from its origins along the banks of the Yellow and Yangtze rivers in China. By the late third century, this dynamic culture had begun to expand among the proto-Chinese peoples in the hilly regions south of the Yangtze River. With growth, however, had come instability and a long period of internal civil war (called, in Chinese history, the period of the Warring States) that was brought to an end only in 221 B.C. with the creation of the first centralized Chinese empire of the Ch'in, under the dynamic ruler Ch'in Shih Huang Ti.

Among those peoples who were affected and later absorbed by the new empire of the Ch'in were the so-called Yüeh (in Vietnamese, Viet) peoples then living throughout the southern coastal provinces of China and down into mainland Southeast Asia. Among the southernmost of these Viet peoples were the so-called Lac Viet, who lived in the lowland marshy areas of the Red River delta. Sometime during the third century B.C., the Lac Viet united with other Viet peoples (sometimes called the Tay Au, or Hsi Ou in Chinese) living in the nearby mountains to found the small state of Au Lac with its capital at Co Loa, not far from the present-day city of Hanoi. What little is known about the kingdom of Au Lac comes largely from Chinese sources. The state was primarily agricultural, and the people tilled the fields with polished stone hoes. Most of the arable land was owned by feudal aristocrats; there may have been some slavery. By Chinese standards, Lac Viet was undoubtedly rather small and unexceptional. According to Vietnamese historical sources, however, the small state had a distinguished ancestry; it was descended from a semi-mythical Hong Bang dynasty, which had ruled over an ancient kingdom of Van Lang for more than two thousand years, beginning in 2879 B.C.

The historical accuracy of such records is difficult to determine, and certainly those parts relating the origins of the Vietnamese peoples to the marriage of a dragon, Lac Long Quan, and a fairy, Au Ca, are apocryphal. Yet historians believe that Van Lang may have been an actual state, and it is not unlikely that the origins of the kingdom of Au Lac can be found in the Dong Son Bronze Age civilization a thousand years earlier.

THE CHINESE CONQUEST

Whatever its origins, the infant kingdom of Au Lac was not destined to survive. In 206 B.C. the short-lived Ch'in dynasty collapsed. In the chaotic situation that ensued, one of the Ch'in military commanders in South China, General Chao T'o (in Vietnamese, Trieu Da), founded a new kingdom of Nam Viet (South Viet, or Nan Yüeh in Chinese), with its capital at Canton. In the process of consolidating his rule, Trieu Da defeated the armies of Au Lac and assimilated the lands of the Red River delta into his own empire. Trieu Da was able to maintain control over his kingdom until his death, but his successors soon ran into conflict with the new Han dynasty that had risen from the ashes of the Ch'in in China, and in 111 B.C. Chinese armies defeated Nam Viet and incorporated it into the growing empire of the Han.

The Chinese conquest had lasting consequences for Vietnam. At first Chinese rulers were willing to apply the principle of indirect rule and governed the peoples of the delta through local tribal chieftains. During the early years of the first century A.D., however, Chinese efforts to assimilate the area politically and culturally into the Han empire intensified. Chinese settlers began to immigrate into the area in increasing numbers, and some were selected to assume a major role in administration. Chinese institutions and customs were introduced as Chinese authorities sought to transform what they considered a semibarbarian society into a more civilized reflection of parent China to the north. This policy of Sinification undermined the social status and political authority of the native feudal magnates, however, and in 39 A.D. led to a revolt by the famous Trung sisters (Hai Ba Trung). Trung Trac and her sister, Trung Nhi, were widows of Vietnamese noblemen who had allegedly died fighting the Chinese. Now they hoisted the banner of rebellion against foreign rule. The revolt was briefly successful, and Trung Trac declared herself ruler of an independent kingdom. But Han armies under General Ma Yüan soon returned to the attack and reincorporated the rebellious areas into the Chinese empire. In despair, the Trung sisters committed suicide by throwing themselves into a river.

For the next several centuries, Vietnam was a part of China, exposed to a concentrated policy of political and cultural assimilation. Chinese administrators replaced local aristocrats in positions of authority, although a few Vietnamese were permitted to occupy subordinate positions in the bureaucracy. The Chinese written language was introduced and became the official language of administration and literary expression. Chinese village rituals and customs replaced the relatively informal social mores practiced by the local Vietnamese. The Confucian classics became the foundation of the educational system in Vietnam. Chinese art, architecture, and music were imported and served as models for Vietnamese creative workers.

From the Chinese standpoint, the effort to integrate Vietnam into the broader world of Chinese culture was simply an extension of the historic attempt to pacify the outer frontier of the Chinese world and bring culture to the barbarian peoples living beyond the bounds of Confucian civilization. As such, the conquest and absorption of the Red River delta was not only a security problem but a consequence of the cultural dynamism and moral imperatives of the Chinese state. For most of the proto-Chinese peoples living in South China, the effort was a success, and the provinces south of the Yangtze River are today an integral part of the cultural world of modern China (although it should be noted that cultural differences between North and South China remain, and even today, Vietnamese intellectuals are occasionally prone to comment on the cultural and ethnic similarities of Vietnamese and South Chinese). In the case of Vietnam, the effort failed. Why this occurred is both a matter of intense pride to the Vietnamese and a source of dispute and fascination among historians. Whatever the reasons, several centuries of Chinese rule were not able to erase the memory of Vietnamese independence, and revolts broke out sporadically in abortive efforts to drive out the foreign invader.

INDEPENDENCE RESTORED

In the early tenth century, the T'ang dynasty, one of the most powerful and advanced in Chinese history, began to disintegrate. Taking advantage of the chaos, a revolt led by Ngo Quyen drove out the Chinese and restored the independent state of Nam Viet, with its capital at the ancient city of Co Loa. But Ngo Quyen died in 944, and for the remainder of the century the country was shaken by civil war. Only the weakness of the new Sung dynasty prevented a reconquest of the area by Chinese troops. In 1010, however, a new Ly dynasty rose and soon proved to be one of the stablest and most glorious in the history of the Vietnamese nation. Under the leadership of several dynamic emperors, notably the founder Ly Thai To and his successor Ly Thanh Ton, the Vietnamese state, now renamed Dai Viet (Greater Viet), consolidated its independence and began to expand beyond the confines of the Red River delta. In that undertaking, the new state learned quickly the benefits of relying on Chinese experience. The political institutions and ideology of Confucian China were retained and put to use in building a centralized state.

Like China, and like most of its neighbors throughout the region, Vietnam was an agricultural society, based primarily on the cultivation of

The famous Linh Mu pagoda, an early nineteenth-century Buddhist pagoda in the imperial city of Hue. (Photo property of the author)

wet rice. In terms of landownership, the system in some ways resembled the feudal system in medieval Europe. In theory, the king owned all land, but much of it was normally awarded to top officials or nobles who were thus able to amass vast feudal manor holdings. Most of these manor holdings were tilled by serfs or, in some cases, slaves, but there was also a class of freeholding peasants based on small plots of land in countless villages throughout the Red River delta or along the coast.

If agriculture was the foundation of the state, commerce and man-ufacturing were not entirely neglected. Handicrafts flourished in the major cities (mainly textiles, ceramics, and wood and metal working), and a trading network developed not only within the country but with the mountain peoples and other states across the South China Sea as well. Like China, however, Vietnam under the Ly was not primarily a seafaring state, and commerce was distinctly secondary to agriculture in national priorities.

China had not abandoned its dream of ruling Vietnam. The Sung dynasty, which ruled until the late thirteenth century, lacked the military prowess to restore Chinese rule over the delta, although the rulers of Dai Viet, in order to avoid provoking imperial hostility, accepted tributary status with the court to the north. In the late thirteenth century, however, the Sung fell to the growing power of the Mongols, who established the new Yüan dynasty in 1279. Under the Yüan, the old threat to Dai Viet rapidly revived. In 1285, the Tran ruler (the Tran dynasty had succeeded the Ly in 1225) refused permission for Mongol troops to cross Vietnamese territory to attack the state of Champa along the coast to the south. To punish such insolence, a Mongol army invaded Vietnam and sacked the capital. But the Vietnamese, under the inspired and astute leadership of one of their greatest national heroes, Tran Hung Dao, mobilized a national war of resistance against the invaders and, after several bloody battles, drove them back across the frontier. Two years later the Mongols returned to the attack but were again dealt a stunning defeat and eventually accepted a Vietnamese declaration of fealty to the Yüan emperor.

By the late fourteenth century, the Tran dynasty, plagued by famine, official corruption, land hunger, and almost constant war with the state of Champa, had begun to decay. In 1400, Ho Quy Ly, the regent for a child emperor, seized the throne. In China, Emperor Yung Lo of the vigorous new Ming dynasty refused to recognize the new dynasty and in 1407 launched an invasion, bringing Vietnam once again under foreign rule. Chinese officials were again imported to fill all high-ranking posts, and a program of comprehensive sinification was adopted to replace all remaining native traditions.

This time, Chinese rule lasted only twenty years. Although early resistance, mounted by a claimant representing the Tran dynasty, failed, in 1418 a more serious threat was mounted by a commoner from Thanh Hoa Province. Le Loi, son of a prosperous landowner and an ex-official who had refused to serve under the Ming occupation, declared himself a new "pacifying king" and, with the aid of the astute scholar and military genius Nguyen Trai, launched a guerrilla movement in the hilly regions of Thanh Hoa Province, south of Hanoi. By 1426, Le Loi felt strong enough to begin a major offensive against Chinese positions in the Red River delta and to lay siege to Chinese troops in the capital. The Ming court sent reinforcements, but they suffered a disastrous defeat. In the winter of 1427, Chinese forces surrendered and were permitted to withdraw. Like most founding emperors, Le Loi of the new Le dynasty set out immediately to solve one of the most persistent problems in Vietnamese society, the inequality of landholdings. Large landowners who had served the Tran or the Chinese were dispossessed by the state, and their land was redistributed among Le Loi's followers, while village commune lands were distributed to the poor. Legal restrictions on peasant rights were eased or eliminated, and rents were reduced. Major efforts were made to increase grain productivity.

The early Le dynasty can be considered a high point in the evolution of traditional society in Vietnam. A series of vigorous rulers reduced the power of the feudal magnates and issued decrees calling for greater equality of landholdings. The influence of Buddhist advisers at court declined, and a strengthened bureaucracy based on Confucian orthodoxy was established. The regime reached its apogee under Le Thanh Tong (1460–1497), during whose reign a new civil code, called the Hong Duc Code, was promulgated to establish the rule of law and systematize the laws and regulations of the empire.

MARCH TO THE SOUTH

One major contribution of the Le dynasty was to solve a long-standing problem in relations with Vietnam's neighbor to the south, Champa. For centuries, the major foreign policy concern of the Vietnamese state had been the danger of invasion from the north. Under the independent dynasties of the Ly, the Tran, and the Le, however, a new frontier opened up to the south. Here, along the central coast, lay the kingdom of Champa. Originally of Malay extraction, the Cham were a seafaring people who since the early Christian era had inhabited the coastal areas of what is today central Vietnam and down into the Mekong Delta. Unlike Vietnam, Champa had been exposed to influence not from China but from India and, after the eighth century, from Islam. If Dai Viet was a classic example of an Asian hydraulic society, Champa was an active participant in the trading network established by Chinese merchants and Arab traders throughout the region of the South China Sea. With the rise of the vigorous Ly dynasty in the eleventh century, tension between the two neighboring states began to increase and eventually led to conflict. On several occasions, Cham armies invaded the southern provinces of Dai Viet and once, taking advantage of the internal decay of the Ly, even sacked the Vietnamese capital. In general, however, the Vietnamese had the better of the struggle and, during the early Le dynasty, gradually advanced south, forcing the Cham to cede territory and move their capital southward. In 1471, Vietnamese troops occupied the Cham capital at Vijaya (in present-day Binh Dinh Province) and reduced the state to a virtual dependency.

Vietnamese expansion to the south provided new lands for a growing population and extended the power of the state but also created new problems. With territorial expansion, combined with the gradual decline of the Le dynasty in the sixteenth century, tensions arose at court and led to the rise of two powerful noble families, the Trinh and the Nguyen. Under weak rulers, land seizures by the wealthy and powerful and official corruption drove desperate peasants to rebellion. Rivalry between the Trinh and Nguyen led to the domination of the former in the North, while the latter were compelled to accept viceroyship over the newly conquered lands in the South, with their capital at Hue.

Internal dissension, however, did not end Vietnamese expansion in the south. On the contrary, the Nguyen completed their conquest of the Mekong Delta and placed the entire area under Vietnamese rule. By now their main rival was the declining Khmer empire of Angkor in Cambodia. In earlier centuries, Angkor had been the most powerful state in mainland Southeast Asia and had held sway over much of the lower Mekong and the area around the Tonle Sap. By the mid-fifteenth century, however, its power was in decline, and when marauding Thai armies sacked the capital near the present-day market town of Siem Reap, the Angkor kingdom abandoned the area near the Tonle Sap and established a new capital at Phnom Penh. During the seventeenth century, Vietnamese settlers, frequently supplemented by armed force, gradually occupied lands from modern Bien Hoa down to the delta of the Mekong. Taking advantage of factionalism at the Khmer court, the Nguyen periodically intervened in internal politics and reduced the disintegrating Khmer state to a virtual dependency of Vietnam, while consolidating their control over the lower Mekong.

THE COMING OF THE WEST

The expansion of the Vietnamese state toward the south in the sixteenth and seventeenth centuries coincided generally with the appearance of a new political and cultural force on the Southeast Asian scene. In 1511, the first signs of the new age of Western adventurism emerged with the arrival of a Portuguese fleet under Admiral Alfonso de Albuquerque at Malacca, on the west coast of the Malayan peninsula. The Portuguese were followed by others, and by the end of the century the Indian Ocean and the South China Sea were teeming with ships flying the flags of Spain, the Netherlands, France, and England.

The motives of the Westerners were diverse. While statesmen viewed the East in terms of imperial grandeur, control over the seas, and national wealth and power, merchants were lured by the promise of riches and a monopoly of the spice trade that had so long been dominated by Arab traders. Men of the cloth viewed the East as the home of millions of heathen souls to be saved. As the process accelerated, such motives often coalesced and intertwined. European governments subsidized the formation of joint stock companies, like the famous Dutch and British East India companies, to exploit the riches of Asia. Catholic missionaries accompanied Spanish, French, or Portuguese fleets on their voyages and frequently combined mercantile activity with their evangelical mission.

Vietnam's first direct exposure to the West came in 1535 when a Portuguese ship entered the Bay of Da Nang on the central coast. Within a few years the Portuguese had set up a trading port at Faifo (now, Hoi An), a few miles to the south, which now became the main port of entry for foreign goods. The Portuguese were soon followed by others, and by early in the seventeenth century traders from several European nations were active at several ports along the Vietnamese coast.

The first Catholic mission to Vietnam came in 1615, when Jesuit missionaries from the Portuguese colony of Macao set up a small mission at Faifo. The French, however, soon became the leaders in the effort. Under the vigorous sponsorship of an ambitious Jesuit scholar, Alexander of Rhodes, French Catholics set up the Society of Foreign Missions to train missionaries to propagate the Christian faith in Vietnam. A significant aspect of Rhodes's work was his desire to train native priests to serve the needs of Vietnamese converts. As a means of facilitating this goal, he devised the first transliteration of the Vietnamese spoken language into the roman alphabet. Although this written script (known as *quoc ngu*, or national language) did not at that time come into general use, French and later Vietnamese missionaries used it to translate the Bible into Vietnamese. As a result of such dedicated efforts, thousands of Vietnamese were converted to the new faith.

Success, however, was short-lived. Missionary activities eventually antagonized Vietnamese authorities, who feared, with some justification, that Christian doctrine would subvert Confucian institutions and beliefs and public loyalty to the emperor. In 1631, the propagation of Christianity was barred in the South; thirty years later, a similar decree was issued in the North. European missionaries were expelled, and a few were executed. A similar decline occurred in commercial contacts. Although by no means a poor country, Vietnam had relatively little to offer in the way of spices and mineral resources. In 1697, the French closed down their small factory at Faifo. Others soon followed, leaving only the Portuguese with a small office.

THE TAY SON REBELLION

Throughout much of the eighteenth century, peasant revolts had underscored rural unhappiness about mandarin corruption, land grabbing by the wealthy, and the general incompetence of the decrepit Le regime. Like peasant jacqueries everywhere, most were disorganized and quickly put down. But in 1771, a rebellion broke out that would eventually overthrow both the Nguyen and the Trinh and lead to the founding of a new united dynasty. The leaders were three brothers from the village of Tay Son in Binh Dinh Province in Central Vietnam, thus providing the so-called Tay Son revolt with its name. Riding in the vanguard of a widespread struggle by impoverished and land-hungry peasants in South Vietnam to alleviate intolerable economic conditions, the Tay Son brothers, like Asian Robin Hoods, ravaged the countryside while seizing the wealth of the rich and giving it to the poor. For several years the revolt was limited to the provinces of Quang Nam, Quang Ngai, and Binh Dinh. But in 1776, the Trinh took advantage of the chaotic situation and invaded the Nguyen domain. In the confusion, the Tay Son rebels seized Saigon. Many of the Nguyen lords were killed, but one, Prince Nguyen Anh, managed to flee to safety to an island in the South China Sea.

Flushed with success, the rebels now attacked the North and overthrew Trinh rule. Promising to restore power to the figurehead Le dynasty, the eldest and most capable of the brothers, Nguyen Huê, now married the daughter of the emperor and declared his fealty to the old dynasty. The emperor, however, distrusted the intentions of the Tay Son rebels and requested assistance from Chinese Emperor Ch'ien Lung. In 1788, a Chinese invasion force crossed the border and seized Hanoi, but Nguyen Huê deposed the Le ruler and declared himself the founding emperor of a new dynasty. In a bitter conflict near Hanoi, the Vietnamese achieved a decisive victory over Chinese forces, who fled in disorder back to China.

Following traditional fashion, the new emperor, under the reign title Quang Trung, set out to solidify his rule by improving conditions in rural areas. Commune lands were returned to the poor peasants, and lands abandoned by their owners during the civil war were put back under the plow. Commercial activity was promoted and good relations were sought with China. But Emperor Quang Trung died suddenly in 1792 at the age of forty, and his two brothers proved to lack his acumen; the empire rapidly began to disintegrate.

The sudden decline of the power of the Tay Son came as a blessing to the remaining survivor of the Nguyen house in the South. After fleeing to Phuc Quoc Island to escape the Tay Son, Nguyen Anh went to Thailand to seek assistance to recover his patrimony, but his first attempt to return was defeated in 1784. Then, however, he was befriended by Pigneau de Behaine, a French bishop stationed at Ha Tien on the Gulf of Thailand. Convinced that French help in restoring Nguyen Anh to power could create an opening for the revival of Catholic missionary activity in Vietnam, Pigneau promised to provide him with assistance. A trip by Pigneau to Paris in 1787 elicited a promise from the French government to support a naval expedition against the Tay Son in return for a promise of trade privileges and the cession of Poulo Condore Island and Da Nang harbor to France. The plan was scuttled by the French viceroy in India, however, who refused to provide the funds for the mission. Undeterred, Pigneau raised the money on his own to purchase two ships and provide weapons and volunteers for an expedition that was launched in the summer of 1789. After the death of Quang Trung in 1792, the insurgents began to make progress, and in 1802, Nguyen Anh seized Hanoi and declared the founding of a new Nguyen dynasty with its capital at Hue, in Central Vietnam. Pigneau, who died in 1799, did not live to see the victory of his protegé.

THE NGUYEN DYNASTY

Pigneau de Behaine's gamble that French assistance to Nguyen Anh would provide an opening for French commercial and missionary interests in Vietnam proved to be unjustified. The new emperor, assigning himself the reign title Gia Long, was reasonably tolerant and permitted French missionaries to operate in Vietnam during his lifetime. He refused to ratify the abortive treaty arranged by Pigneau in Paris, however, and French hopes for improved trade relations between the two countries were not fulfilled. After Gia Long died in 1820, his successor Minh Mang continued and in some ways extended this restrictive policy toward contact with the West. Bright and dedicated, the new emperor was a devout believer in Confucian orthodoxy, and although interested in mastering Western technology, he feared the effects of European ideas on traditional culture in Vietnam. During his reign, the propagation of Christianity was sternly forbidden and missionaries and their converts were persecuted. A few who persisted were executed.

The dynasty's effort to solve Vietnam's chronic social and economic problems had only indifferent success. Despite attempts to control land concentration and official corruption, conditions in rural areas did not improve significantly from the declining years of the Le, resulting in sporadic peasant unrest. Such problems were intensified by internal dissension at court and the widespread unpopularity of the Nguyen dynasty in the North, where memories of the civil war ran deep.

THE FRENCH CONQUEST

Throughout the first half of the nineteenth century, commercial, military, and religious circles in France had attempted to goad the French government into adopting a more active policy toward Vietnam. Such

The Imperial Palace at Hue, built in the early nineteenth century and patterned after the Forbidden City in Peking. (Photo property of the author)

voices became even more vocal at mid-century, when periodic executions of French missionaries in Vietnam aroused a public outcry. For the most part, government leaders had resisted these pressures, but by the late 1850s it had become difficult to maintain such an attitude. Commercial interests, concerned at increasing British control over Burma and the possible loss to the British of the "China Market," agitated for an aggressive policy to bring Vietnam under French influence and to open up the "soft underbelly" of China to French economic exploitation. Religious organizations, angered over Hue's persecution of Catholic missionary activity, demanded protection for French missionaries and Christian converts in Vietnam. In 1857, the government ordered a French fleet to seize the central Vietnamese port city of Da Nang and to compel the Vietnamese court to accept French demands.

The attack, launched in the summer of 1858, did not achieve these objectives. A predicted revolt against the imperial government in the rural areas along the central coast did not materialize, and European troops were pinned down in the city and unable to advance northward to threaten the imperial capital. With his troops ravaged by disease, the French commander, Admiral Charles Rigault de Genouilly, decided to evacuate the city and resume the attack further south at Saigon, which the French seized the following February. In succeeding months, French troops extended their control into neighboring areas after bitter fighting. Defeat in the South, coupled with a spreading revolt led by Le pretenders in the North, led the court to seek peace, and in the spring of 1862, French and Vietnamese negotiators reached agreement on a treaty that ceded three provinces in the South and the island of Poulo Condore to France. Three port cities were opened to French commerce, and Christian missionaries were granted freedom to propagate their religion in Vietnam.

The seizure of three provinces in the South was only the first step in a process that led before the end of the century to the conquest of the remainder of the country and the creation of an Indochinese Union including Vietnam, Laos, and Cambodia. In 1867, French units under Governor Benoit de la Grandière seized the remainder of the South and transformed the area into the French colony of Cochin China. In the meantime, the French had assumed Vietnamese rights in Cambodia and turned it into a protectorate. For more than two centuries, Thailand and Vietnam had clashed repeatedly over dominance in Phnom Penh, with each relying for support on factions within the Khmer court. In the early nineteenth century, Vietnam had turned the disintegrating state into a virtual protectorate, but resistance to Vietnamese domination led to a revolt, and in 1846, an agreement between Vietnam and Thailand placed the area under their joint suzerainty. In the Treaty of Saigon, signed in 1862, the Nguyen court renounced its claims over Cambodia, claims that were assumed a few months later by France.

The seizure of Cochin China and Cambodia did not satisfy the dreams of French expansionists. The French conquest of the South had not opened up the vast potential market of South China to French commercial exploitation, and militant elements in Saigon and Paris agitated for vigorous action to bring the North under French rule and put France in an advantageous position to dominate the China market.

In 1873, an opportunity to extend French influence to the North appeared when a French adventurer, Jean Dupuis, who had been running guns up the Red River into South China, encountered difficulties with local authorities. When the Vietnamese authorities attempted to control his activities, he mobilized a small military force of Europeans and Asians, seized parts of Hanoi, and then appealed to the governor of Cochin China in Saigon, Admiral Jean-Marie Dupré, for assistance. Dupré, who viewed the situation as an opportunity to compel the court to accept a French protectorate over the remainder of Vietnam and French authority in all of Cochin China, dispatched a small detachment of French troops under the command of an ex–naval officer, Francis Garnier. Ostensibly, Garnier's responsibility was to extract Dupuis from Hanoi, but Garnier—an imperialist in the mold of Cecil Rhodes—joined forces with Dupuis and seized the Hanoi citadel. Garnier himself was killed in a brief skirmish with imperial troops in December. In Paris, however, reaction to Saigon's unilateral effort

The River of Perfume, Hue's sacred river, at dawn. (Photo property of the author)

to seize the North was hostile, and after the government had informed Saigon of its opposition to an occupation of the North, French troops were withdrawn in return for the court's recognition of French sovereignty over all Cochin China.

In the mid-1880s, the French completed their conquest of Vietnam. Pressure in France to adopt a more aggressive policy to counter British advances in Burma continued to rise, and in early 1882, reacting to the arrival in the North of Chinese troops in response to a plea for help from the court at Hue, Captain Henri Rivière was dispatched with 200 men to Hanoi. Arriving in April, he seized the citadel and consolidated French control over the entire lower delta. Rivière was later killed in a skirmish with pirates, but Paris had already decided to take further military action to bring the court to heel and to force it to accept French suzerainty. Taking advantage of the death of Emperor Tu Duc, Paris ordered additional troops to the delta. Resistance from Chinese and Vietnamese forces was soon broken, and in August 1883, the dispirited court acceded to French demands and signed a treaty establishing a French protectorate over the remainder of the country. In a separate treaty, China renounced its claims to a tributary relationship with Vietnam. Less than a decade later, the new French "balcony on the Pacific" was completed by the establishment of a protectorate over the kingdom of Laos.

CONCLUSION

To those acquainted with the history of the Vietnamese people, the relative ease with which the Nguyen court succumbed to the French is somewhat puzzling. Why, after a tradition of centuries of staunch resistance to invasion from the north, did the Vietnamese so readily accept the new rulers from the West? Part of the answer may be sought in the domestic political situation. Vietnam had the misfortune of encountering intense Western pressure at a time of serious internal weakness. Since the decline of the Le dynasty in the late sixteenth century, the country had faced serious internal problems. Expansion to the south had eased the heavy pressure on the land in the Red River delta, but it had not solved the problems of official corruption or concentration of land in the hands of the wealthy. Peasant unrest had become a familiar part of the political landscape and continued to cause internal instability well into the middle of the nineteenth century. Furthermore, expansion had led to a growing split within the ruling elite, resulting in the de facto division of Vietnamese society into two separate and mutually antagonistic regions in the North and South for several generations. The rise of the Nguyen dynasty had not brought a solution to this problem either, and regional factionalism continued during the nineteenth century beneath the superficial unity of the Nguyen dynasty.

The internal divisions and tensions within Vietnamese society were exacerbated by the cultural challenge from abroad. Although the official attitude toward the West at court was tinged with hostility, fear, and at least initially, a whiff of Confucian contempt for barbarian ways, it did not take long for perceptive members of the ruling elite to observe that Western civilization was equal or perhaps in some respects even superior to Sino-Vietnamese civilization in Vietnam, particularly as the latter was facing a severe internal crisis. For many Vietnamese intellectuals concerned over the fate of their nation, fear of the West was soon tempered by the realization that, in order to survive, Vietnam might be compelled to abandon its traditional heritage and adopt many of the attributes of Western culture.

3

The Roots of Revolution

THE NATURE OF FRENCH COLONIALISM

By the end of the nineteenth century, the colonial edifice in Indochina was firmly in place. An Indochinese Union, comprising five separate territories—the protectorates in Tonkin (North Vietnam), Annam (Central Vietnam), Cambodia, and Laos and the colony of Cochin China. At the top of the administrative hierarchy in the new union was a governor-general appointed from Paris to make policy for the entire region. To assist him were lower-ranking officers responsible for each of the five territories—*résidents supérieurs* in each of the protectorates and a governor in Cochin China. In addition, French *résidents* were placed at the provincial level in the protectorates to provide advice to native administrators. In the central provinces of Annam, the emperor and his bureaucracy were permitted to retain a modicum of their quondam administrative authority. But in the North, the authority of the emperor was emasculated by making the *résident supérieur* the official representative of the court.

From the beginning, there was little question that the primary objectives of French colonial policy in Indochina were economic. For commercial interests, of course, the main purpose of colonialism was simply to register economic gain—to exploit the natural resources of the area and to open up new markets for the manufactured goods of the home country. For government officials in Paris, Hanoi, or Saigon, the perspective was somewhat more complicated, but not markedly at variance with the mercantile view. Although they were not blind to the seductive lure of commercial profit, for officials in Paris the main purpose of the French colonial venture in Southeast Asia could only be to enhance national security and prestige. There was no necessary contradiction between such objectives. In the prevailing wisdom of the day, nations, like living species, operated by the law of natural selection. Only the fittest nations survived, and those that could not adapt to changing conditions would be left behind in the brutal struggle for survival. For turn-of-the-century Europeans, national survival was directly linked to the possession of a colonial empire, which provided not only political and military power and influence but also the economic wealth that was itself the foundation of national strength.

But if there was no question of the ultimate objectives behind the French colonial effort, the public view of the colonial enterprise was quite another matter. Like most other contemporary practitioners of the colonial experiment, the French placed considerable emphasis on the moral aspect of colonialism—what in English-language countries was often summed up in the well-known phrase the "white man's burden." The lure of economic profit was, all things considered, the most crucial factor in provoking the French imperialist effort in Asia, but for millions of ordinary French citizens the primary justification for colonial rule was the civilizing mission (*mission civilisatrice*)—the obligation of the advanced peoples of the world to bring the benefits of modern civilization to the primitive peoples of Asia and Africa. In an earlier age, this sentiment had usually been cloaked in religious terms—to bring the word of the one true God to the heathen. By the end of the nineteenth century, the civilizing mission of French colonial rule could as easily be couched in secular terms: Commercial exploitation would bring Asian societies into the world market. This would lead not only to their economic enrichment but ultimately to the development of a modern society based on the concepts of representative government and individual freedom.

It was one thing to proclaim the existence of a French civilizing mission in Indochina. It was quite another to know how to carry it out. What were the responsibilities of the colonial power in Indochina? Were the colonial peoples to be exposed to the full panoply of Western values and institutions? Or should they be allowed to pick and choose in order to produce a viable synthesis of foreign and indigenous concepts? Could, indeed, the Vietnamese be transformed into—in the picturesque French phrase—*"français de couleur"*? Such questions were of more than academic interest. They went to the heart of the question of the nature of man. Was human nature universal? Were Asian peoples destined to repeat the path to industrial development and democracy now being trod in the West? Or, as Rudyard Kipling had proclaimed, were East and West divided by irreconcilable cultural and philosophical cleavages?

Moreover, there were potentially serious contradictions between the publicized goal of the white man's burden and the more pragmatic objective of exploiting the economic resources of the colonial territories for the benefit of the home country. How could the interests of the colonial peoples be adequately protected when the primary objective of the colonial regime was to serve the commercial needs of the metropole? Would the colonial government promote the growth of an indigenous manufacturing and commercial sector in Indochina when the products of such a sector might compete against manufactured goods imported from France? Could the social and economic welfare of Indochinese workers and peasants be served when it was clearly in the interests of the French economy that prices of raw materials imported from Indochina be kept to a minimum? Finally, why should the French promote the capacity of the peoples of Indochina to create and operate democratic institutions when, in the end, such a society must inevitably wish to restore its independence?

Such questions underlined the ambiguities in French colonial policy and ultimately caused its undoing. From the beginning, French colonial strategy was marked by ambivalence, and a coherent statement of political and social objectives in Indochina was never realized. From the beginning, too, the civilizing mission was subordinated to the more immediate goal of commercial profit.

Early colonial administrators in Cochin China, motivated primarily by the practical objective of facilitating the economic exploitation of the area, had attempted to minimize the impact of the French presence on the native population of Indochina. Where possible, the support of local elites was solicited to create the necessary conditions for efficient exploitation of the economic resources of the colony.

By the early years of the twentieth century, this policy, called "association," had come increasingly under criticism. The attack came from diverse sources. In part it came from France, where liberal elements contended that the policy of association simply milked the colonies for their economic resources without in turn providing them with the benefits of Western civilization. A similar charge came from within Vietnam, where some intellectuals complained that the French were not living up to their promise to bring the benefits of Western civilization to the native population.

Ultimately, such criticism led to a change in colonial policy. In the early twentieth century, the position of governor-general was occupied by a number of progressive colonial administrators who expressed French determination to carry through its *mission civilisatrice* in Indochina. Under the guiding hand of such enlightened figures as Paul Beau and Albert Sarraut, the French government began to devise reforms designed to introduce the local population to the benefits of Western civilization and to establish, as one of them declared in a moment of exuberance, a "politics of collaboration." The results were somewhat less than the early promise. The colonial regime set up legislative assemblies at the provincial level in Annam and Tonkin (a Colonial Council dominated by French *colons* and limited in its authority had already been established in Cochin China before the end of the century). These bodies, however, were only consultative and restricted in their membership and franchise and hardly represented a serious effort to initiate the Vietnamese people into democratic practice. Although some consideration was given to setting up a legislative body to provide political representation for the entire population of the Indochinese Union, the proposal never left the drawing board.

Similar problems plagued French policy in the field of education. While liberal administrators attempted to set up a new system to introduce the native population to the values and institutions of the modern West, the system was haphazard and often contradictory in both theory and practice. The small colonial elite received an education based roughly on the Western model, but the mass of the population received only an indifferent exposure to Western culture and institutions, and for lack of funds, many young Vietnamese in rural areas received virtually no education at all. If education was a measure of the seriousness of the colonial effort, French practice fell far short of promise.

Above all, performance of the colonial regime was judged in the area of economic and social progress. The primary objective of colonialism, of course, was to provide financial profit to the home country and to its citizens operating in Indochina. On the other hand, one of the major justifications of French colonial rule was that it would improve the standard of living of the local population and increase the productive capacity of society and its ability to compete effectively within the international economic order. As one French colonial administrator, Paul Reynaud, remarked in the early 1930s, it was quite obvious that most Vietnamese would prefer independence. The best way for the French to justify their presence was to demonstrate that economic and social benefits resulted from colonial rule.

The centerpiece of the colonial argument was that French colonial rule would create a modernized commercial and manufacturing sector, improve transport and communications, and generally improve the local standard of living. Along these lines, apologists for the colonial regime pointed out that under French rule there was general economic progress in Vietnam. In the big cities of Hanoi, Haiphong, Saigon, and Da Nang, as well as in smaller provincial capitals and market towns like Vinh, Nam Dinh, and Qui Nhon in the Center and My Tho and Can Tho in the Mekong Delta, a young and vigorous commercial and manufacturing sector gradually emerged. Most of this activity was in the area of light industry: textiles, paper, sugar, matches, bicycle assembly, and food processing. There was little in the way of heavy industry, although the coal mines along the coast north of Haiphong are worthy of note. Defenders of the regime also pointed with pride to progress in transport and communications. Under French rule, bridges were built over the major waterways, railroads were constructed from Hanoi to Saigon and from Hanoi north to the Chinese border and thence onto Kunming, and what many described as the best system of metalled roads in all of Southeast Asia was established.

Perhaps the greatest contribution made by the French in rural areas was the expansion of the amount of land under cultivation. Swampy and frequently inundated by salt water, the lower Mekong Delta was generally unfit for the cultivation of wet rice during the precolonial period. The French drained many of the marshlands and built a series of canals that put thousands of acres under cultivation for the first time. They were also active in piedmont areas and in the *terre rouge* (red lands) along the Cambodian border. Here new cash crops for the export market, like coffee, tea, and rubber, were cultivated in plantations owned by the French but worked by Vietnamese laborers hired from the crowded villages of the North. In the early years of the twentieth century, rubber became, after rice, the second major source of export earnings in Indochina.

How effective such measures were in increasing the productive potential of the economy and raising the standard of living of the native population is a matter of dispute. Defenders of the colonial regime frequently pointed to the steady growth in rice exports as an indication that the French presence had a beneficial impact on the living standard of the mass of the rural population. At the height of the export boom, in the mid-1930s, as much as 300,000 metric tons of milled rice was exported from Vietnamese ports each year. Critics charged, however, that such statistics were seriously misleading and that in actuality living conditions in rural areas may have declined during the period of colonial rule. Higher taxes, French monopolies on the production and sale of salt, alcohol, and opium, and the creation of a market economy that led to rising land concentration and rural tenancy all combined to make life more difficult for many peasants and to drive many below the level of subsistence.

This is not the place to attempt a definitive assessment of the question, for statistics can often be misleading. There are indications that rural standards of living, at least in Cochin China, may have risen between 1900 and 1930 but then declined during and after the world Depression in the 1930s. And although thousands of acres of new land were opened up by drainage of the marshy areas in the Mekong Delta, much of this land was held by absentee landlords who leased out small parcels of land to poor peasants from Annam and Tonkin for high rents, sometimes as much as 50 percent of the annual harvest. It was, perhaps, the commercialization of agriculture that had the most disruptive impact on living conditions in rural Vietnam. This, of course, is a pattern familiar to all societies in an early stage of capital and technological advancement. The commercialization of agriculture forces excess laborers from the villages into the cities in a desperate search for jobs. The fortunate ones obtain employment in factories, ships, and coal mines, or on plantations, sometimes working in abysmal conditions. Others, living adjacent to the cities, keep one foot in the village, the other in the factory, working the fields at harvest time and seeking employment in the cities during the off season.

This process had occurred during the early stages of the industrial revolution in Europe and has been repeated in other parts of the world recently. In Europe, the process of agricultural modernization, although tragic enough in its consequences for those who suffered personal hardship as a result of it, eventually led to the rise of industrial societies based on the concepts of representative democracy. Land concentration and capital investment in rural areas led to a more efficient system of agriculture. Surplus workers in the cities provided the cheap labor that, combined with the increase in capital and technological advancement, fueled the emergence of modern capitalism. Unfortunately, in Vietnam the consequences were not so beneficial. In good part, this was a direct result of colonial policy. The French did not encourage the development of an indigenous commercial and manufacturing sector. To the contrary, commerce and manufacturing in colonial Vietnam tended to be dominated by European interests or by foreign immigrants such as the Chinese and Indians. Moreover, government policy attempted to discourage the development of local industries that might compete with French goods by a tariff policy that encouraged French imports. In effect, Vietnam was forced to undergo the painful stresses of agricultural modernization without the benefit of rapid industrial growth in the cities.

Here, of course, was one of the fundamental weaknesses of colonialism as a vehicle for the modernization of preindustrial societies. The implied or stated promise of colonial policy was to undertake needed measures to bring about social and economic change and political democracy, but such objectives frequently conflicted with the economic priorities of the ruling power and its citizens. When such conflicts took place, of course, the latter normally took precedence. France, like most colonial powers, was a democracy that was ultimately responsible to its domestic constituency in France and the European population in Indochina. Because the interests of the Vietnamese were inadequately represented in Paris, these interests tended to be ignored.

SOURCES OF NATIONALISM AND COMMUNISM

The Vietnamese response to the French conquest had been surprisingly weak in view of the long tradition of national resistance to foreign aggression. Whether the reasons for that weakness can be ascribed to personal factors (e.g., the incompetence and vacillation of Emperor Tu Duc) or to the endemic weakness of the dynasty itself (like the Manchu dynasty in China, the Nguyen had the misfortune to encounter the full thrust of Western imperialist aggression at a time of internal division and social unrest) is not a question appropriate for consideration here. But it is clear that the Vietnamese defeat at the hands of the French was at least partly the result of the failure of the court to mobilize resistance to foreign aggression within society at large.

That is not to say that resistance to foreign rule was totally lacking. In fact, a relatively substantial movement of opposition to the French emerged at the grass-roots level, among civilian and military officials, urban residents, and even among peasants in the village. Much of this was disorganized and sporadic, however, and suffered from lack of support from the court. Indeed, after the Treaty of Saigon, the emperor, fearful of French wrath, expressly forbade resistance activities and attempted to quell them in areas under his control. In some instances, local elite groups raised the flag of rebellion despite lack of approval from the court. The most worthy of mention was the guerrilla movement organized by the patriot leader Phan Dinh Phung in the hills of Central Vietnam, a movement that was not finally quelled until Phung's death in 1896. In general, however, such spontaneous resistance was ineffectual and, lacking either organization or the capacity to counter the technological superiority of French firepower, was put down by the French with relatively little difficulty.

By the opening of the twentieth century, then, the French colonial regime was firmly in place. Some Vietnamese managed with few compunctions to live with the new situation. A new class of native "collaborators" sprang up to cooperate with the foreigners and facilitate the operations of their new regime. Some became low-level functionaries of the bureaucracy—clerks, translators, village officials, and mandarins in areas still ruled by the imperial court. Others became members of a new class of economic middlemen—local employees of the colonial enterprises, foremen in the rubber plantations and coal mines. Others, while not directly tied to the regime or to the enterprises of the Europeans, nevertheless benefited directly from their presence—lawyers, agronomists, engineers, architects, and the members of that small but vocal group, the affluent commercial and manufacturing bourgeoisie.

For such elements, of course, the colonial presence represented their livelihood. Many of them were attracted to the glittering quality of Western civilization and adapted quickly to it, learning the French language, dressing in French clothes, eating French food, and if they could afford it, living in French-style houses. Collectively, this class would perform the role of middlemen between the French colonial regime and the mass of the population and would be the most visible evidence to apologists of colonialism that the *mission civilisatrice* was succeeding.

Yet if the major source of support for the French colonial regime came from a new bureaucratic, commercial, and professional class in the cities, it was from the cities, too, that the first major threat to the stability of the regime ultimately began to emerge. The first wave of resistance to French rule had come primarily from the traditional scholar-gentry class, motivated by Confucian loyalty to the Vietnamese state and hostility to the foreign and revolutionary doctrines coming from the West. By the end of the nineteenth century, that source of traditionalist opposition to foreign rule had begun to decline. Even members of the traditional elite had come to see the impossibility of restoring precolonial society and the need to adopt Western values and institutions as a means of coping with the challenges of the modern world. With that recognition, the first shoots of modern nationalism began to appear, and it was in the cities, above all, that this process began to take place. The quickening pace of commerce and industry in the cities led to the rise of a new urban class. Composing this new petty bourgeoisie were shop clerks, petty functionaries in the bureaucracy, schoolteachers, journalists, and students. Throughout the colonial world it has characteristically been among this class of urban intelligentsia that the first stirrings of modern nationalism have begun to appear. Such was the case in Vietnam. Living in the cities, educated in the new Franco-Vietnamese school system, this class made up the first generation of Vietnamese to have a first-hand understanding of the nature of Western culture and its impact on Vietnamese society. Having absorbed the doctrine of progress, certainly one of the primary attributes of the modern Western outlook on life, many of them had developed rising expectations about their personal futures and were quick to discern the yawning gap between the promise and the realities of the colonial experiment. Many, indeed, had come from families of elite status within the traditional society and soon sensed the frustration of blocked access to positions of wealth, prestige, and influence.

For most, the Western concepts of democracy, science and technology, and material affluence had considerable appeal. Few indeed wished to return to the now discredited doctrines and practices of traditional Sino-Vietnamese society. Their reaction to Western culture was thus inevitably somewhat ambivalent. Admiration for the progressive aspects of Western society, and a firm desire that the future of Vietnam should follow a similar path, were colored by the conviction that the path to that bright future (in both personal and national terms) was obstructed by the colonial presence.

The emotional and intellectual outlet for the frustrations and aspirations of Vietnamese educated youth was thus focused on a new and heightened sense of nationhood based on the vision of a democratic and economically advanced society. The first clear sign of this new sense of nationalism began to appear during and immediately following World War I. In all three regions of Vietnam, small factions dedicated to the eviction of the colonial regime began to appear among radical youth in the cities. In some cases, such groups were little more than student organizations agitating for economic or political reforms, or small coteries of urban intellectuals vacillating between reformist agitation and violent revolution.

The French authorities were quick to respond to such agitation, and demonstrations in Saigon and other major cities were broken up and their perpetrators placed in jail. When student riots took place, schools were closed. Publications considered hostile to the regime were shut down, and all others were exposed to vigorous official censorship. For a while, such preventive efforts appeared to take the heart out of the opposition. But in the last years of the 1920s a sense of professional commitment began to emerge with the formation of political organizations dedicated to the achievement of total independence. Even at this early stage, however, the nascent nationalist movement showed signs of incipient weakness. Most nationalist organizations were factions rather than parties; often they were identified with a region or an individual rather than imbued with a sense of common national interest. Some, like the sects in the South, sought regional autonomy more than the eviction of the French. There was disagreement, too, over ultimate goals. Although the majority of participants undoubtedly sought independence, some were dedicated to violent revolution while others hoped to achieve their goals through reformist measures. A few would tolerate or even seek a continuing tie with France.

Perhaps a more serious obstacle to the effectiveness of the nationalist movement was its inability to build a base among the mass of the population. The nationalist parties in the 1920s were composed primarily of radical urban youths, with a sprinkling of older patriotic figures; few had close ties with peasants and workers. As a result, such parties suffered from the typical weaknesses of elite groups. For the most part, their goals reflected the aspirations of the educated middle class—increased political rights, equal pay for equal work, democratic freedoms, female emancipation, and so on. Although not unsympathetic to the poor—many of their programs called for lower taxes, equality of landholding, and the right of collective bargaining—they tended to concentrate on political issues that had little meaning to the average Vietnamese. And in the tradition of fledgling revolutionary organizations, they tended to see the final uprising as an affair of a few rather than the result of a patient mobilization of the force of the mass of the population.

The failure of the nationalist parties to prepare for a mass struggle to overthrow the colonial regime was not simply a consequence of inadequate understanding or execution by patriotic intellectuals. Until the late 1920s, neither peasants nor workers had become politically aroused in the nationalist cause. Rural discontent had broken out sporadically in the years since the French conquest—notably a series of peasant riots against high taxes and mandarin corruption in the provinces south of Hue in 1908—but on the whole peasant discontent had been focused on economic rather than on political issues. The situation was similar with the small Vietnamese working class. A Vietnamese proletariat had begun to appear early in the century in the factories, the shipyards, and the coal mines run by the French and by the decade following World War I numbered nearly 200,000 men. The first signs of worker organization appeared in the early 1920s when Ton Duc Thang, a radical nationalist recently returned from France, began to organize secret labor unions in the factories and on the docks in Saigon. For a few years overt activity was quelled, but with the onset of the Depression in the late 1920s, worker strikes became increasingly frequent. Most were staged primarily for economic objectives—higher salaries, shorter hours, paid vacations, and improved working conditions—but they were a sign of increasing activism within the growing laboring class.

It was in these conditions that the Communist party made its appearance in Vietnam. The founder of the party was the young patriot Ho Chi Minh, then known under the earlier pseudonym of Nguyen Ai Quoc (Nguyen the Patriot). Son of a patriotic official in Nghe An Province in Central Vietnam, Ho Chi Minh was educated at the prestigious National Academy in Hue but apparently left school before graduation and took employment on a French ocean liner as a cook's helper. After several years at sea, he settled in Paris after the end of World War I and became active in radical circles. In 1920, he joined the French Communist party (FCP) and three years later was summoned to Moscow to receive training as an agent of the Comintern. In late 1924, he returned to South China and formed a proto-communist organization among Vietnamese radicals in exile called the Revolutionary Youth League. Fiercely dedicated, an astute organizer with a seductive and charismatic personality, Ho Chi Minh had good success in winning support from the radical youth in Vietnam, and by the end of the decade, membership in the organization had reached more than one thousand. In 1930, after a brief split caused by policy disagreements, the league was transformed into the Indochinese Communist party (ICP).

The party appeared at a significant juncture in the colonial era. After several decades of relatively peaceful conditions, in 1930, serious disturbances took place in both urban and rural areas. The immediate cause of the unrest was the world Depression. Plant closings exacerbated existing anger over salaries and working conditions and led to strikes in several factories in cities throughout Vietnam. Similar unrest broke out at rubber plantations near Bien Hoa in Cochin China. By midsummer, the agitation had spread to rural areas in the central provinces of Nghe An and Ha Tinh. In September, rioting peasants seized power in local villages, terrorized local officials, and incited by Communist activists, set up so-called soviets and in some cases distributed commune land to the poor. The French reacted swiftly, dispatching a unit of legionnaires to the rebellious districts and bombing a procession of angry peasants marching toward the provincial capital of Vinh. By the spring and summer of 1931, the revolt had been quelled, and thousands of participants, including most of the leadership of the Communist party, were in prison. To the Comintern leadership in Moscow, the so-called Nghe-Tinh revolt must have seemed the harbinger of revolution throughout Asia, as the impoverished masses rose to overthrow their colonial masters. If so, the hope was to be seriously disappointed. With most of their leadership dead or in prison and their apparatus within Vietnam a shambles due to government repression, the ICP and other radical nationalist parties were unable to pose a serious threat to French rule for a decade. The masses were quiet if sullen. For several years, the resistance movement in Vietnam came to a virtual standstill.

THE COMING OF WORLD WAR II

The precarious stability of the French colonial regime was brutally shattered by the Pacific crisis and the expansion of Japanese power into Southeast Asia at the end of the 1930s. Since early in the century, many

Japanese politicians had felt a mild proprietary interest in the anticolonial movements in Southeast Asia and particularly in Vietnam. Between 1905 and 1908, Japan had permitted Vietnamese and other Southeast Asian radical groups to establish headquarters in exile in Japan, and some politicians had implied that Tokyo might encourage revolutionary struggles for independence in colonial areas. In 1908, however, Japanese policy shifted when Tokyo reached an agreement with France and the United States on mutual spheres of influence in Asia, and radical organizations were ordered to leave Japan.

In the late 1930s, Japanese interest in Southeast Asia revived. Expansion into Soviet Siberia had been thwarted by the pact signed by Tokyo's ally Germany with the Soviet Union in August 1939. Plans for domination of China had been sidetracked by unexpectedly strong resistance from Chiang Kai-shek and his government, now holed up in its mountain capital of Chungking. Anxious to put the "China incident" to an end and lured by the promise of rich mineral resources in colonial Southeast Asia, Japanese military strategists in 1940 adopted a new southward strategy directed at incorporating the European colonies in Southeast Asia into a new Japanese-directed "Greater East Asia Co-prosperity Sphere."

The first impact of the new policy was felt in Indochina in the summer of 1940 when Tokyo demanded that the French government prohibit the shipment of goods to China from Tonkin and provide Japan with military and economic privileges in the northern provinces of Indochina. After some hesitation, during which time Governor-General Georges Catroux sought in vain the promise of military assistance from the United States to counter a possible Japanese invasion of the area, the colonial regime eventually acceded to the Japanese demands. By the summer of 1941, Japan had expanded its presence into Cochin China and, under the cover of the now intimidated French Vichy government, seized control of the area. The fiction of French sovereignty was temporarily retained, but in fact the Japanese had become masters of Indochina.

In the last analysis, the primary benefactors of the Japanese occupation of Indochina were the Communists. The nationalist parties were divided over how to respond to the new situation. A few, like the Vietnamese Nationalist party (VNQDD), which had been a significant force in Tonkin since 1927, declared their hostility to both the Japanese and to the French and maintained their headquarters for the duration in South China. Others, including several smaller nonviolent parties in Saigon and the Cao Dai sect, accepted Japanese promises to bestow independence on colonial peoples in Asia and decided to cooperate with the new rulers. For the Communists, there was no question that the Japanese, along with the French, were to be treated like an enemy. Indeed, to Ho Chi Minh, recently returned to the area after several years in the Soviet Union, the war and its consequences in Indochina represented a great opportunity. If, as Ho predicted, Japan went to war with the United States and eventually lost, its defeat could create a vacuum in Vietnam at the end of the war that the Communists might hope to fill before the arrival of Allied occupation forces to accept the surrender of Japanese troops.

In the spring of 1941, the ICP Central Committee met in a small mountain village near the Chinese border and inaugurated a new revolutionary strategy to seize power at the end of the Pacific war. The political centerpiece of the new strategy was the establishment of a new united front, called the League for the Independence of Vietnam, Vietminh for short. In order to attract patriotic elements from all social classes, the Communist direction of the new front would be disguised. Radical social issues, such as the nationalization of industry and the collectivization of agriculture, would be avoided, and a moderate program would be adopted calling for social reforms and democratic freedoms. The primary focus of the new front would be on the struggle for independence.

Supplementing the new political approach was a new military strategy. Borrowing from the experience of its fraternal party in China, the ICP turned to the strategy of people's war to mobilize support from peasants and workers, set up liberated base areas in isolated areas of the country, and then, through a combination of guerrilla tactics and popular uprisings, seize power in both rural and urban areas at the end of the war. For the next four years, the Communists painstakingly built up the new Vietminh Front in villages throughout North Vietnam. Guerrilla forces were created in the mountains adjacent to the Chinese border and, in 1944, the Vietminh leadership set up the first units of what would eventually become the Vietnamese Liberation Army.

In March 1945, the Japanese occupation authorities, suspicious of growing support for the Gaullist Free French movement among French civilian and military officials in Indochina, deposed the French colonial regime and granted a spurious independence to a pro-Japanese puppet government under Emperor Bao Dai. The Japanese coup improved Communist prospects for victory at war's end. Not only was the French regime now dismantled, but the Japanese did not bother to fill the vacuum left by the destruction of the French administrative apparatus in rural areas. Into that vacuum, the Vietminh would be free to move.

THE AUGUST REVOLUTION

On August 14, 1945, Japan surrendered to the Allies. At approximately that moment, the Communists appealed to their supporters to rise and seize power in Vietnam. Within two weeks, forces under the Vietminh Front had seized control of most rural villages and cities throughout the North, including Hanoi, where President Ho Chi Minh announced the formation of the Provisional Democratic Republic. In the Center, forces under Communist direction seized the imperial capital of Hue and compelled the abdication of Bao Dai. In Cochin China, the Vietminh combined with other nationalist parties in forming a Committee for the South, which claimed to voice the legitimate aspirations of the population.

It had been a masterful performance. With an army of only a few thousand poorly armed guerrillas, the Communists had seized control of most of the country under the noses of the Japanese occupation authorities. The keys to success, as Ho Chi Minh had pointed out to his colleagues, were the elements of initiative and surprise. Power would have to be seized in the interval between the surrender of the Japanese and the arrival of Allied expeditionary forces (the British in the South, the Nationalist Chinese in the North) as called for by the Potsdam conference in August. If the Vietminh could present the Allies with a fait accompli, the new provisional republican government might obtain recognition as the legitimate representative of the wishes of the Vietnamese people.

The Communists came within an eyelash of succeeding. The August Revolution was a brilliant success. In less than two weeks, the North and Center were almost entirely in Communist hands, in a virtually bloodless takeover. The Japanese were lured into taking a neutral attitude toward the situation, and the noncommunist nationalists, for the most part, were ineffective or still in South China. Only in Cochin China was the Vietminh forced to share power. Here, where the influence of moderate nationalism and the sects had been high since before the war, the Vietminh played an influential but not a dominant role in the Committee for the South.

In September, Allied occupation troops began to arrive in Vietnam. In the North, the Chinese military command had relatively little interest in the political situation and proved willing to deal with Ho Chi Minh's new government, although it pressed Ho to broaden its base by including in the cabinet members of rival nationalist parties. This Ho Chi Minh was willing to do, and in late autumn an agreement was reached calling for the formation of a coalition government with Ho as president and a prominent nationalist, Nguyen Hai Than, as vice-president. National elections were scheduled to be held in January 1946. In the meantime, at Ho Chi Minh's insistence, the social and economic policies of the new government were basically moderate—only major industries and utilities were nationalized, taxes were reduced, and a mild program of land reform was instituted.

The Communists were less successful in the South. Not only did local nationalist groups and French residents pose greater resistance to Vietminh domination of the new Committee for the South, but the commander of the British expeditionary forces, General Douglas Gracey, was sympathetic to the restoration of French colonial rule and, in defiance of the agreement at Potsdam to avoid intervention in the local political situation, disarmed the Vietminh and other nationalist groups and turned power over to the French, whose military units began to arrive in October. During the fall of 1945, the Vietminh were driven from the city into the countryside, where French troops gradually pacified most of the area and

Ho Chi Minh as president of the D.R.V. in 1946. The accompanying text is an appeal to the population to vote in the January elections for the new National Assembly. (Photo courtesy of *Vietnam* pictorial)

returned the villages to French administration. For the moment, local Vietminh forces were unable to counter French moves and were reduced to sporadic guerrilla action. In effect, within three months of the end of the war, Vietnam had been divided into two hostile zones—a Communist North and a French South. The ultimate shape of a generation of conflict had begun to take form.

For several months, the French and the Communist-dominated government in Hanoi attempted to avoid war. In March of 1946, Ho Chi Minh signed a preliminary agreement with the French representative in Indochina, Jean Sainteny, calling for French recognition of Vietnam as a "free state," with its own army, parliament, and finances. In return, the Vietnamese government would agree to accept a continuing French cultural, economic, and political presence in Vietnam and to join the projected French Union. French troops could be stationed in the North to protect French interests and residents. Because the two negotiators could not agree on whether to include Cochin China in the new free state, a plebiscite was called for to allow the local population to determine the future status of the colony. Ho Chi Minh had only with difficulty persuaded the party's Central Committee and the cabinet (which included a number of militantly anti-French nationalists) of the need for a compromise. In the end, however, Ho's arguments were undoubtedly persuasive. The Vietnamese government in Hanoi was now isolated on the global scene (the United States, which had earlier expressed some reservations about the return of the French, had now moved perceptibly toward the French position, while the Soviet Union, the Vietminh's major potential supporter, was preoccupied with events in Europe and inclined to counsel the ICP to moderation) and not yet strong enough to achieve its ultimate goal of independence by armed force. While a free state was considerably less than the Communists wanted, it would give them time to consolidate their strength and prepare for a further advance in the near future.

In June, full-scale negotiations began at Fontainebleau to work out remaining differences and reach a final settlement. By then, however, the preliminary agreement itself was in peril. Each side accused the other of bad faith, but the major source of difficulty emanated from Saigon, where hard-line elements within the colonial community, encouraged by the new high commissioner for Indochina, Admiral Thiérry d'Argenlieu (the new title replaced the prewar position of governor-general), set out to sabotage the Ho-Sainteny Agreement, which d'Argenlieu had publicly labeled a "Munich." In April, d'Argenlieu convened a separate conference consisting of pro-French and anticommunist elements in Cochin China in the mountain resort town of Dalat. Predictably, the conference rejected membership in the projected free state governed from Hanoi and declared its preference for the establishment of a separate republic of Cochin China that would make separate arrangements with Paris.

In the meantime, a new government had taken office in Paris that showed itself less receptive to a compromise in Indochina. When formal negotiations got under way at Fontainebleau in June, the French position had hardened. Despite pleas from Ho Chi Minh, who warned that failure to achieve an agreement would only strengthen the hand of militants in the Hanoi government, French delegates took a hard-line position at the talks, and in late summer the negotiations broke down and the Vietnamese delegation returned to Hanoi. Ho Chi Minh, convinced that the Vietminh was not yet strong enough to risk war, remained in Paris and in September signed a "modus vivendi" that called for a cease-fire and a resumption of talks early the following year.

During the fall it became increasingly apparent that war could not be avoided. As tensions rose, bloody clashes broke out in the North between local Vietnamese forces and French troops stationed in the area. Ho Chi Minh attempted to keep the channels of negotiation open while strengthening the Communist role in the government and ordering preparations for military conflict. In November, disagreement over control of customs authority led to a brutal French bombing of the native quarter at Haiphong. As incidents increased in December, the French military command in the North demanded that French troops be given responsibility for law and order. Convinced that war was unavoidable, the Vietminh launched a surprise attack on French installations in Hanoi on December 19. While local forces engaged in a holding operation, main force Vietminh units gradually withdrew to prepared base areas in the countryside and prepared to resume guerrilla war.

THE FIRST INDOCHINA WAR BEGINS

As the Franco-Vietminh conflict began, the Communists were not in an enviable position. Their military forces were small and lacked the firepower to pose a serious challenge to the French. Aid from their socialist allies would be limited. The U.S.S.R. was distant and more concerned over the prospects of a Communist government in Paris than those of a successful revolutionary struggle in far-off Indochina. The Chinese Communist party (CCP) was fully occupied in North China with its own civil war against the forces of Chiang Kai-shek. Even within Vietnam, the situation was ambiguous. Increasing evidence that the Communists were the dominant force behind the Vietminh Front and the D.R.V. had alienated many moderates and made them reluctant to support the front in its struggle against French colonialism. In an effort to take advantage of this situation, the French negotiated with ex-Emperor Bao Dai (in late summer 1945, he had, with some reluctance, caved in to Vietminh pressure and abdicated the throne, accepting in its stead the sinecure of supreme political adviser to the provisional republican government) to accept the position of chief of state in a new French-supported "Associated State of Vietnam." In 1949, Bao Dai accepted this arrangement, although, according to the Elysée agreements, the new state possessed only limited powers. Vital issues dealing with both internal and foreign policy remained in the hands of the French. The "Bao Dai solution" did provide an alternative to Ho Chi Minh's government, but most nationalists viewed it as simply a creation of French colonialism.

During 1947, the Vietminh were reduced to a struggle for sheer survival. Guerrilla units hid in the mountains of the Viet Bac, or in the Central Highlands or Plain of Reeds further to the south, while the party leadership urgently concentrated on building up the strength of the revolutionary forces. By 1948, Vietminh strategists felt sufficiently confident to move cautiously into highly populated lowland areas, to intensify recruitment efforts, and to launch sporadic attacks on French military outposts and exposed villages and district towns. Gradually, Vietminh forces were beginning to approach parity in numbers with the French.

VIETNAM ENTERS THE COLD WAR

The year 1949 was of pivotal significance for the future course for the war. On the battlefield, signs of stalemate were beginning to appear. The momentum of French military attacks on Vietminh strongholds was beginning to ebb, and French military strategy increasingly concentrated on protecting populated areas from Communist attacks. Public support for the war in France was beginning to slacken, and voices calling for an end to the war were on the increase. On the other hand, the Vietminh, although undoubtedly stronger than at the beginning of the conflict, still lacked the firepower to pose a significant military threat to French rule in Vietnam. Moreover, the formation of the Bao Dai government had weakened the Vietminh claim to represent the legitimate national interest of the Vietnamese people. While the Associated State hardly attracted enthusiastic support in nationalist circles, it did provide a potential alternative to Ho Chi Minh's movement, which was now increasingly viewed as dominated by the Communists.

Under such circumstances, both sides groped for a breakthrough that would give them an advantage in the lengthening conflict. For the Vietminh, the Communist victory in China in the fall of 1949 brought a surge of optimism through the party's ranks. Since before the Pacific war, the CCP had given some assistance to its Vietnamese comrades. During the civil war in China, however, ties were limited. But the victory of the forces of Mao Tse-tung in the fall of 1949 raised hopes for a vast increase in Chinese support for the Communist cause in Vietnam. The following January, Vo Nguyen Giap, commander of Vietminh forces and a top party member, traveled secretly to Peking for arms aid talks with the new People's Republic of China, and two months later Ho Chi Minh signed a formal agreement providing for Chinese military assistance to the Vietminh. The P.R.C. formally recognized the D.R.V. as the sole legitimate government in Vietnam. A few days later, the Soviet Union followed suit.

Preparations to take advantage of the new opportunity were soon in evidence. During the summer of 1950, French intelligence reported an ominous buildup of Vietminh forces along the Chinese border. In the fall, the insurgents launched a major offensive against French border posts in the area. The attack resulted in the first major French defeat of the war. The French decided to abandon a string of bases along the frontier and concede Vietminh control over the entire Viet Bac, thus giving the Vietminh easy access to China and possession of a liberated base area adjacent to the densely populated and strategically critical Red River delta. Any hopes that the French had of destroying Vietminh power were now virtually eliminated.

The French response to the heightened threat from the Vietminh was to seek increased aid from the United States. Since the end of World War II, the Truman administration had stayed aloof from the conflict in Vietnam. At first, admiration for Ho Chi Minh and for the Vietminh as an anti-Japanese guerrilla force and traditional antipathy to French colonialism had made some Americans (including a number of military officials on the spot) sympathetic to the Vietminh cause. The Truman administration was unwilling to risk antagonizing or weakening the French, however, and refrained from placing pressure on Paris to abandon its claim to Indochina. By 1947, the Communist complexion of Ho's government had become increasingly apparent, and sympathy gradually gave way to hostility. Still, it was viewed as a French, not an American, problem.

The rise of the Cold War in Europe and concern over the regional impact of a Communist victory in China began to change minds in Washington. In 1950, the administration approved a military assistance program for Indochina. Although the bulk of the aid was designed to go to the Vietnamese National Army, recently created by Paris as a means of transferring some of the burden of the war from France to the Vietnamese, at French insistence U.S. aid was channeled through the French. U.S. officials expressed some vocal criticism of the French failure to perfect Vietnamese independence under the Bao Dai government but refrained from exerting strong pressure on Paris for fear that the French would abandon what was now increasingly viewed as a Cold War struggle between the forces of communism and those of the free world.

The indirect entry of China and the United States into the Franco-Vietminh conflict not only brought the struggle into the vortex of the Cold War but also led to an increasing militarization of the war. In early 1951, Vietminh forces, now strengthened by rising quantities of arms from China, launched a major military offensive against French posts on the fringes of the Red River delta with the apparent hope of breaking through to Hanoi. Vo Nguyen Giap, however, had underestimated the resourcefulness and determination of the new French military commander in Indochina, General de Lattre de Tassigny. De Lattre, who had won respect for his military prowess during World War II, had been appointed high commissioner and commander in chief of French military forces in Indochina in December 1950. Newly arrived when the Vietminh offensive broke, de Lattre reacted quickly, ordering air strikes against advancing Vietminh troops and transferring units from other areas to the beleaguered city of Vinh Yen, in the upper Red River delta. De Lattre's action salvaged the situation for the French and blunted the force of the Vietminh attack. Later offensives north and south of Hanoi had no greater success, and by spring, the Vietminh had abandoned their campaign.

NEGOTIATIONS AT GENEVA

For the next two years, Vietminh strategists avoided the risk of open confrontation with French units in Indochina, preferring instead to launch small-scale attacks on isolated French posts in the Northwest, in Laos, and in the Central Highlands. Such tactics were hardly a recipe for total victory, but they permitted the Vietminh time to build up its forces for a future offensive in lowland areas. Moreover, by maintaining pressure on the battlefield, Vietminh strategists hoped to provoke growing public discontent in France with the war. The logjam began to break in the fall of 1953. For years, the French had spurned Ho Chi Minh's offer of peace talks. Now officials in Paris sought not to win the war but to find an honorable way to end it. When government sources in Paris suggested a negotiated settlement to end the conflict, Ho Chi Minh responded. In a November interview with the Swedish newspaper *Expressen*, he declared a willingness to explore proposals for peace with the French. Early the following year, the two sides agreed to discuss the Indochina issue at an international conference to be held at Geneva in May. Joining the French, the Bao Dai government, and the Vietminh at the conference table would be representatives of the great powers, including the P.R.C., the Soviet Union, Great Britain, and the United States, as well as representatives from Vietnam's neighbor states in Indochina, the kingdoms of Laos and Cambodia.

The D.R.V. attitude toward a negotiated settlement has long been a matter of dispute. It has frequently been asserted that the Vietnamese were pressured to come to the conference table by the Soviets and the Chinese, each anxious for its own reasons to end the conflict. There is probably some truth to this contention. Information from several sources confirms that many party leaders were unhappy at the decision to accept a compromise settlement. Realism, however, prevailed. Not only would the Vietminh find it difficult to achieve a military victory without active Soviet and Chinese diplomatic and material support, but without a settlement, U.S. military intervention was likely. The ever practical Ho Chi Minh probably persuaded his colleagues that a compromise settlement was the best that could be hoped for at the moment. The Vietminh did not enter the negotiations from a position of military weakness; on the eve of the conference, after a six-week siege, the French post at Dien Bien Phu in the mountainous Northwest fell to a Communist assault. The Vietminh attack had been made possible by massive shipments of arms from China; it is probable that such aid was Ho Chi Minh's price for accepting negotiations.

With their morale drained by the long conflict and the tragic fall of Dien Bien Phu on the eve of the conference, the French had no heart for continuing the war, and in June Pierre Mendès-France became prime minister on a pledge to bring the conflict to an end within thirty days. A month later, French and D.R.V. representatives agreed on a cease-fire dividing Vietnam into two separate regroupment zones, the Vietminh in the North, the French and the supporters of the Bao Dai government in the South, with the two zones divided at the Ben Hai River, on the seventeenth parallel. Vietnam was to be neutralized, and neither zone was permitted to join a military alliance. The size of the military forces in the two zones was to be restricted to existing levels, and an International Control Commission (ICC), composed of Canada, India, and Poland, was to supervise the provisions of the agreement.

Neither the D.R.V. nor the Bao Dai government, however, was willing to accept a permanent division of the country into two separate states divided by ideology. To resolve that problem, the conference delegates drew up a political accord declaring that the cease-fire line was a provisional one and "should not in any way be interpreted as constituting a political or territorial boundary." The agreement called for general elections to be held in both zones in July 1956 in order to obtain an expression of the national popular will on the issue of the future of Vietnam. Consultations on such elections were to be held between representatives of the two zones in July 1955.

The Geneva Conference settlement was designed to permit an honorable withdrawal of the French from Indochina, to remove the area from the arena of great power competition, and to permit a political settlement of the crisis. Only the first goal was attained. One reason for this was the attitude of the United States. The Eisenhower administration had been reluctant to take part in the negotiations from the beginning. Secretary of State John Foster Dulles had attempted to persuade Great Britain and France to join with the United States in a grand alliance to fight and win the war, but London and Paris preferred to await the results of the Geneva Conference. Washington had then agreed to participate in the talks with some reluctance. At Geneva, Dulles reluctantly acceded to the division of Vietnam into separate zones but made it clear that the United States could not accept a solution that provided for the possibility of a total takeover of Vietnam by the Communists. Unhappy with the provisions of the political accords, Secretary Dulles indicated that Washington could take no more responsibility for the conference. In the end, the United States refused to sign, or even verbally consent to, the political accords, and the U.S. delegation merely "took note" of the accords and promised "to refrain from the threat or use of force to disturb them." It reiterated its position that the unity of Vietnam should be sought through elections supervised by the United States.

Agreements on Laos and Cambodia settled the conflicts in those areas and established the independence of the new royal governments in those countries. In Laos, the Communist Pathet Lao movement allied with the Vietminh was granted two provinces in northeastern Laos as a regroupment zone, and the two sides were instructed to negotiate a political settlement to integrate the Pathet Lao area into the royal Lao administration. The small Communist movement in Cambodia, popularly named the Khmer Rouge (Red Khmer), received no recognition or regroupment zone, and the final agreement simply called for the departure of foreign troops from Cambodian soil.

In later years, the failure to activate the political provisions of the Geneva Agreements understandably was the source of considerable controversy with respect to the issue of responsibility for the later resumption of the conflict. Some blamed the accords themselves for their vagueness and legal ambiguity. Did the accords specifically require that national elections promised by the ICC be carried out? Was the Government of Vietnam (G.V.N.), which had publicly indicated its disagreement with several of the provisions and would later refuse to be held to them, legally bound to carry out the political protocol? Had in fact the conference really intended elections to take place, or was the political protocol merely a

polite fiction (as some U.S. observers contended) to save the face of the
D.R.V.? To what degree was the United States bound by the accords?
Indeed, if the United States was not bound by them, how could the area
be isolated from the Cold War?

This is not the place for a definitive evaluation of the accords and
their legal standing, but a few brief points are in order. There is no doubt
that the ambiguity of the agreement sowed the seeds of future disagreements
and ultimately led to renewed conflict. Under the circumstances, however,
it may well have been the only way to end the war and indeed to avoid
a widening conflict. It is often the essence of diplomacy to use ambiguity
in order to obtain an agreement that otherwise would not be possible.
The French were willing to depart but would not have been willing to
accept a total defeat. The Communists were willing to accept a compromise
but not to give up all their objectives. The United States had threatened
to take matters into its own hands if not satisfied that the negotiations
provided an opportunity for the development of a Vietnam free from
Communist control. Although the results, from Washington's standpoint,
were not entirely satisfactory, the Eisenhower administration appeared
willing to live with them. In such circumstances, the agreement was a
gamble that with the removal of foreign troops and the establishment of
cease-fire, political factors would take effect and lead to an internal solution.
That they did not is less an indication of the failure of the delegates than
a measure of the depth of the ideological and political bitterness that had
marked the conflict from its earliest years and would continue to fan the
fire of discontent well into the future.

4

A Nation Divided

The Geneva Agreement did not end the Vietnamese conflict. It merely served as a watershed between two phases of the conflict—the anticolonial and anti-French phase before 1954 and the civil war and the anti-American phase afterward. The political and ideological chasm between the two sides was probably too deep and too bitter to be resolved through a purely political solution. To make it worse, the Vietnam question had now increasingly become a part of the Cold War and could not be resolved without affecting, in one way or another, the interests of the great powers and the international power balance. If and when the conflict resumed, it would do so on a more intense and dangerous level.

In the South, the Geneva Agreements led to the departure of the French and their replacement by the United States. During the negotiations in Geneva, John Foster Dulles had stated at a press conference in Washington that once the accords had been concluded, the United States could begin to help build up the noncommunist regimes in South Vietnam, Laos, and Cambodia. Although the U.S. attitude toward the projected national elections was apparently somewhat ambiguous, there is little doubt that policymakers in Washington soon came to view the new Government of Vietnam in the South as a keystone in the emerging U.S. strategy for the defense of Southeast Asia from communist aggression and feared the possibility of a Communist victory in those elections. Washington's options were limited. The two zones of Vietnam, plus Laos and Cambodia, were prohibited from joining alliances and limited in the size of their military force levels. The United States could thus not formally incorporate the new noncommunist states into the defense alliance system formed at Manila in September, the Southeast Asia Treaty Organization (SEATO). To circumvent this legal restriction, the SEATO pact members created a so-called umbrella clause, according to which the three noncommunist Indochinese states could be protected by the provisions of the alliance even though they were not officially members of the organization.

THE DIEM REGIME

The de facto integration of the G.V.N. into the SEATO alliance system was only a formal confirmation of the fact that the United States was now committed to stabilizing the situation in South Vietnam in an effort to create a viable state that could halt the further expansion of communism in Indochina. For the moment, the nature of that effort would be primarily political. The key to success, above all, would depend on Washington's ability to locate new political leadership that could provide a measure of stability and direction and the basis for the rise of a strong and viable new noncommunist society in the South. Bao Dai, the new chief of state, was considered to be lacking in competence, too pro-French, and tainted by his imperial past. Francophile elements in Saigon were viewed as hopelessly addicted to the characteristic French political disease of factionalism and lacking an adequate commitment to nationalism and democracy. To save South Vietnam, a new political leadership with a strong commitment to a noncommunist nationalism would be required.

The result of that effort was the emergence of Ngo Dinh Diem. Descended from an elite family with connections at the old imperial court in Hue, Diem had been active in Vietnamese politics prior to the Pacific war and had briefly served in Bao Dai's first cabinet in 1933 as minister of the interior. Diem was viscerally anti-French, however, and resented Bao Dai's willingness to collaborate with the colonial regime; he had resigned his position after a few months and refused further cooperation with the emperor. Diem, a devout Catholic and an admirer of Confucianism, was equally opposed to the Communists. He refused an offer by Ho Chi Minh in 1945 to cooperate with the Vietminh and during the Franco-Vietminh conflict abstained from involvement with either government, spending much of the war abroad, including a stay at a Catholic seminary in the United States. Here he came to the attention of the Eisenhower administration.

It would be too much to describe Diem as a creature of the United States. Diem was headstrong and independent and noted for his integrity and dedication to Vietnamese nationalism. But it is clear that he was appointed prime minister in the summer of 1954 primarily as a result of U.S. pressure on Bao Dai. Diem's contempt for Bao Dai and the pro-French politicans around the head of state led quickly to mutual antipathy, and in 1955 he arranged for a plebiscite between the two of them for chief of state. In the vote, in which there was considerable suspicion that Diem's supporters had stuffed the ballot boxes, he won an overwhelming victory.

Diem also moved decisively against the sects and other pressure groups that might challenge his authority and soon centralized power in his own hands. At first, the Eisenhower administration took an ambivalent view of Diem's hard-line approach to his potential political rivals and appeared nervous that he would alienate important sectors of Vietnamese opinion. On the other hand, the vigor of his efforts earned admiration, and by late 1955, Washington was firmly on his side. Because of the new restrictions on military force levels and foreign involvement, the U.S. commitment was a limited one, contained in a personal letter dated October 1, 1954, from President Eisenhower to Diem. In that letter, Eisenhower promised assistance to help the G.V.N. in "developing and maintaining a strong, viable state, capable of resisting subversion or aggression through military means." It was qualified by the statement that the United States would expect that the aid "would be met by performance on the part of the Government of Vietnam in undertaking needed reforms."

President Eisenhower's letter to Diem had emphasized the U.S. desire to see the creation of a strong and viable state in South Vietnam. There had been considerable pessimism in U.S. intelligence circles regarding the capacity of the Saigon government to survive a concerted onslaught by the Communists in the postwar period, and Diem's rapid and vigorous assertion of power was gratifying. Yet more would be needed to transform South Vietnam into a bastion of the free world than mere force. Diem would need to establish a regime able to respond to the collective aspirations of the population and to earn international recognition as a legitimate representative of Vietnamese nationalism. And he would have to move with dispatch to resolve some of the social and economic problems that had plagued Vietnam since before the imposition of French rule nearly a century earlier. To assist him in this effort, U.S. advisers were sent to Vietnam to help the new regime in building a political system based on democratic Western traditions. A constitution was approved calling for the creation of a political system based on a combination of the presidential and parliamentary models.

Diem, of course, remained president. During the next few years, he continued to consolidate his control. As a mainstay of his regime, he relied to a considerable degree on the 2 million Catholics in the South, and many were selected for positions of influence and responsibility within the government. Catholic villages (Catholics composed more than two-thirds of the approximately 900,000 refugees who fled south after the Geneva Agreements) were built in the suburbs of Saigon to provide the capital with a protective belt against possible attack by Communists in the countryside. Others were settled in Rural Development Centers established in the piedmont areas adjacent to the Central Highlands. To maintain loyalty to the regime, Diem's brother Ngo Dinh Nhu was charged with setting up Leninist-style progovernment organizations such as the secret Can Lao (Personalist Labor) party and mass front organizations to enlist the support and participation of the population. To strengthen the government's hold over rural villages, the tradition of local autonomy in electing village officials was abolished and village leaders were appointed by and responsible to the central government.

Through such techniques, Diem attempted to consolidate his control over the government in the South in order to begin to tackle the deeper and more intractable problems in the economy. Arguably, the most serious problem was the unequal distribution of arable land. Policies adopted under the colonial regime had resulted in the concentration of land in the rich Mekong Delta in the hands of a few landlords, many of them absentee owners living in Saigon and charging exorbitant rents to their tenants. According to generally accepted statistics, throughout the country as a whole, 2.5 percent of all landowners owned approximately 50 percent of all the cultivable land. Some of this land had been confiscated and distributed to poor peasants in areas where the Vietminh had established a revolutionary administration before the Geneva Conference. After peace was restored, the landlords returned and seized their land, often charging the peasants back rents. With U.S. assistance, Diem launched a land reform program to reduce inequities in land holdings and to win the support of the rural population. The program, however, was faulty both in design and in implementation. In many cases, peasants were asked to buy land that had previously been given to them under Vietminh occupation. In others, landlords ignored provisions in the law restricting rents to 25 percent of the crop and continued to charge high rents, with peasants too intimidated to protest. Most damaging of all was that the government program was not sufficiently rigorous. Landlords were allowed to retain up to 100 hectares (about 250 acres) of rice land under their ownership—in a society where the average peasant holding was less than one hectare. In the end, less than one-third of the land that had been earmarked for transfer was actually purchased by the peasants.

By the end of the decade, the promise engendered by the early years of the Diem regime had rapidly dissipated. Although a man of personal integrity and decency, Diem found it difficult to act as the head of a democratic government. Intolerant of criticism, Diem, with the active assistance of his brother Nhu, cracked down on all potential sources of opposition within South Vietnamese society. Newspapers were censored and politicians hostile to the regime were harassed and sometimes arrested. Diem was particularly fearful of the Communists. A "denounce the Communists" campaign was inaugurated, and roving tribunals moved from village to village seeking out those guilty of collaboration with the Vietminh. Many of those tried and convicted of treasonous activities may actually have been followers of the Communists (several thousand had remained in the South to maintain the revolutionary apparatus), but there were widespread reports that the campaign suffered from corruption and that many innocent Vietnamese were forced to pay bribes to avoid prosecution or were falsely accused by others seeking personal revenge.

The regime's heavy-handed suppression of all resistance and its intolerance of potential sources of opposition soon led to widespread alienation. Southerners resented alleged domination over society by northern and central Vietnamese; the sects and the mountain minorities resented Saigon's efforts to place their areas under the administrative control of the central government; the overseas Chinese resented attempts to compel them to adopt Vietnamese citizenship; Saigon intellectuals disapproved of the regime's suppression of free speech; peasants were antagonized by the false promises of the land reform program; and Buddhists resented Diem's policy of favoring the nation's minority Catholic population. In effect, Diem's potential base of support among the population was gradually eroded; increasingly he, and his regime, were isolated.

THE SECOND INDOCHINA WAR BEGINS

After the close of the Geneva Conference in 1954, there was strong concern in Saigon and in Washington that the Communists would shortly resume the revolutionary war to complete their takeover of all of Vietnam. In fact, contrary to general belief at the time, the Communists had no intention of resuming the revolutionary struggle in South Vietnam, at least in the years immediately following the restoration of peace. In the first place, the party needed time to recover from the war and to begin the long and arduous march to socialism in the North. The final months of the war, including the attack at Dien Bien Phu and related attacks in Laos and in the Central Highlands, had been costly and exhausting, and it would undoubtedly take time before the Vietminh armed forces and the new "rear base" in the North could be transformed into an effective instrument for the liberation of the South. An equally persuasive reason for avoiding an early return to military conflict was the attitude of the D.R.V.'s foreign allies. Both Moscow and Peking, each for its own reasons, had been anxious to end the struggle in Indochina. The new post-Stalin Soviet leadership under Nikita Khrushchev wished to minimize the risks of military confrontation with the United States and to put competition on a new economic, political, and ideological basis. China had embarked on a major effort to modernize the economy and needed time to prepare for socialist construction. A resumption of war in Vietnam would threaten the security of China and could force it into a direct confrontation with the United States. It is likely that both Moscow and Peking warned Hanoi that their support would be limited if war resumed.

Given such circumstances, it seems probable that the Communist leadership in Hanoi placed its hopes in the mechanism created by the Geneva Accords, which called for unification through elections in 1956. Although it is not improbable that there was some skepticism in Hanoi that the elections would ever take place (there were frequent references in the world press to the possibility that Saigon would refuse to hold consultations as called for by the accords), D.R.V. leaders adopted a public attitude of optimism that the provisions of the Geneva Accords would be adhered to. If not, party strategists appeared to believe that, given the intrinsic weakness of the noncommunist nationalist forces in Vietnam, the Saigon regime would collapse of its own accord or be compelled to accept a coalition government that would include the Communists and their supporters. To handle such contingencies, the party left a small apparatus of supporters in South Vietnam to prepare for elections, for political agitation, or for the possibility of a return to armed struggle. The remainder, perhaps numbering between 50,000 and 100,000, went to the North. Many were youths, often the sons and daughters of Vietminh supporters who, on arrival in the North, were enrolled in cadre schools, where they were trained in guerrilla and propaganda techniques for a possible future return to the South.

In the summer of 1955, Ngo Dinh Diem announced that the Saigon government would not hold consultations on elections with the D.R.V., claiming that any elections held in the North would not be fair and, furthermore, that as the G.V.N. had not signed the accords, it could not be held responsible for them. The Eisenhower administration, although somewhat concerned at the possible propaganda backlash from such an outright refusal to abide by the agreement, supported Diem's position. Saigon's refusal to hold talks on elections did not immediately change Communist strategy toward the South, and for the next few years, D.R.V. leaders in Hanoi continued to take the official position that a peaceful solution to the problem of national unification needed to be found. For the moment, no major shift in strategy took place, and the slogan of the day was to "build the North, and look to the South."

But as the new decade approached, two related factors combined to force a reappraisal of this position. First, the efforts of Diem's security forces to eradicate the Communist menace in the South led to heavy losses of personnel and in some key areas to the virtual destruction of the revolutionary apparatus. Second, it was becoming increasingly clear that Diem's policies were creating serious discontent among key groups in the South. By the late 1950s, local party leaders in the South were pleading to the central leadership in Hanoi that Saigon was ripe for the plucking if only the party would take the lead in focusing the unrest. Otherwise, the revolutionary movement might be too weakened by Diem's repressive policies to take action.

In early 1959, the Central Committee, after several months of hesitation, approved a policy calling for a more active strategy in the South. Party leaders were still reluctant to return to armed struggle, not only because they were not certain that it was required, but also out of concern over the possible U.S. reaction. To avoid provoking Washington, a policy combining political activity with low-level armed struggle was adopted. The key was to use the "political force of the masses" in demonstrations and protests against G.V.N. policies. In selective cases, assassination of "enemies of the people" was approved, while intensive efforts began to build up the revolutionary forces for a possible return to war.

One way to minimize the risk of U.S. involvement, and to maximize the revolutionary appeal in the South, was to disguise the leading role of the Communists and of Hanoi in the movement. For that reason, a maximum effort would be needed to give the impression that the movement was composed of and directed by southerners. In actuality, the movement would be directed from Hanoi. To provide such guidance, several party officials of Central Committee rank were assigned to direct the movement in the South and to communicate periodically with the Politburo. To provide additional direction, a number of southerners who had been trained in the D.R.V. after Geneva were infiltrated into the G.V.N. to serve as leading cadres in the movement.

To create the vehicle for the new insurgency movement, the party turned to the technique that had been used with such success against the French. A broad alliance called the National Front for the Liberation of South Vietnam (NLF) was established in the winter of 1960-1961. The presidium of the front was to be composed of representatives of a wide variety of groups opposed to the Diem regime in the South, including peasants, workers, intellectuals, the sects, the Buddhists, and the mountain minorities. There was no hint of northern involvement in the new organization, and its program, carefully avoiding any identification with Marxist doctrine, stressed such popular concerns as democratic freedoms, "land to the tiller," independence (from U.S. imperialist domination), and a policy of neutrality leading to peaceful unification with the North.

In general, the party's strategy was relatively successful. During the early 1960s, the Diem regime, under the pressure of rising political discontent and a series of low-level attacks by the revolutionary forces (labeled by the Saigon regime the Viet Cong, or Vietnamese Communists), continued to weaken. Characteristically, Saigon overreacted. In an effort to increase government control over rural villages and thus dry up the sea in which the guerrilla fish must swim, the G.V.N. forced unwilling peasants to leave their home villages and to settle in so-called agrovilles, development centers in rural areas to concentrate the rural population in a secure area and provide the basis for sustained economic growth. The crackdown on all forms of political opposition against the Diem regime was intensified, particularly in the cities, increasing the restiveness of the country and leading to an abortive coup launched by rebellious elements in the armed forces.

But if the Communists had correctly foreseen the growing weakness of the Diem regime, they were less perceptive in their estimate of the U.S. reaction. Hanoi had hoped that Diem could be overthrown without increased U.S. involvement. But the new Kennedy administration, which had come into office in January 1961, did not follow the Communist script. Anxious to impress the Kremlin leadership with an image of U.S. toughness after the Bay of Pigs fiasco in Cuba, Kennedy deliberately chose to adopt a tough stand in Vietnam even while recognizing the growing weakness of the Diem regime. During Kennedy's first year in office, several high-level officials from the new administration visited South Vietnam to evaluate the situation on the spot and discuss future strategy with Vietnamese leaders. By the winter of 1961-1962, Kennedy had committed the United States to increase aid to the Saigon regime, but only on condition that Diem's own performance improve.

A crucial element in the Kennedy strategy was the adoption of a new approach to the growing insurgency in South Vietnam. Where the Eisenhower administration had tended to interpret the threat to the G.V.N. primarily in terms of a possible armed attack across the demilitarized zone similar to what had taken place a decade earlier in Korea (thus leading to the assumption that the South Vietnamese armed forces—Army of the Republic of Vietnam [ARVN]—should be organized in conventional main force units), leading elements in the Kennedy administration countered that Saigon needed to adopt a counterinsurgency strategy to deal with the problem of a local war waged by guerrillas at the village level. The plan called for a breakdown of ARVN forces into smaller units trained in counterguerrilla techniques in order to protect the rural population from the insurgency. The keystone of the program was the so-called strategic hamlet. Similar in concept to the agrovilles but smaller in scope, the strategic hamlets were to be based on existing village organizations, which were to be strengthened to provide security against Communist attacks. In order to provide guidance in carrying out the new program and to boost South Vietnamese morale, the Kennedy administration also approved an increase in the number of U.S. advisers in South Vietnam. By 1963, the number of Americans in South Vietnam had risen to more than 15,000.

In theory, the Kennedy program was well conceived and sensitive to the realities of the situation in Vietnam. It had corrected past misconceptions of the nature of the war and attempted to fashion a new approach that dealt with the real threat from within the country. It attempted to provide assistance and guidance to the Saigon government without actually Americanizing the war (a proposal to introduce a division of U.S. combat troops was rejected by the president). It focused on the need of the Diem regime to improve its own capacity to deal with the threat of insurgency and to meet the needs of the population. But the program could be effective only if the Saigon regime demonstrated its ability and willingness to carry it out. In fact, this was the weakest link in the entire program. In the early 1960s, the Diem regime became increasingly isolated from the population. As opposition grew, the government reacted with ferocity. Harassment of the opposition was intensified, and several anti-Diem figures were arrested. In rural areas, the strategic hamlet program was characterized by corruption, official arrogance, and sloppy execution and soon ran into difficulties. Peasants were frequently forced to join the new organizations against their will and to provide labor without compensation. The new hamlets were often just existing villages surrounded by barbed wire.

Security was difficult to maintain, and many were attacked and destroyed several times by insurgency forces. By 1963, the program, initially worrisome to the Communists, had lost momentum and was being widely criticized.

By the summer of 1963, the Diem regime was beginning to disintegrate. Alleged government favoritism to Catholics had alienated Buddhist elements, and public protests, sometimes organized by professional Buddhist associations in Hue and Saigon, were put down with brutality by the police. Unrest even reached into the upper ranks of the armed forces, where plotting against the government reached epidemic levels. In Washington, the Kennedy administration was increasingly dismayed at the rapid deterioration of the Saigon regime and warned Diem that U.S. support could not continue unless the situation improved. Diem responded by expelling U.S. reporters whose accounts of conditions in the South were increasingly critical and by threatening to make a separate peace with the Communists.

By now, many policymakers in Washington were convinced that the war could not be won unless Diem was replaced. When in late summer dissident elements within the armed forces privately queried U.S. officials in Saigon as to whether the United States would support an overthrow of the Diem regime, Washington, after some hesitation, gave an affirmative answer. Although the administration did not wish to become openly involved in a coup, it promised privately that it would support a new government that would agree to continue the war effort. In November, a coup launched by several high-ranking military officers overthrew the Diem regime. Diem refused an offer of asylum at the U.S. Embassy and, with his brother Nhu, sought refuge in Saigon's neighboring city of Cholon. When his hideout was discovered, he surrendered but was executed with his brother on the way back to Saigon.

Washington's decision to support the coup d'état against the Diem regime represented a gamble that a new government would be able to unite the country more effectively against the threat of the insurgency. In the beginning, there was a glimmer of hope. A Military Revolutionary Council was formed under the leadership of a popular general of southern origin, General Duong Van "Big" Minh. The new government was greeted with an outburst of popular enthusiasm by a populace relieved at the fall of the increasingly detested Diem regime. The new regime rejected overtures from the Communists to explore a negotiated peace and declared its determination to continue the struggle against the insurgent forces in cooperation with the United States.

But the buoyant optimism soon evaporated. Duong Van Minh, although affable and personally popular, appeared to lack leadership ability, and the new government soon fell prey to internal squabbling and factionalism. Violent riots between Catholic and Buddhist groups erupted in the streets of Saigon. In the field, combat operations suffered as military commanders, responding uneasily to the chaos in Saigon, refrained from aggressive operations against the insurgent forces.

The Communist leadership in Hanoi reacted to the overthrow of the Diem regime with caution. Uncertain of the intentions of the new government in Saigon, it tentatively offered negotiations. When these were rejected, it increased military pressure in the countryside to test the mettle of its new adversary. By December, it had become apparent that the new regime intended to pursue the struggle with continued and perhaps enhanced support from Washington. At a plenary session that month, the Central Committee approved a proposal to escalate the level of conflict in the South in the hope that the new Saigon government could be toppled rapidly before it was stabilized with U.S. help. The level of infiltration from the North was significantly increased, and in 1964, the first main force units of the People's Army of Vietnam (PAVN) began to stream south. For the first time, the struggle in the South began to take on the signs of an open military confrontation. Hanoi's main risk was that a further deterioration of security in the South would lead to increased U.S. involvement, something that neither Hanoi nor its allies in Moscow and Peking desired. In a circular to other communist parties, the Central Committee contended that U.S. intervention was improbable, but worth risking.

The rising level of Communist activity led to a further crumbling of the G.V.N. position in the South and to growing concern in Washington. The military council of "Big" Minh fell and was replaced by a series of short-lived regimes composed of military officers or civilian politicians. Reflecting the anarchy in Saigon, security in rural areas deteriorated, and by the winter of 1964-1965 most of the countryside was in Communist hands. U.S. officials in Saigon were predicting that without significantly increased U.S. involvement, South Vietnam would fall in less than a year.

It was the misfortune of President Lyndon Johnson, who assumed office in November 1963 after the assassination of John Kennedy, to be faced with the problem that had been feared by three of his predecessors: What should be done if the Saigon regime could not hold? Party leaders in Hanoi hoped and predicted that, faced with a deteriorating situation, the United States would withdraw its advisers or negotiate a settlement, as it had done in China in the late 1940s, in Korea in 1953, and in Laos in 1962. Yet here, as in 1959 and 1960, Hanoi had misread U.S. intentions. Unlike his predecessor, Lyndon Johnson apparently gave little serious consideration to the possibility of a U.S. pullout and reacted to the crisis by raising the level of U.S. involvement. In August 1964, on the pretext of a North Vietnamese attack on U.S. naval craft off the North Vietnamese coast, Johnson ordered air attacks on Communist military installations along the northern coast and then requested a resolution from both houses of Congress giving him the right to take action to protect U.S. forces in the area.

Armed with the powers provided by the Tonkin Gulf Resolution, Johnson now responded vigorously to the deteriorating situation by ex-

Tanks rumbling through downtown Saigon during an abortive effort to overthrow the government in February 1965. (By Wilbur E. Garrett, © 1965 National Geographic Society)

panding the U.S. military role in the conflict in South Vietnam. When insurgent units attacked a U.S. advisers' camp at Pleiku, killing several U.S. servicemen, the administration announced a program of retaliatory bombing of vital targets in North Vietnam. Eventually this policy of tit-for-tat attacks turned into a series of sustained bombing raids throughout the North under the name Operation Rolling Thunder. American dependents were evacuated, and during the spring and summer, U.S. military units began to arrive in South Vietnam and for the first time took part in combat operations against insurgency forces in the Central Highlands and along the central coast. The primary objective of the U.S. units, according to the strategy of the commander, General William Westmoreland, was to undertake "search and destroy" operations to blunt the momentum of the insurgency and to drive the guerrillas back from the lowland villages into the mountains and along the frontier, thus depriving them of recruits and provisions. In the meantime, ARVN forces could be released for pacification operations to secure local areas and clean out pockets of guerrillas in the heavily populated provinces in the Mekong Delta and along the central coast.

Critics charged that Johnson, by approving an escalation of U.S.

Civilian and military leaders in Saigon at the height of the instability in early 1965. At the far left in the front row is General Nguyen Van Thieu, soon to become president of South Vietnam. Second from right is General William West- moreland, commander of U.S. forces in Vietnam. Behind Westmoreland is General Nguyen Cao Ky. (By Wilbur E. Garrett © 1965 National Geographic Society)

military involvement, had ignored the primarily political character of the war. Administration spokesmen retorted that they were only responding to a military escalation already undertaken in the South by Hanoi. Both sides had now decided that success on the battlefield would have a lot to do with determining the political realities in South Vietnam. Washington policymakers were not blind to the importance of political factors, however, and were aware that the determination, cohesiveness, and capacity for leadership of the G.V.N. would be crucial in determining victory or defeat.

To respond to that challenge, in 1966 the administration began to try to bring some order to the political and economic situation in the South. Since the fall of the Diem regime in 1963, the political situation in Saigon had been in virtual chaos. Over a period of less than two years, several governments had arisen and quickly collapsed. Finally, in the early summer of 1965, a new regime composed of younger military officers under Generals Nguyen Cao Ky and Nguyen Van Thieu came to power in Saigon. Somewhat to Washington's surprise, the new government began to demonstrate an ability to stabilize the situation.

After an initial period of hesitation and doubt about the capacity of the new leadership, the Johnson administration attempted to take advantage of the promise of renewed stability in Saigon. In 1966, a conference of top officials from Washington and Saigon convened in Honolulu to discuss measures to increase political stability in Saigon and to win popular support for the new government. U.S. officials promised more assistance to help the G.V.N. solve its burgeoning economic and social problems. The Saigon generals promised to move with dispatch toward the creation of a representative government with the trappings of Western democracy. A constituent assembly was to be elected in 1966 to write a constitution and schedule national elections. In these elections, held in 1967, Nguyen Van Thieu was chosen president, with Ky as his vice-president. Similar reforms were undertaken in the area of economic and social policies. Perhaps the most pressing problem was that of land reform. For years the issue had lain dormant as officials in Washington and Saigon refused to concede that peasant economic discontent was at the root of Communist popularity at the village level. By the late 1960s, the importance of the land question was more widely recognized, and in 1969 the G.V.N. pushed through a "land to the tiller" law that in effect assigned ownership of farmland to the tenant without payment. Owners were to be compensated by the government.

The main objectives of the new U.S. strategy were twofold: (1) to strengthen the G.V.N. so that it could gradually develop the capacity to defend itself and (2) to demonstrate to the Communists in Hanoi (and to aspiring insurgency movements elsewhere) U.S. capacity and resolve to prevent successful national liberation struggles throughout the Third World. The success or failure of the first objective would be determined only after the U.S. departure from Vietnam. The validity of the second assumption, however, would soon be put to the test. The U.S. escalation did not result in a major change in Hanoi's strategy in the South. Indeed, Hanoi's war planners concluded that the U.S. challenge must be met head-on and defeated. To back down, to retreat to a defensive posture of sporadic guerrilla war—as was apparently advised by Peking—would only cause the revolutionary forces to lose their momentum and suffer a decline in morale and would make a future victory that much more difficult. To defeat the U.S. strategy, the Communists would be compelled to maintain the pressure on the battlefield and to maximize U.S. casualties in order to reduce public support for the war in the United States.

The strategy was an extremely costly one. Because the liberation armed forces could not hope to match the enemy in firepower (despite increased military assistance from Moscow and Peking), they would have to rely on the power of numbers and the advantages of stratagem and surprise. For several months, Hanoi strategists attempted to maintain the initiative on the battlefield. U.S. "head count" figures of more than 300,000 Communist casualties a year were probably exaggerated, but there is no doubt that Hanoi's losses were high. To maintain force levels, Hanoi found it increasingly necessary to introduce regular force units from the North, and infiltration rates reportedly reached more than 100,000 a year. Because access to the villages in the South was increasingly restricted by U.S. and ARVN sweep operations, the local apparatus was unable to recruit effectively and had to use fillers from the North. This in turn led to morale problems and growing antagonism between northerners and southerners within the movement. Because revolutionary units had been driven from the rich lowlands into the mountains and along the Cambodian border, provisions were short and had to be imported from the North. U.S. bombing raids along the Ho Chi Minh Trail through Southern Laos made overland shipments difficult, and supplies were increasingly brought in through the new Cambodian port of Sihanoukville.

Hanoi could hardly hope for a clear-cut military victory over the United States and ARVN forces in the South. Its best hope was to achieve sufficient military success to destabilize the Saigon government and force a change of government that could produce leaders willing to pursue a negotiated settlement. Alternatively, battlefield failures might undermine public support for the war effort in the United States and force Washington to withdraw or seek peace. Signs of disenchantment with the war in the United States were increasingly apparent in 1967 as university campuses erupted in hostility to the conflict. To intensify such discontent, the Communists would require a major success on the battlefield.

TET

Planning for a major military offensive apparently began in the late summer or early fall of 1967. At approximately the same time, U.S. observers noticed heightened enemy activity in the northern provinces just below the demilitarized zone (DMZ) where Westmoreland had ordered the construction of a string of U.S. firebases to interdict Communist infiltration across the DMZ. Throughout the remainder of the year, Communist pressure in the area grew in intensity resulting in a prolonged attack on the U.S. firebase at Khe Sanh, a rocky hill a few miles south of the DMZ. General Westmoreland ordered the base reinforced, and it was able to hold despite a lengthy siege.

There was considerable speculation at the time that the Communist buildup near the DMZ signaled an attempt to create a U.S. "Dien Bien Phu" in the north. Other observers suggested that it might have represented an effort by Hanoi strategists to divert U.S. attention from areas more vital to the South. In all likelihood, Communist strategy was flexible and designed to take advantage of whatever opening U.S. moves created. In any event, in late January 1968, during the annual Tet (New Year's) holiday, Communist forces throughout the country attacked major cities, provincial and district capitals, and rural villages in a nationwide offensive. Approximately 80,000 troops took part in the assault. The most prominent

Saigon, the "pearl of the Orient," during the Vietnam War. (By Wilbur E. Garrett © 1965 National Geographic Society)

areas of attack were Saigon and the imperial capital of Hue. In Hue, the attacking forces seized most of the city and the imperial citadel and held on to it for three weeks until finally driven out after street-by-street attacks by U.S. and South Vietnamese forces. In Saigon, Communist sapper units and suicide squads assaulted several vital military and government installations. Communist success was brief but had maximum psychological impact. One squad managed to penetrate the grounds of the walled U.S. Embassy compound in downtown Saigon and occupied the ground floor of the chancery for several hours before they were killed. Other units managed to hold out for several days in Cholon before they were suppressed.

In the countryside, the impact of the offensive, although less spectacular, was longer lasting. Attacks on several provincial capitals were driven back only after heavy U.S. bombardments, which in some cases caused considerable damage and loss of life. In rural areas, the pacification program was seriously disrupted and G.V.N. control over many areas was reestablished only several months later.

Some Western observers claimed that the Tet offensive had been a failure. General Westmoreland, citing heavy Communist losses, contended that Tet had been a severe defeat for Hanoi's forces, who did not achieve their goal of destroying the Saigon regime. Others, however, pointed to the psychological impact of the offensive on public opinion in the United States and to the ultimate effect on U.S. policy as an indication that the offensive had been a striking success. The truth was probably somewhere in between. Communist casualties in the attack were indeed heavy—by some estimates up to one-half the entire assault force—and it would be several years before Hanoi would be able to recoup its losses to launch a second offensive of similar size. Moreover, revolutionary successes in rural areas turned out, for the most part, to be ephemeral. Within a year, ARVN troops had seized most of the areas lost to the insurgent forces and resumed pacification operations. But there is no question that Tet resulted in a significant shift in U.S. war strategy. By mid-spring, the Johnson administration had become persuaded that further military escalation in pursuit of total victory was not worth the cost either on the battlefield or on the domestic scene in the United States and had reluctantly decided to seek a negotiated settlement. It remained only to find a means of coming to the conference table.

The route to the conference table had been a tortuous one. Diplomatic exchanges about possible peace talks had been in the air throughout the early 1960s, but without concrete results. In effect, neither side had wanted to begin negotiations until relatively favorable military and political conditions had appeared, leading to the possibility of a diplomatic victory. Since 1965, both sides, while wishing to appear willing to begin peace talks, had refused to make the necessary conditions to bring the other to the conference table. Washington had rejected Hanoi's Four Points, which appeared to require the resignation of the Thieu regime. The D.R.V., on the other hand, had refused to open talks without a cessation of the U.S. bombing of the North. After the Tet offensive, both sides modified their positions, and when President Johnson agreed to stop the bombing (although he refused to put the commitment in writing), the last stumbling block was removed and talks could begin.

In the presidential elections of 1968, Richard Nixon won a narrow victory over the Democratic candidate, Hubert Humphrey. Nixon's election did not significantly change the direction of U.S. policy in Vietnam, despite the new president's claim that he had a "secret plan" to end the war. In fact, the policy of the new administration toward the war was substantially a continuation of that adopted by President Johnson after the Tet offensive, with some elaborations. Nixon's strategy, in effect, was to attempt to find a compromise settlement to the war while strengthening the South Vietnamese government and armed forces so that they could defend themselves if negotiations did not succeed. In negotiations, Nixon would offer the Communists a legitimate political role in the South, provided that they withdrew their PAVN units to the North and accepted the presidency of Nguyen Van Thieu. In the meantime, U.S. combat units would be gradually withdrawn over a four-year period (the target date for full withdrawal was June 1972, only a few months prior to the next presidential elections), while ARVN forces would be strengthened to take over the primary burden in the war. The process of "Vietnamization" would begin slowly but would accelerate as conditions permitted. It was, indeed, a clever strategy, provided that the American public had the patience to permit the war to continue for several more years. In the last analysis, of course, its ultimate success would be based on the assumption that, at some future date, Saigon would be able to stand on its own.

Such a compromise settlement was a step forward from the hard-line position taken by the Johnson administration before the Tet Offensive, but it had little immediate appeal to Hanoi. The removal of U.S. forces was of little benefit so long as Thieu remained president and North Vietnamese units were called upon to withdraw from the South. A better settlement could be achieved by waiting for the departure of the bulk of the U.S. troops and then launching a second major offensive to destroy or at least seriously weaken the Thieu regime. During the months following the opening of peace talks in Paris, then, no significant progress was registered, as both sides concentrated on strengthening their military and political position in South Vietnam. With Communist forces weakened by the losses suffered at Tet and U.S. strategy shifting perceptibly from an offensive to a defensive position, the level of conflict gradually subsided, although military operations continued on both sides.

THE INVASION OF CAMBODIA

In March 1970, the neutralist Cambodian regime of Prince Norodom Sihanouk was overthrown and replaced by a new military government, under General Lon Nol, more sympathetic to the United States. The sudden change of government significantly affected the situation in neighboring Vietnam. For the Communists, it represented both opportunity and danger. For years, the revolutionary forces fighting in the South had used the eastern border provinces of Cambodia as a sanctuary and as a conduit for the shipment of weapons, men, and supplies into South Vietnam. The Sihanouk government had reluctantly tolerated such activities in order to placate Hanoi, whose power and ultimate intentions were greatly feared in Phnom Penh. There was a small communist movement, the Khmer Rouge, in Cambodia, but under Hanoi's guidance it had refrained from a policy of armed struggle in order to avoid provoking Sihanouk to revoke his tacit toleration of Vietnamese use of the border area. But the new government was unsympathetic to Communist use of the border provinces. Less than a week after seizing power, Lon Nol demanded that all Vietnamese forces be withdrawn.

For the Nixon administration, the new situation offered temptation. For several years Washington policymakers, reluctant to antagonize Sihanouk, had rejected appeals by General Westmoreland in Saigon to permit U.S. and ARVN forces to launch attacks to clean out the sanctuaries. Now the situation had changed, and in April, Nixon approved a proposal to launch an invasion of the Cambodian eastern provinces. The invading forces, consisting of both U.S. and South Vietnamese units, met with little resistance and advanced virtually unmolested into Cambodia, as Communist forces simply retreated before the allied advance. But Hanoi did not remain powerless in the new situation. When Lon Nol demanded Communist evacuation of the border provinces, Hanoi decided that Cambodian neutrality was of no further benefit and began to train Cambodian guerrillas in an attempt to stir up civil war and overthrow the Phnom Penh regime. To provide leadership and firm guidance over the movement, several hundred Cambodian Communists who had resided in North Vietnam since the Geneva Conference were returned to Cambodia to direct the struggle. For good or ill, Cambodia had become a pawn in the crisis in Southeast Asia.

The Cambodian invasion had an equally noteworthy impact in the United States. While the Nixon administration predictably defended its action as a means of cleaning out the sanctuaries, reducing the likelihood of a new Communist offensive, and thus permitting a further reduction in U.S. force levels in Vietnam, opponents of the war argued that the invasion had simply widened the war and made it more difficult to resolve. Protests against the war on college campuses escalated to new heights.

Whether or not the invasion of Cambodia impeded a new Communist offensive and accelerated the rate of withdrawal of U.S. forces from South Vietnam is a matter of dispute. What is clear is that conflict in South Vietnam continued at a low level during succeeding months while U.S. force levels in Vietnam gradually declined. On the other hand, the insurgency movement in Cambodia grew steadily, and peace was nowhere in sight. Hanoi was still hoping to achieve a breakthrough on the battlefield in South Vietnam to stimulate antiwar sentiment in the United States and force the administration to the conference table. This may well have been what party strategists had in mind when they planned a new military offensive to be launched over the Easter holidays in 1972. The attack was carefully timed to take place when U.S. force levels would dip below 100,000 for the first time since 1965. Not coincidentally, it would also occur during the opening stages of the 1972 presidential election campaign in the United States. The Easter Offensive—like its predecessor in 1968—thus had both military and psychological dimensions.

There were some significant differences in approach from Tet, however. Unlike in 1968, the Easter Offensive would take place almost entirely in rural areas. Cities would be attacked only if the probability of success was high. Second, in contrast to 1968, when few PAVN units were committed to the battle, North Vietnamese troops would play a major role in the fighting in an attempt to deal a severe and perhaps fatal blow to the ARVN. If the ultimate objective of the Easter Offensive was to destroy Saigon, it did not succeed, but it came close. Heavy Communist attacks in the northern provinces led to the virtual disintegration of some of the newer and less experienced ARVN divisions in the area. Only the tenacity of the tougher ARVN 1st Division and U.S. aerial bombing managed to prevent panic and an outright defeat. One Communist commander contended that only logistical weaknesses prevented a spectacular victory. As it was, Communist territorial gains were limited and casualties were high. But the ARVN's ability to survive alone—the keystone of the Nixon Vietnamization program—was put once again into serious question.

The Easter Offensive did not lead immediately to a major breakthrough in the peace talks. But during the next few months, the U.S. position began to show signs of a new flexibility. The major sticking points in the negotiations had always been Hanoi's refusal to accept Thieu, who had been reelected virtually without opposition in 1971, as head of a post-settlement government (Hanoi offered to accept members of the government but not Thieu himself) and the U.S. refusal to negotiate a settlement and a departure of U.S. forces without a corresponding removal from the South of the 200,000 North Vietnamese forces (a presence Hanoi had never admitted). Now Henry Kissinger suggested to the D.R.V. negotiator Le Duc Tho that if Hanoi accepted Thieu, a settlement need not require the withdrawal of PAVN units from the South. Hanoi did not immediately respond, but in September Tho indicated that a compromise along such lines might be feasible. For the next several weeks, both sides worked feverishly to hammer out an agreement. Tentative agreement was reached in November, and Kissinger announced, prematurely as it turned out, that "peace was at hand." When Saigon (which had not been consulted) resisted, the U.S. insisted on renegotiating several points. Hanoi, now suspicious, refused, and Nixon ordered a resumption of the bombing of the North over the Christmas holidays in order to bring the North Vietnamese to terms. Final agreement was reached in early January, and the treaty, with Thieu's reluctant acquiescence, was signed on the twenty-third. It called for a cease-fire in place and the removal of remaining U.S. fighting forces. The division of territory under the control of the NLF and the government was to be decided in negotiations between the two sides. The Thieu government remained in power but a new "administrative structure" (U.S. negotiators had refused to describe it as a "coalition government") was to be established within three months to prepare for elections and a new government in South Vietnam. This so-called National Council of Reconciliation and Concord was based on a tripartite formula, with representatives from the Provisional Revolutionary Government (P.R.G.—formed by the Communists as an alternative to the G.V.N. after the Tet offensive), the Thieu regime, and neutral forces.

FROM PARIS TO SAIGON

Like the Geneva Accords two decades previously, the Paris Agreement did not end the Vietnam War. It simply served to facilitate the removal of U.S. troops and to return the conflict to the two rival forces in Hanoi and Saigon. That in itself was no mean accomplishment. With the Cold War rivalry over Vietnam removed, the likelihood that the conflict there could lead to a major great power confrontation was sharply reduced. But the internal competition between the two sides continued and indeed intensified. In the months following the cease-fire, negotiations on a future political structure and a military settlement quickly broke down amid mutual recriminations. It would be idle at this point to attempt to single out the guilty party, as the breakdown was the product of a generation of accumulated mistrust and hostility. The Thieu government did not carry through on its commitments and harassed Communist forces. On the other hand, the Communists clearly used the cease-fire to improve their military position in the South. At first, they had hoped that the overthrow of the Thieu regime could be achieved without a return to armed struggle. But Thieu's refusal to carry out the agreement and his efforts to reduce the amount of territory under P.R.G. control through armed action soon changed minds in Hanoi. In 1974, party leaders approved a major strengthening of their military capabilities in the South and, in the autumn, adopted a proposal to launch a major offensive in the South early in 1975, with the hope of completing a takeover of the entire country the following year. There was some hesitation caused by concern about the possible U.S. response. Richard Nixon had promised Thieu that the United States would respond vigorously if Hanoi broke the agreement. In order to test the U.S. reaction, Hanoi's campaign would open with partial offensives along the Cambodian border and in the Central Highlands. If the U.S. response was weak and the attacks were successful, then a major offensive would open in the highlands and in the northern provinces and last until the onset of the rainy season in May.

In any event, the success of the campaign exceeded Hanoi's highest hopes. The first stages, in Tay Ninh Province, resulted in the seizure of the provincial capital. When Thieu elected not to attempt to retake it and Washington (where Gerald Ford had replaced Richard Nixon as president the previous August) did not respond, the second stage was launched in mid-March in the Central Highlands with a major offensive against Ban Me Thuot, the largest city in the area. The government in Saigon was taken by surprise, and the ARVN forces in the area fled in panic. Other heavy attacks by PAVN forces in the north threatened major population centers and induced President Thieu to abandon virtually all the northern provinces to the Communists in the hope of stabilizing the G.V.N. position further south. In the panic that ensued, the entire north was lost, including the major urban centers of Hue and Da Nang and much of Saigon's armed forces.

The arrival of North Vietnamese tanks before the Independence Palace in Saigon, April 30, 1975. (Photo courtesy of *Vietnam* pictorial)

Flushed with success, Hanoi decided to press for total victory before the end of the dry season. In Washington, the Ford administration tried to push a $1 billion military aid program through Congress, but gave no sign of reintroducing U.S. forces into the war. Communist forces poured south from the Central Highlands and along the coast and by mid-April were approaching the outskirts of Saigon. Others were advancing from Tay Ninh toward Tan Son Nhut Airport. For a brief period, hard-pressed ARVN troops held up the Communist onslaught at Xuan Loc, but the effort to stabilize the front failed. In its last days, the Saigon regime attempted desperately to contact Hanoi to seek a compromise settlement, but party leaders were now convinced that total victory was within their grasp and remained silent, even after Thieu had resigned and Duong Van Minh, who, it had long been rumored, was more acceptable to the Communists, had taken over the presidency. By the last week of April, Communist forces were poised on the edge of the city while Saigon's resistance crumbled and helicopters evacuated Americans from rooftops to aircraft carriers waiting offshore. On the thirtieth, North Vietnamese units streamed into the city along the main thoroughfares, encountering little resistance. In Saigon, the party's followers surfaced with flags, leaflets, and microphones to provide enthusiasm along the route. After three decades of bitter struggle, the long Vietnamese conflict had come to an end.

The victory of the Communists in Vietnam has been ascribed to various causes. The strategic and organizational genius of the Communists, the weakness and factionalism of their rivals, the military and political misjudgments of the French and the Americans—all these played a significant role in the final outcome. It is fruitless to seek a single explanation for the tragedy of Vietnam. But it is important to recognize that, above all, the results of the war were a consequence of the political, social, and cultural realities within Vietnam. The United States did not militarily lose the war. Certainly the Paris Agreement in 1973 was not the product of U.S. defeats on the battlefield. To the contrary, U.S. military superiority had significantly blunted Communist momentum in the late 1960s, the Tet Offensive notwithstanding. The U.S. failure, above all, was in not being able to overcome the disparity between the political capacities of the Communists and those of its own ally in Saigon. To the end, the deeper meaning in the war was that, without outside intervention, the Communists would have triumphed with ease over their noncommunist rivals.

Could a different strategy, or a higher level of commitment in Washington, have altered the final result? Life does not permit us to relive history. Perhaps a more vigorous U.S. effort to transform South Vietnamese society would have resulted in the emergence of a stronger sense of local commitment to a separate, noncommunist Vietnam. Such a strategy, however, would have aroused charges of neocolonialism and might well have provoked widespread resentment of the United States in the South. Possibly a more aggressive military strategy would have ultimately broken the Communists' will to resist. Certainly the United States possessed the power to destroy North Vietnam. Such a policy, however, risked nuclear confrontation with Moscow or all-out war with China. Moreover, there is serious doubt that U.S. public opinion would have supported such a brutal resolution of what was viewed by most as a problem of only limited importance. The military solution might have worked, but the potential costs were dangerously high.

The fact is that there was no easy U.S. solution for what was, in the last analysis, a Vietnamese problem. In the end, the only unused options for the United States—escalated involvement, a high risk of war with the Soviet Union—were those that, for one reason or another, the American people were probably unwilling to adopt. Recognition of this fact came gradually and painfully and culminated in the Paris Agreement in 1973 and the U.S. disengagement that followed it. The rapid Communist victory two years later served to confirm the estimate.

5

Politics and Government

One of the key objectives of U.S. foreign policy during a generation of involvement in Vietnam was to build an independent state based on the Western democratic model. This objective had first been set forth by the Truman administration when, in 1949, it had attempted to persuade the French to create democratic institutions and to promise ultimate independence to the Vietnamese in return for U.S. military assistance against the Vietminh. It was reasserted following the Geneva Conference in 1954, when the Eisenhower administration provided advisers to help the South Vietnamese government of Ngo Dinh Diem construct a political system based on representative institutions. The effort continued into the middle and late 1960s, when the Johnson administration pressured the military regime led by Generals Nguyen Cao Ky and Nguyen Van Thieu to establish a legal basis for their rule. This resulted in a new constitution and national elections in 1967. In the end, the experiment was a failure. Neither the Diem regime nor that of Thieu and Ky was able to build the foundation of a political system with a sense of legitimacy and a broad base of popular support within the country. The rapid collapse of the G.V.N. under the onslaught of the Communist military offensive in the spring of 1975 was only the most visible evidence of this failure.

The failure of South Vietnam to develop a Westernized political system has often been attributed to Washington's insistence on emphasizing anticommunism over democratic practice and military concerns over political and social development. Although such a view probably has some validity, it is certainly an oversimplification. The failure of democracy in Vietnam is the product, above all, of deep-seated historical and cultural factors within Vietnamese society. It is instructive to note, for example, that of the new nations in Southeast Asia that emerged from colonial rule after World War II—virtually all of which adopted some form of representative political system based on Western models—only two are still working democracies. All the rest have abandoned democratic practice and turned to authoritarian rule by either military or civilian elites. The hopes of many that independence would lead to the rise of democratic

71

societies in Southeast Asia have been sorely disappointed, at least for the time being.

In retrospect, it is clear that both Western and Asian proponents of liberal democracy were overoptimistic about the ability of newly independent societies in Asia to install systems of government that in the West had taken generations, even centuries, to evolve. Not only were these new states faced with severe class divisions and intimidating economic and social problems sufficient to strain even societies with long experience with democratic practices, but, equally serious, many of the human values and behavioral patterns that underlay democratic political systems in the West were unfamiliar to the native populations in Southeast Asia and frequently ran directly counter to the political and social traditions inherited from the past. It is little wonder that in many new states the democratic experiment was quickly aborted.

THE DYNAMICS OF VIETNAMESE POLITICAL TRADITION

The failure of Western political models to succeed in modern Vietnam can best be understood as the consequence of a process that has taken place in varying forms throughout the region. To understand the evolution of Vietnamese political tradition and practice in the modern day, then, it is necessary to begin with an analysis of the institutions and values of the premodern period and of how they have been affected by Vietnam's entrance into the modern world.

As the earlier chapters on Vietnamese history have shown, the political institutions of Vietnam were shaped, above all, by two millenia of continual contact with China. Within the context of Asian political thought and practice, the Chinese political system generally identified as Confucianism can be described as a relatively advanced stage in the process of secularization and rationalization that has taken place in recent generations throughout human society. Unlike the political systems of many societies in Southern Asia, often identified with the Indian *devaraja*, or god-king concept, Confucianism established a clear distinction between the realms of religion and politics. The *devaraja* concept fused the sacred and profane into the single emperor-divinity; Confucian political thought denied the divine quality of the monarch. Like monarchs in Western tradition, Confucian rulers were assumed to be mortal men who ruled by divine right. By reason of their talent and virtue, they had received a "mandate of Heaven" to govern ordinary men. There was, of course, a magical or religious quality about the Confucian ruler that helped him to establish and maintain a charismatic form of authority over his subjects. But the ruler was expected to adhere to established rules of behavior (in Chinese, known as the *Tao*, or the Way) that were, in effect, a set of common laws above the king. And there was an implicit right of revolution in cases where the ruler failed to live up to his obligations to society.

In the selection of the ruling elite as well, Confucianism represented a step beyond the systems used elsewhere in Southeast Asia. Most states in Asia selected the ruling class strictly from the hereditary aristocracy; Confucian practice called for the selection of officials through a sophisticated process of civil service examinations. In practice members of noble families often achieved positions of influence in the bureaucracy, even in China, and favoritism and nepotism often played a role in the selection process, but the system was undoubtedly a major advance in the process of creating a system based on the concept of rule by merit. Moreover, it created a sense of class fluidity and upward mobility absent in societies with more rigid class distinctions. In turn, the bureaucracy developed a sense of professionalism and expertise that tended to limit the arbitrary power of the ruler. While emperors and even dynasties came and went, the bureaucrats often remained.

Confucian institutions were probably first introduced into Vietnam shortly after the Chinese military conquest in the third century B.C. Although relatively little is known about Vietnamese political practices under Chinese rule, it seems highly probable that Confucian doctrine played a considerable if not dominant role. In any case, when independence was restored in the tenth century A.D., the new state adopted a number of Confucian practices as a means of legitimizing the monarchy and strengthening the centralizing power of the state. At first, Confucian institutions were compelled to compete with rival ideologies, such as Buddhism and indigenous cults, as the central force underlying the political system. During the first centuries after independence, Buddhist monks played a major role as advisers at court, and aristocratic families dominated higher positions within the bureaucracy. Gradually, however, Confucianism became increasingly influential as strong monarchs saw it as a means of improving efficiency and strengthening their position as the dominant force within Vietnamese society. Under the dynamic rule of Emperor Le Thanh Tong (1460–1497) Confucianism became official doctrine, and a new legal system, labeled the Hong Duc Code, was promulgated to regularize laws and regulations on the Chinese pattern.

The adoption of Confucianism undoubtedly had some benefits for Vietnamese society. It encouraged the development of efficient administrative practices and of a rational government hierarchy throughout all levels of society. It promoted the transformation of a social order dominated by a powerful and arrogant hereditary aristocracy into one based at least partly on merit; it provided a system of social ethics based on hard work, service to the community, personal rectitude, and benevolence. In a word, Confucianism well served the needs of a hydraulic society in which such qualities were a prerequisite for social order and economic prosperity.

The beauty of Confucian theory, however, was not always effectively translated into practice. The emperor, surrounded by eunuchs and sycophants, was frequently isolated at court, while the system was often rigid and unresponsive to the needs of society unless prodded by a humane and activist ruler. Bureaucrats displayed a tendency toward arrogance and self-seeking, while even Confucian scholars, the keepers of the moral law, often ignored the content of the Confucian classics and lapsed into ritualism and a pedantic concern for style rather than content.

This tendency was particularly marked during the later Le dynasty. Weak rulers and internal factionalism led to the dominance of princely families at court and to a general breakdown in the effectiveness of Confucian institutions in Vietnamese society. The ineffectiveness emanating from the court encouraged corruption within the bureaucracy and the increasing concentration of land in the hands of the wealthy in rural areas. By the eighteenth century, signs of the incipient disintegration of the political and social bonds of the traditional culture were clearly evident. The brief reign of Emperor Quang Trung and then the rise of the Nguyen dynasty at the end of the century restored a measure of internal unity but did not arrest the progressive decline of Sino-Vietnamese society, despite the manifest effort of Vietnamese monarchs to return to the purity of Confucian institutions.

THE IMPACT OF THE WEST

The weaknesses of the Confucian system were brought into high relief by the French conquest. The failure of the court to respond effectively to the threat from abroad and the visible signs of Western material superiority convinced many thoughtful Vietnamese that Confucian institutions were irrelevant to current conditions and that, in order to survive, Vietnam would have to borrow liberally from the West. The rapid collapse of official resistance to the French and the toadying behavior of many court officials toward the new rulers, accentuated by the cavalier treatment of the traditional monarchy by the colonial regime (during the early years of colonial rule, the French replaced emperors virtually at will), served to accelerate the demise of the traditional system and to undermine public confidence in its validity as a framework for the Vietnamese society of the future.

In general, this process was encouraged by the French. For supporters of the view that France had a *mission civilisatrice* in Indochina, one of the primary assumptions was that the outmoded Confucian political system had to be replaced by representative institutions from the West. In actuality, as noted above, French policy was inconsistent in carrying out political change. The court was permitted to retain its authority in Annam, and in Tonkin the colonial regime was often slow to take steps to introduce or replace traditional practices with Western ones. Even in the colony of Cochin China, the French appeared reluctant to move expeditiously toward the creation of a political system reflecting Western models. As a result, the pressure to introduce representative democratic institutions came more from within Vietnamese society, among intellectuals familiar from travel or study with European civilization, than it did from the regime. By the first decade of the twentieth century, progressive members of the traditional scholar-gentry class had already begun to call for the abandonment of old ways and the transformation of Vietnamese political institutions and practices along Western lines. To such prominent intellectual figures as Phan Chu Trinh (1872–1926), son of a military official from Quang Nam Province, the main stumbling block to the creation of a prosperous and independent Vietnam was not the French colonial regime—which, in his view, could actually become the means of national salvation—but the decrepit monarchy in Hue. To avid Westernizers like Trinh, the Vietnamese should take advantage of the French presence to force the colonial regime to introduce major changes in Vietnamese society and institutions that would lead to the ultimate creation of a representative government with fully democratic institutions. The primary weakness of Trinh's program was his estimate of the sincerity of the French commitment to its civilizing mission. Although a reformer rather than an advocate of armed struggle, Trinh was arrested in 1906 and forced to live in exile in France until the final year of his life. His fate understandably discouraged many thoughtful Vietnamese from the belief that national salvation could be achieved in concert with French rulers.

The class for whom Western political ideas were a major source of attraction, however, was the rising urban middle class. Living directly in the shadow of the colonial regime, often educated in French schools and engaged in occupations created by the Western presence, the Vietnamese middle class tended to combine resentment of colonial rule with admiration for Western culture. This ambivalence was clearly reflected in the various nationalist organizations that blossomed during the decade following World War I. While virtually all such parties or factions were passionately concerned with the issue of independence and national identity, they voiced such aspirations in terms familiar to Western political culture and looked forward to a future Vietnam based on political ideals and institutions imported from the West. Some were sensitive to the problem of adopting ideas so unfamiliar to the native political culture. Phan Chu Trinh, duplicating similar efforts by reform-minded Confucian scholars in turn-of-the century China, attempted to devise a synthesis of Confucian ethics and Western political and social institutions that could ease Vietnam's entry into the modern world. Others, like the scholar and journalist Pham Quynh, expressed publicly their doubts that Western democratic ideals were relevant to Vietnam and sought alternatives that could harmonize the traditional values of an agrarian community with those of the material civilization penetrating from the West. Others still appeared to accept the relevance of Western values and institutions to Vietnamese society in a relatively uncritical manner and failed to see that Western democratic ideals and institutions, so symbiotically linked to the Western capitalist tradition, had little immediate relevance in a society still predominantly agrarian and unfamiliar with the techniques of popular political participation.

It is one of the ironies of our day that the philosophy of Karl Marx, which Marx himself had devised for application primarily in the capitalist societies of the West, now has its primary appeal as a vehicle for rapid social change in the developing societies of the Third World. The attractiveness of Marxism to Third World intellectuals and political leaders is quite understandable. For societies suffering from the collapse of traditional institutions and values, Marxism offers a persuasive alternative to Western capitalist democracy as an appropriate tool in the nation-building effort.

This was certainly the case in Vietnam. Where Western liberal democracy emphasizes the individual as the foundation of political society, Marxism stresses the subordination of the individual to the overall needs of the community, a view familiar to the Confucian mind. Where liberal democracy is gradualist in orientation and stresses the decentralization of power, Marxism provides a dynamic approach to problems of social change and stresses the need for popular mobilization, centralized leadership, and a coherent ideology, all features attractive to radical intellectuals who have lost their faith in the Confucian world view. In effect, Marxism serves not only as a developmental ideology but also as a form of political religion, providing an explanation of history, a doctrine of good and evil, and the promise of a future paradise on earth.

Marxist doctrine made its appearance in Vietnam in the years immediately following the Bolshevik revolution and World War I. At first, vigorous censorship by the colonial regime prevented knowledge of the explosive doctrine from being disseminated among restive Vietnamese intellectuals seeking a solution to the intimidating challenges of social change. By the late 1920s, however, Marxism had become a familiar item on the Vietnamese intellectual scene and, to many, a persuasive alternative to the Western democratic model. With the formation of Ho Chi Minh's Revolutionary Youth League in 1925 and the ICP five years later, an organization devoted to the realization of the Marxist utopia in Vietnam had come into being.

For the next several decades, the doctrines of Western liberal democracy and Marxism competed to fill the vacuum left by the gradual demise of the traditional Confucian order. Vietnamese Marxists, placing the issue in class terms, interpret the competition as a struggle between two classes—the bourgeoisie and proletariat—for the leadership of the Vietnamese revolution. Although this interpretation is by no means wholly invalid, it is an oversimplification that does little credit to the complexity of the issue. The strongest support for liberal democratic and capitalist ideas came from the emerging commercial and manufacturing bourgeoisie, but support for Marxism did not come primarily from the Vietnamese proletariat. In fact, although the young Communist movement did in time manage to build a base of support within the small but growing Vietnamese working class, its major source of support in the early years came from what is often called the urban petit bourgeois intelligentsia. To this mixed class of students, teachers, journalists, lower-level officials, clerks, and disappointed job-seekers (many of whom came from traditional elite families), Marxism was an attractive alternative to liberal democracy.

It was only after Marxism had taken firm roots within the petit bourgeois intelligentsia that, through the efforts of Ho Chi Minh and the ICP, it began to spread to the working class and the impoverished peasantry. In Vietnam, the roots of this appeal were partly patriotic (in the sense that Marxist doctrine was viewed by nationalists as a revolutionary strategy for seizing power from the French) and partly social revolutionary (in the sense that the committed Marxist saw the Marxist-Leninist model as the best means of rectifying the inequities of the traditional system and organizing a new system of production, distribution, and ownership after the seizure of independence). Specialists might dispute the comparative importance of these two factors in the growth of the Vietnamese Communist movement, but it is indisputable that both played a significant role in its growing popularity. By World War II, Marxism was becoming an increasing force in Vietnamese politics and culture and a serious rival of Western liberal democracy.

For a generation, the proponents of Western liberal democracy and Marxist social revolution labored under the common handicap of French repression. Until the end of World War II, French officials appeared almost equally suspicious of all Vietnamese patriots, whether they were proponents of a form of liberal democracy or of Marxism-Leninism. It was only after the war, under the pressure of the Franco-Vietminh conflict, that the colonial regime turned with some reluctance to moderates as a means of preserving the French presence and preventing the victory of communism in Vietnam. Thus was born the "Bao Dai formula" and the Associated State of Vietnam (see Chapter 3).

THE REPUBLIC OF VIETNAM

In 1954, Ngo Dinh Diem fell heir to the Bao Dai experiment and with U.S. support set up a Republic of Vietnam in the South based on the Western liberal democratic model. For more than two decades, under the leadership of Diem and that of his successors until the collapse of the Thieu regime in the spring of 1975, the South Vietnamese political elite, composed of moderate nationalists, an affluent urban middle class, landed elements in rural areas, and the civilian and military bureaucracy, attempted unsuccessfully to establish a political system based, in practice as well as in theory, on the Western democratic model. Whether this failure is a consequence of faulty U.S. policies, of pressure imposed by intimidating social problems and the persistent destabilizing efforts of the Communist-led insurgency movement, of poor political leadership, or of objective conditions antipathetic to Western democratic practice within Vietnam is a matter of considerable disagreement and can be only briefly alluded to here. U.S. policy undoubtedly had an impact on domestic politics in Vietnam but was probably not a decisive factor in the failure of the democratic model. Washington's persistent emphasis on the overriding importance of the survival of an anticommunist regime in Saigon undoubtedly led U.S. policymakers to give priority to military and security issues over democratic practices. On the other hand, successive U.S. administrations consistently pressed the Saigon regime to broaden its popular base and to strengthen its image of legitimacy in the international arena. That Saigon was unable or unwilling to do so cannot be ascribed solely to U.S. policy.

Was the failure simply an accident of poor leadership? Certainly the failure of the Diem regime can be attributed, at least in part, to Diem's failure to comprehend the essential meaning of the democratic process and the vision of a pluralistic society. Under the veneer of his commitment to republican institutions, Diem was at heart a traditional figure, more comfortable in the world of Confucian hierarchy and enlightened despotism than in the rough-and-tumble arena of democratic politics. In actuality, in some respects the Diem regime borrowed more from Leninist organizational techniques—such as the formation of an elitist party, the formation of a broad progovernment national front, and the creation of functional mass organizations—than from the Western democratic model. It is significant that the regime was equally unsuccessful with either.

Many U.S. policymakers (and anticommunist elements in Saigon) were optimistic that, with Diem removed, a viable state built on democratic institutions could be created in South Vietnam. The rise of the military regime of Nguyen Cao Ky and Nguyen Van Thieu in the summer of 1965 provided a basis for the conviction that the period of musical chairs that had followed the fall of Diem was at an end. In 1966, the Johnson administration began to pressure the new leadership to replace the existing system of military rule through the Armed Forces Council and the Directorate, composed of ten generals and nineteen civilians, with a more legitimate source of authority.

The process began in September 1966 with the election of the 117-member Constituent Assembly. After several months, that assembly drew up a new constitution, the final draft of which was issued in March 1967, providing for a presidential system and a two-house legislature. The Directorate and the Armed Forces Council accepted the document without change, and it was promulgated as the new constitution of the republic in April. The system was designed to provide the republic with the strong government considered necessary to cope with the challenge of nation-building and internal civil war. The president, who was to be elected by popular vote for a four-year term and was eligible for a single reelection, had substantial power to promulgate laws, initiate legislation, serve as the supreme commander of the armed forces, determine national policy, and preside over the Council of Ministers. He was also empowered to declare a national state of emergency, although such a decree had to be approved by the National Assembly within twelve days. In time of war, he could appoint province chiefs, subject to approval by a two-thirds vote of the lower house, or National Assembly. Although the president was in effect both head of government and chief of state, the constitution provided for a prime minister, who was appointed by and could be removed by the president, to assist him in executive duties. The Assembly could also force the resignation of the prime minister by a two-thirds vote.

The legislative branch consisted of the National Assembly and the Senate, both elected by universal suffrage and direct ballot. Deputies in the lower house were to be elected for a four-year term from separate constituencies; senators served for six years and were elected at large by list under a plurality system. The Assembly voted on legislation, ratified treaties, and determined the declaration of war and the opening of peace talks. It could override a presidential veto by an absolute majority vote, and its members had the traditional legal protections against arbitrary arrest. Other interesting aspects of the system were an independent judiciary, including a supreme court that was empowered to decide on appeals from lower courts and on the constitutionality of all laws and decrees, a bill of rights, and an inspectorate, an agency to oversee the operations of the administrative branch. Political parties were of course permitted, but an article of the constitution declared that "the Republic of Vietnam opposes communism in any form" and prohibited all publicity for communism.

In form, then, in 1967 the Republic of Vietnam became a democratic society. National elections in September resulted in the election of Nguyen Van Thieu as president and Nguyen Cao Ky as vice-president. A new legislature was elected in September and October. During the following eight years the regime generally managed to operate within the bounds of legality, although in several ways the system did not work effectively. Political parties were permitted to operate, so long as they espoused moderate social programs, supported the war effort, and posed no threat to the supremacy of the Thieu regime. Those who advocated neutralism or a compromise settlement of the war, however, were frequently harassed and sometimes arrested. Such practices are hardly unusual in developing societies. What was disquieting was the inability of the government to establish a popular base of support and the failure of the system to produce political parties that could compete effectively to voice popular social objectives on a national scale. Unlike the Diem regime, which had at least attempted (albeit with limited success) to articulate a general philosophy of development (that murky synthesis of Confucian and progressive Catholic thought known as Personalism) and create a popular base of support through the formation of mass organizations and the progovernment National Revolutionary Movement, President Thieu was surprisingly slow to follow the pattern familiar elsewhere in the Third World of setting up a national popular front to support government policies.

Significantly, however, the potential opposition was equally disorganized. Most of the parties operating in the National Assembly were cliques and factions based on regional or religious interests rather than nationally organized political parties. The legislature appeared to be a mere congeries of diverse interests, and members found it difficult either to coalesce behind the government or in support of an organized opposition. President Thieu, in effect, was operating in a political vacuum. Despite widespread discontent with many of his policies, he was reelected in 1971 with virtually no opposition; he then attempted with mediocre success to reorganize the party systems on a national basis and to set up a progovernment democratic party.

In sum, the Republic of Vietnam under Nguyen Van Thieu was democratic in form but not in content. Although some of the blame can be ascribed to overall social conditions and the pressures of war, the failure of the system to evolve over a period of two decades suggests that the origins of the problem were deep-seated. In fact, the root of the problem lay in the inability of Saigon political elites to adapt Western political techniques to the Vietnamese environment. Unlike the Communists, who after years of careful analysis had worked out a strategy for revolution and nation-building that combined the theoretical and practical tenets of Marxism-Leninism with the political and cultural realities of Vietnamese society, the political elites in Saigon approached the problem in a perfunctory and disjointed manner. Western institutions were applied—sometimes, admittedly, at U.S. insistence—with little thought to their relevance in a Vietnamese context. Saigon's efforts to build a foundation for a Western political system at the village level, though often well-meaning, were plagued by inefficiency and corruption, and throughout most of the life of the G.V.N., the bulk of the population felt little sense of commitment to the government in Saigon. Political practice in Saigon represented an uneasy amalgam of techniques inherited from Confucian tradition, French colonial rule, and poorly assimilated ideas of Western democracy. The fault was probably partly Thieu's and partly Washington's. But it is hard to avoid the conclusion that another factor was the difficulty of grafting a set of political institutions designed for an advanced industrial society based on deep-rooted democratic cultural traditions on an agrarian society faced with severe social and economic problems, a disciplined and well-organized insurgency movement, and little experience with democratic practices.

Thus, it may have been unrealistic to expect that South Vietnam, under such conditions, could put into practice a democratic system patterned after that of the United States. Given the recent history of societies throughout the region, that may well be the case. What was needed was an approach that could more effectively adapt modern political techniques to the still traditional world of the village. Although the U.S. democratic experience may by no means be wholly irrelevant to such needs, it seems doubtful that the United States, with its vastly different cultural traditions and realities and its ignorance of Vietnamese history and culture, could form a useful model for that effort. The answer would have to come from within.

THE MARXIST ALTERNATIVE

While politicians in Saigon were groping with the challenges of social development and civil strife in the South, the Communists under Ho Chi Minh were attempting to apply their alternative in the North. Their first opportunity had come in September 1945, when the party had seized power in Hanoi at the head of the Vietminh Front at the end of the Pacific war. During the succeeding months, Ho Chi Minh's provisional government had put in place a set of institutions that, on paper, did not differ substantially from those of Western liberal democracies. Not only did the party adopt such major tenets of Western representative government as elections by secret ballot, separation of powers, a multiparty system, and a constitution with a bill of rights, but it gave the impression of a willingness, at least in form, to share power with its noncommunist rivals. The adoption of the Western-style balance of power between an executive, legislative, and a judicial branch, of course, conforms to Leninist practice. Although Lenin, like Marx, had scorned Western liberal assemblies as "talking shops," he had found it useful to adopt the forms of liberal democracy in the new Soviet state, even though their usage was to be markedly different.

The willingness of the Vietnamese Communists to share power with other parties, on the other hand, was a departure from Leninism and reflected above all the fact that, at least at the outset, the ICP was too weak to govern on its own. Until the party was strong enough to feel secure about its control over the levers of government, and about the support or acquiescence of the mass of the population, it would eschew use of the Marxist dictatorship of the proletariat. In fact, during the Franco-Vietminh war, the party maintained political dominance over the government, while on paper, it was only one of several cooperating parties within a coalition based on the common objective of achieving independence. Indeed, between the fall of 1945 and the Second National Congress in 1951 the party was publicly disbanded, although it continued to operate in secret.

The Geneva Conference, which returned the Communists to power in the North, relieved them of the necessity of disguising their political dominance. Returning to Hanoi in October, the party now consolidated its power throughout the North and inaugurated a people's democratic dictatorship following the model used five years earlier by the CCP in

The mausoleum of Ho Chi Minh in the heart of Hanoi. (Photo courtesy of *Vietnam pictorial*)

China. Two small puppet parties, the Democratic party and the Radical Socialist party, were permitted to continue in operation, but the dominant role of the Communist party, now renamed the Vietnam Workers' party, was no longer disguised. Most key positions in the government were now occupied by top party figures, including such posts as president (Ho Chi

Minh), prime minister (Pham Van Dong), minister of defense (Vo Nguyen Giap), and minister of foreign affairs (Nguyen Duy Trinh). Party leaders were concerned, however, to build a broad popular base of support and to avoid unnecessarily alienating moderates at home and abroad at a time when the national revolution had not yet been completed. Therefore, although the government authorities did not permit any open opposition to their rule, for a period they tolerated the qualified free expression of opinion by nonparty intellectuals, similar to the famous Hundred Flowers campaign then taking place in China. As in China, however, some intellectuals used this opportunity to criticize the party and its policies, leading the authorities in 1958 to crack down on the dissidents and to shut down their organ, the literary journal *Nhan Van* [Humanities].

During the late 1950s, the regime also attempted to strengthen and extend the administrative structure by making it elective at all levels of government and prepared a new constitution to carry North Vietnamese society to the next stage of socialism. A committee to draft the new constitution was set up in 1956, and the new charter, to replace the original one approved in 1946, was ratified by a unanimous vote of the National Assembly in December 1959. The new constitution retained many of the political institutions that had been in operation since the August Revolution in 1945, but it made a number of innovations appropriate to the new situation. In recognition of the need for strong central authority and of the somewhat unique role of the party's founder and leader, Ho Chi Minh, it created a strong presidency. Article 66 gave the president the power, "when necessary," to attend and preside over meetings of the cabinet of ministers. Thus, as in South Vietnam, although the system provided for both a president and a prime minister, the former was in effect both chief of state and leading executive. The president also headed the new National Defense Council, which included among its members the prime minister, the minister of defense, the minister of public security, and several key military officers.

The new constitution retained the unicameral National Assembly first set up after the August Revolution. Its members (including eighteen seats for delegates elected in 1946 to represent the population of the South) were elected by universal suffrage on the basis of one deputy for every 10,000 voters in urban areas and one per 30,000 in the countryside. In theory, the Assembly was the sovereign body in the state. In practice, it served as a rubber stamp to ratify decisions already taken by the executive branch. Its directing body, the Standing Committee, possessed considerable authority, however, and not only directed the work of the Assembly but also was empowered to oversee the operations of the prime minister and the Government Council (equivalent to the cabinet). The new constitution broadened and strengthened the role of the judicial system and the Supreme Court and also established the People's Procuratorate, the duties of which were to oversee the execution of government and party directives.

Below the central government, the regime put in place an elective administrative structure at all levels down to the basic unit, the village. At first, regional divisions above the level of province, which had been created to facilitate military operations during the Franco-Vietminh conflict, were retained, but eventually they were abolished, leaving only two levels, the province (*tinh*) and the district (*huyen*), between the central government and the village. At each level, elected executive and legislative bodies patterned after the structure at the top were established. At the village level, local people's councils (*hoi dong nhan dan*) were elected; they in turn would then elect from their members an administrative committee (*uy ban hanh chinh*) to handle executive decisions between sessions of the people's council. To guarantee local conformity with central regulations, all decisions could be vetoed by the higher echelons.

THE ROLE OF THE PARTY

Since its formation in 1930, the Communist party has viewed itself as the leading force in the Vietnamese revolution. At times, as in the 1930s, and in the D.R.V. after 1954, this vanguard role has been openly proclaimed. At others, as during the Franco-Vietminh conflict and during the second phase of the war in the South after Geneva, it was carefully disguised in order to maximize support for the revolutionary movement. But, as in all Marxist-Leninist societies, the role of the party in guiding society through various stages to the final stage of communism is a key tenet that can under no circumstances be abandoned. This does not mean that the party is the sole political organization in the D.R.V. As in China and Eastern Europe, the Communist party in North Vietnam permitted the existence of small noncommunist parties as a testimony to the multiclass "people's" character of the Vietnamese revolution. But power, in Hanoi, has clearly resided in the VWP and its leadership. The Communist party is not only the representative of the leading social class, the proletariat; even more important, it is the guardian of the purity of Marxist-Leninist doctrine, the guiding ideology of the state, the vehicle of social and political change, the central force of the revolution.

A key component in the party's ability to retain its dominant political role within the D.R.V. lay in its capacity to maintain inner cohesion and centralization of purpose and authority. The means of achieving such unity lies in the Leninist concept of democratic centralism, according to which the party makes its decisions by a democratic process but enforces absolute obedience throughout all echelons of the party once a final decision is made. As described in a party directive cited by Douglas Pike: Decisions are made at "committee meetings by majority vote and individual Party members must then obey. The minority obeys the decision of the majority. The lower echelons obey the decisions of the upper echelons. All elements obey the Central Committee . . . one shout and a thousand echoes."[1]

In effect, the Leninist principle creates a well-disciplined and cohesive party responsive to policy direction from the leadership. Party discipline is rigorously enforced; members and the apparatus as a whole can retreat quickly into clandestinity when the necessity arises. Party organization is designed to maximize centralized authority and efficiency. In theory, the supreme body of all communist parties is a national congress, with its members selected by party organizations at all echelons. In Vietnam, congresses are scheduled to take place every five years, but in practice they have been convened on an ad hoc basis to ratify decisions of vital importance already reached by the Politburo and the Central Committee. The Central Committee is a smaller executive organization elected by the National Congress from among its members to initiate and execute party policy during the long intervals between congresses. In early years, when the party was small and found it difficult to operate because of French repression, the Central Committee was often composed of fewer than 10 members and was the de facto decision-making body within the party. As the party grew larger, however, the Central Committee itself grew progressively larger and more unwieldy, and a smaller Politburo on the Soviet model was created to allow key party leaders to handle day-to-day issues between plenary sessions of the Central Committee. In recent years, the Central Committee has risen to 116 members and 36 alternates; the Politburo contains 13 members and 2 alternates.

The direction of the party, then, is in the hands of a small number of top leaders concentrated in the Politburo. That leadership has been remarkably stable. Indeed, few Communist parties have been as successful in maintaining unity under conditions of high tension as has the Vietnamese. The current leadership first began to take shape just before and during World War II, when party leadership was in the hands of Ho Chi Minh and a number of his younger colleagues, including Pham Van Dong, Vo Nguyen Giap, and Truong Chinh. During the years following the end of the war, that inner-party elite was gradually expanded to include Nguyen Chi Thanh, Pham Hung, and the current general secretary, Le Duan. Throughout the Vietnam War this group retained control over the party, despite some minor adjustments and the death of Ho Chi Minh in 1969. Once elevated to a position of leadership, few fell into disgrace. In 1956, Truong Chinh was removed from his position as general secretary because of failures in the land reform program. But he retained his position in the Politburo and was eventually assigned to the influential governmental post of chairman of the Standing Committee of the National Assembly. The post of general secretary, temporarily left vacant, was formally filled in 1960 by a rising new star, Le Duan. Throughout a generation of war, however, there were remarkably few changes in the party's top leadership.

This is not to say that there was no controversy within the top organs of the party over domestic and foreign policy, or over the strategy to be followed in the South. Indeed, internal party sources concede that virtually every major decision made during a generation of conflict was accompanied

Ho Chi Minh reading the Political Report to the Third National Congress of the Vietnam Workers' party in September 1960. To his right is the current general secretary of the party, Le Duan. Behind Duan is Minister of Defense Vo Nguyen Giap. To Ho's left is Truong Chinh. (Photo courtesy of *Vietnam* pictorial)

by vigorous discussion and sometimes serious disagreement within the Central Committee and the Politburo. During the war, it was rumored that there were recognizable pro-Peking and pro-Moscow factions within the party leadership. Recent evidence suggests that this is improbable. Top party figures often found it convenient to favor Moscow or Peking according to the needs of the moment, but, for most if not all party leaders, dedication to the cause of Vietnamese unification and survival took precedence over loyalty to China or the Soviet Union. If factions did exist, they probably reflected differences over strategy in the South or over the degree of priority to be assigned to domestic concerns or the issue of national unification. What is most striking in all of this is the degree to which party leaders maintained a solid front against outside threats over a period of several decades.

The party's dominant role in Vietnamese society was out of proportion to its size. With a membership of a little more than 1,000 at the opening of World War II, the ICP had reached about 5,000 at the time of its seizure of power in the August Revolution. During the Franco-Vietminh conflict it expanded rapidly, and at the time of the Second National Congress it numbered a reported 500,000 members. Growth brought problems, however, as a number of unqualified and opportunistic elements had entered the organization during its years of rapid expansion. In the years after

Geneva, membership stabilized and a rectification campaign was launched to cleanse the party of impure and incompetent members. In 1956, the recruiting slowly resumed. Recruitment is undertaken primarily through youth organizations directed by the party, such as the Party Labor Youth Group and the Young Pioneers. During the 1950s, when recruitment virtually ceased during the rectification campaign, few youths entered the party, and at the time of the Third Congress in 1960 only about 10 percent of party members were under 26. When active recruitment resumed, vigorous efforts were made to lower the average age of party members, and by the late 1960s, according to one source, more than three-quarters of all members were under 30.

Similar efforts were made to increase the number of women and workers in the party. The percentage of female party members increased from slightly more than 9 percent in 1960 to about 20 percent five years later. Similar increases took place in the percentage of workers and poor peasants in the party, although workers are still a clear minority in the party and the upper levels are dominated by members of middle-class origin. In the early years of the league and the ICP, most recruits were intellectuals of petit bourgeois or landed gentry origins. Active recruitment of workers during the 1930s, and of peasants after the formation of the Vietminh Front in 1941, gradually changed the class balance of the organization, but the recruitment of workers has persistently been hindered, not only by the small size of the working class in Vietnam, but also by the fact that during both the Franco-Vietminh conflict and the later revolutionary struggle in South Vietnam, most workers lived in urban areas occupied by the enemy. At the time of the Third Party Congress in 1960, the party was still primarily rural or petit bourgeois in origin, with workers accounting for an estimated 5 percent of total party membership. The lack of worker representation was particularly noticeable at top levels where urban intellectuals have been dominant since the early years of the party.

THE MASS ASSOCIATIONS

Because of the small size of the Communist party in relation to the population as a whole, the relationship between the party and the mass of the population is a crucial one and a determining factor in the party's ability to mobilize popular support for its goals. In Vietnam, the key link between party and masses is the so-called mass association. Mass associations are organizations grouping individuals by sex, religion, or occupational function, what in a Western society might be termed "interest groups" or "pressure groups." The concept of the mass association goes back to Lenin, who viewed the formation of such organizations as a means of mobilizing various elements in the population to help the Communist party to realize its goals. The embryo of such organizations appeared at the time of the league and the formation of the party in 1930; Comintern directives had instructed the league in the late 1920s to recruit actively and to organize support groups among workers, peasants, youth, and so on. But the development of the mass association as a key element in party strategy dates from 1941, when party leaders decided to form so-called National Salvation Associations among workers, peasants, students, women, and even intellectuals and artists to support the Vietminh Front. The associations were arranged on a vertical basis, with branches at the local level linked to higher echelons up to a central organization. At all levels, the associations were linked to the front organization dominated behind the scenes by the party.

During the Franco-Vietminh conflict and the war in the South, the mass associations played a significant role in winning mass support for the revolutionary movement. Thousands of Vietnamese were involved in the Vietminh Front, its successors in the North, and the NLF through the mass associations without being active members of the party or in many cases even being aware of the party's guiding role within the movement. Organizations representing functional interests as well as religious groups representing Buddhists, Catholics, and even the sects gave the party the capacity to recruit actively at the base level of Vietnamese society. In times of peace, the mass associations provided the party with a means of mobilizing the masses in support of its political and social goals and a means of permitting the various elements in the populace to express their aspirations within the system. In Maoist parlance, the mass associations are a key component in the concept of the "mass line" (from the masses, to the masses), by which the party represents the interests of the population and mobilizes it in support of party policies.

THE ARMED FORCES

Because of the violent and protracted character of the Vietnamese revolution, the military has consistently played a crucial role. The Vietnamese National Army, formed by the French during the conflict with the Vietminh, was a significant factor in politics during the Bao Dai regime and later under the government of Ngo Dinh Diem in South Vietnam. Top army officers were directly responsible for the overthrow of the Diem regime in 1963, and from that time until the end of the war in 1975, military figures such as Nguyen Van Thieu, Nguyen Cao Ky, and Duong Van Minh dominated the South Vietnamese political scene under the veneer of a civilian elected government. In the Republic of Vietnam, where a cohesive political movement based on resistance to communism never really materialized, the armed forces served as virtually the only organized and certainly the dominant force in Saigon politics. On the surface, the military did not have equivalent influence within the Communist movement. Since the formation of the first armed propaganda brigades in December

1944, the Communists have followed the familiar Maoist maxim that the party controls the gun. Within the party, as in the D.R.V. itself, the armed forces were firmly subordinated to civilian authority. Throughout the long years of struggle, first against the French and later against the United States, the armed forces appeared totally loyal to the party leadership, which exercised its authority over the armed forces, within the party, through the Central Military Conference (which was under the Central Committee), and in the government, under the National Defense Council, chaired by the president.

This does not mean that the military lacked influence within the party. The party's civilian leadership was perfectly aware, after the adoption of a rural approach in the early 1940s, that armed struggle would be a key element in revolutionary strategy, and throughout the generation of struggle that lay ahead, military needs were consistently given high priority. A number of the top figures became career military officers and presumably represented the interests of the armed forces in party meetings. The most prominent undoubtedly was Vo Nguyen Giap, the commander of the first armed propaganda units on their formation in 1944 and later minister of defense of the D.R.V. Other key military figures were Nguyen Chi Thanh, commander of Communist forces in the South until his death in 1967, the minority generals Chu Van Tan and Le Quang Ba, and Van Tien Dung, commander of the final offensive against the Saigon government in 1975 and currently minister of defense of the Socialist Republic of Vietnam (S.R.V.).

Throughout the war, such prominent military figures undoubtedly played a major role in decision making, and several have served in the top councils of the party. There is no evidence, however, that there was a recognizable military faction within the Central Committee or the Politburo or that military figures have dominated the party, as was the case briefly in the Chinese Communist party after the Cultural Revolution in China. Up to the present, the party's tradition of civilian leadership has appeared to remain unshaken. From another perspective, however, the D.R.V. has become one of the most militarized societies in Asia. During the Vietnam War, military conscription took most young males of draft age. Women and those males who were not in the armed forces were mobilized to serve in artillery or bomb-defusing units or, in the countryside, to form self-defense militia units to defend their villages against saboteurs or possible enemy attack from the South. Military units stationed in the North were assigned duties in economic construction, planting and harvesting, or repairing bomb damage. It was, as the slogans of the day confirmed, a totally mobilized society—"all for the front lines" and "every citizen a soldier." The end of the war in 1975 probably brought optimism that the North Vietnamese army, one of the largest in the world, could be rapidly demobilized and returned to peacetime activities. By 1978, however, such plans had to be abandoned. Border conflicts with China and Cambodia, both of which led to war the following year, forced the regime to build up its military forces to wartime levels. Once again, Vietnamese society was forced to gear up for war. Civilians and soldiers were mobilized to build "combat villages" along the Cambodian border and along the northern frontier with China. In the aftermath of the 1979 war with China, the regime called for transforming each district into a self-sufficient military fortress to defend itself against outside attack.

The prominent role of national defense in Vietnamese society today can be explained as a natural consequence of a generation of struggle to achieve unification and of regional conflicts in recent years. The ability of the regime and the party to maintain the primacy of civilian rule throughout the crises of the last generation is impressive and a testimony to the inner cohesion of the party leadership. But the constant mobilization of the population to realize the objectives set by the party is bound to take its toll on popular morale. This, indeed, is what the regime is now finding as it attempts to use such time-tested techniques to mobilize the people of Vietnam to build a prosperous and strong peacetime society.

UNIFICATION

The fall of Saigon in the spring of 1975 brought to a close a generation of civil war and introduced the sweet smell of victory to Hanoi. For the Communists, however, success brought dilemmas as well as opportunities. How quickly should the South be integrated with the North? Should an additional period of separate existence be contemplated, as had been suggested in D.R.V. and NLF propaganda during the war, in order to reassure southerners that they would not be crushed under the heels of hard-bitten cadres sent down from the North? Or should assimilation be achieved rapidly on the assumption that prolonged separation would only exacerbate the delicate problems that the future integration of the two zones into one Vietnam would entail?

There is some evidence that for a brief period after the fall of Saigon, party leaders in Hanoi hesitated over such questions. By midsummer, however, the decision had been taken to move expeditiously toward unification. In the fall, a joint meeting of northern and southern leaders reached agreement to realize political and administrative unification during 1976. Elections for a joint National Assembly, in which almost half the deputies represented the population in the South, were held in April. The People's Revolutionary party (PRP), which had represented the southern branch of the VWP during the war, was abolished and the members integrated into a new nationwide Vietnamese Communist party (VCP), which replaced the VWP at a national congress (the fourth in the party's history) in December of 1976. The NLF was dissolved, and its local organizations in the South were absorbed into the National Fatherland Front, a successor to the Vietminh Front in the North. Finally, in the summer of 1976, the formal unified Socialist Republic of Vietnam was established with its capital at Hanoi.

The decision to move rapidly toward unification was laden with risks, but party leaders probably felt that they had little choice. The violence of the reunification struggle had seriously depleted the stock of experienced and dedicated cadres in the South. Replacements would have to be brought down from the North to handle the complex problems of postwar reconstruction and the consolidation of revolutionary authority. The economy, now in a perilous state because of war damage, the flight of farmers to the cities, and the drying up of foreign aid, would have to be gradually nurtured back to health. This could better be done, in the eyes of party leaders in Hanoi, if administrative unity had been achieved. In sum, the longer the delay in unification, the more potential problems could be expected for the long-term political, social, and economic objectives of the regime.

Under its new rulers, South Vietnam was gradually integrated with the North. A new revolutionary administration was established at all levels with the aid of northern cadres and units of the PAVN. A comprehensive survey of the southern population was carried out, and those considered potentially hostile to the regime (such as military officers, government officials, high-level employees of foreign firms, and so on) were instructed to report to "reeducation camps" for indoctrination. Some were kept only a few weeks and then returned to society. Others were sent to work camps for extensive periods. According to foreign reports, several hundred thousand remained in such camps a number of years after the end of the war, a statistic that was vigorously denied by the authorities.

There was relatively little open resistance in the South to the new administration. A few hostile elements fled to the hills and attempted to continue the struggle. In general, however, the population appeared to acquiesce in the new situation, if not with enthusiasm, then with curiosity or resignation. To many foreign visitors, the population in Saigon appeared to adjust rapidly to the presence of northern cadres in the streets and sometimes even to ignore them. Hanoi would find that it would not be easy to change the profligate and corrupt ways of its new charge.

Indeed, the problems of peace soon began to impose new strains on the system. Attempts to impose government policies in minority areas in the Central Highlands reportedly caused discontent and the recreation of the dissident movement FULRO, which had caused Saigon difficulties in the 1960s. There were reports of the creation of a national resistance front of diverse antiregime groups somewhere in the Mekong Delta. Although it was unlikely that such groups posed a serious threat to the survival of Communist rule in Vietnam, they were an ominous sign of growing opposition to government policies.

Problems within the population at large reflected weaknesses within the body of the party. For a generation, the party had been the heart of the revolution. The willingness of its members to sacrifice for the cause of reunification had been a crucial factor in its success. By the late 1960s, however, there were signs of strain in the almost legendary internal strength of the party. Weariness at the seemingly endless war affected northerners and southerners alike. In the North, press reports of arrogance, laziness, and corruption among party members had become increasingly frequent. Inner-party documents show that similar problems were plaguing party cadres in the South. By 1974, the party called for a rectification campaign to cleanse the organization of its internal impurities.

Victory in the South only added to the problem. In order to cope with the dearth of cadres in the South, party leaders were compelled to introduce northerners into the southern administration. Many, accustomed to the personal privations and the puritanical lifestyle in the North, were seduced by the relatively affluent and hedonistic conditions in the South. Others, accustomed to the "guerrilla mentality" of life in the bush, found it difficult to develop bureaucratic skills and an effective manner of dealing with the masses. Articles in the official press cited cases of flagrant corruption and favoritism. Others were critical of bureaucratic incompetence or arrogance. The problem reached crisis proportions in 1978, when stringent economic reforms nationalized businesses and confiscated property and led thousands of Vietnamese, many of them overseas Chinese, to attempt to flee the country. Many who managed to escape abroad claimed that government officials were accepting bribes of up to $3,000 or $4,000 to grant exit permits and arrange for transport by junk or freighter to other countries in Southeast Asia. Some charged that the government was officially involved in the traffic and was attempting to fleece the allegedly wealthy overseas Chinese of their savings before driving them out of the country. Hanoi vehemently denied the latter charge but conceded that many officials had accepted bribes from those desiring to leave Vietnam.

By the late 1970s, party leaders had become convinced that a stringent purge of the party membership was required to purge the organization of its impure elements. According to Le Duc Tho, the Politburo official in charge of party organization, many party members had committed serious errors such as corruption, favoritism, and oppression of the masses. During succeeding months, the party began to issue new membership cards. Only those who received cards would continue to be members. There were rumors that up to two-thirds of current members, by now numbering well over 1.5 million, might be purged. At the Fifth Congress of the VCP, held in April 1982, however, it was announced that only 86,000 members of the party had been expelled. In the meantime, a recruitment program to bring new blood into the organization was initiated. According to one report, 90 percent of the 370,000 new members were under 30 years of age; 70 percent had served in the armed forces. Clearly, the leadership was hoping that the younger generation, which had formed the foot soldiers of the revolution in its later stages, would now help to build a new socialist Vietnam.

Troubles within the ranks of the party did not leave the top unscathed. For a generation, the party leadership had maintained its internal unity in the face of the intimidating problems of insurgency and war. The problems of peacetime would be more difficult to surmount. In December 1976, at the Fourth Party Congress, several members of the party, including Politburo member Hoang Van Hoan, were deprived of their posts. At the time, reports speculated that Hoan, a member of the party since its founding and one-time ambassador to the People's Republic of China, may have stepped down because of age. It later became clear that the move had political implications. In the summer of 1979, Hoan defected to China while traveling to East Berlin, ostensibly for medical reasons. On arrival in Peking, Hoan charged that VCP General Secretary Le Duan had established a party dictatorship and was ruthlessly suppressing all forms of dissent within the organization. While refraining from predicting an imminent revolt against the current leadership, Hoan asserted that discontent with Le Duan and his policies was rising within the party and would eventually result in his overthrow.

Hoang Van Hoan's charges are difficult to substantiate without further evidence. Clearly, however, tension within the party leadership has escalated in recent years. Signs of strain have periodically appeared in the official press, notably since the summer of 1978, when editorials in *Nhan Dan* conceded that there had been major differences over policy and caustically predicted that there would be further defections of weak elements within the party. It seems likely that both domestic and foreign policy issues have been involved. The purge of Hoang Van Hoan and other lesser party figures in 1976 was probably connected with the deterioration in relations with China, and more recent statements in the official press confirm that some elements within the party would prefer a more even-handed policy between China and the Soviet Union. At the same time, the economic difficulties that have plagued the regime since reunification have apparently resulted in serious differences within the party leadership over the pace of advance toward socialism (for further discussion, see Chapters 6 and 8).

A second major problem facing the postwar VCP is the age of the party leadership. Virtually all the top party leaders are in their late 60s or older, and in 1981 the average age of the twelve most senior members of the Politburo was over 70. Top party officials have been aware of the need to introduce younger figures into positions of leadership, but as in China and the Soviet Union, generational change at the summit of the party has proved difficult. At the Fifth Party Congress, held in late March and April 1982, several party veterans, including Vo Nguyen Giap and Nguyen Duy Trinh, were dropped from the Politburo and replaced by younger men. Yet it is worthy of note that the veteran leadership of Le Duan, Pham Van Dong, and Truong Chinh remains intact (only Vo Nguyen Giap has been removed), suggesting that in difficult times continuity is considered to be of primary importance.

A similar process of cautious change has taken place in the ranks of the government. In early 1980, after months of rumors and speculation, there was a major shakeup in the cabinet. A total of nineteen cabinet posts changed hands, including the replacement of veteran Foreign Minister Nguyen Duy Trinh by his deputy, Nguyen Co Thach; of Minister of Interior Tran Quoc Hoan by Pham Hung; and of Minister of Defense Vo Nguyen Giap by General Van Tien Dung, mastermind of the brilliant spring 1975 military offensive in the South. A number of capable younger officials were moved into positions demanding technological competence. Several other changes took place between 1980 and 1982. Some of these changes were undoubtedly due to reasons of health, for some of the major figures relieved of their posts have been rumored to suffer from serious illness. Others may have been removed as a result of criticism that too many top party officials simultaneously occupy top positions in the government. Above all, however, it is likely that the changes represent a desire to inject new blood, capable of handling the complex challenges of a postliberation world, into the government leadership.

At the same time, further changes in government have appeared with the approval of a new constitution for the S.R.V., which was ratified by the National Assembly in December 1980. The new charter, which is designed to carry Vietnamese society into a period of socialist industrialization in coming decades, provides for the creation of a new Council of State (similar to the Presidium in the Soviet Union) to serve as a collective chief of state. The position of chief of state has been a problem in Hanoi since the death of Ho Chi Minh in 1969. Ho was succeeded by his vice-president, the old labor organizer Ton Duc Thang. Because of Thang's age and relatively limited influence in party ranks, the position declined to one of no more than ceremonial importance. Thang died in March 1980 and was briefly replaced by Nguyen Huu Tho, the long-time chairman of the NLF in the South. The new Council of State replaces the head of state in the 1960 constitution. It is empowered to "decide on important matters concerning the building of Socialism and National Defense" and to "supervise the implementation of the laws, decrees, and resolutions" of the S.R.V. The size of the council was to be determined by the National Assembly. In the early summer of 1981, it was announced that party veteran Truong Chinh had been named chairman of the Council of State and thus had become the de facto head of state. By this choice, the S.R.V. indicated that it would not follow the practice in the Soviet Union, where Party Secretary Leonid Brezhnev was also chairman of the Presidium, but would continue the policy of collective leadership, avoiding the concentration in one person's hands of power in both party and state that had first been established during the life of Ho Chi Minh.

Is a serious split within the party and government leadership a serious possibility in the near future? There seems little doubt that tensions have been at a high level in recent years as Hanoi attempts to confront the challenges of the postwar era. On the other hand, unity against the common enemy has always managed to prevail over disagreement concerning specific policies. Indeed, it is likely that the current leadership has developed a sort of "siege mentality" to protect itself through internal cohesion against the storms that have battered it from without. Hoang Van Hoan's charges notwithstanding, the historical record suggests that party leaders recognize the vital importance of maintaining a solid front in the face of external danger and will make every effort to maintain that record in coming years.

CONCLUSION

For a generation, the domestic representatives of two dynamic political ideologies struggled for supremacy in Vietnam. Although it might be an overstatement to characterize the G.V.N. under Ngo Dinh Diem and Nguyen Van Thieu as a practicing democracy, it is not too much to say that the fall of Saigon in 1975 symbolized the triumph in Vietnam of communist doctrine and practice over those of Western bourgeois democracy.

What internal factors can explain the triumph of communism over the forces of Western-style democracy in Vietnam? To analyze the problem, one must break it into two parts: (1) the failure of Western democracy and (2) the success of communism. The first is easier to explain than the second. The fact is that democratic political systems established in several Southeast Asian countries following World War II have not fared well in recent years. Lacking the cultural heritage that made democratic institutions possible in the West, plagued by economic imbalance, political factionalism, and ethnic unrest, most collapsed or were overthrown by military coups d'etat. Today few survive. Placed in this perspective, the failure of democracy in South Vietnam appears less the consequence of political failure in Washington or Saigon than the product of conditions endemic throughout the region. For the cultural obstacles to democracy in Vietnam were at least as strong as they were elsewhere in the region, if not stronger. The presence of an experienced and determined revolutionary movement with its roots deep in the colonial era only compounded the problem.

But if the failure of Western democracy in Vietnam can be ascribed to generic causes throughout the region as a whole, the triumph of communism cannot. Indeed, except for Cambodia and Laos, societies that were clearly influenced by the events taking place in Indochina as a whole, Vietnam is the only case in Southeast Asia in which the national liberation struggle was led to victory by the Communist party. Elsewhere, the failure of democratic institutions usually resulted, often by default, in the rise of the military. In Vietnam, the Communists not only provided a viable alternative to Western bourgeois democracy or military rule, but they grasped power, after a generation of bitter struggle, by their own efforts.

To explain the unique conditions that brought about the Vietnam exception, then, attention must be directed above all to the internal conditions that led to Communist success. As noted earlier in this chapter, Marxism had a particular appeal among patriotic intellectuals in colonial Vietnam. As revolutionary experience in both China and Vietnam has demonstrated, it was apparently relatively easy for the sons and daughters of the traditional scholar-elite to transfer their allegiance from the now discredited Confucian tradition, itself more a secularized social and political philosophy than a metaphysical religious system, to a dynamic "political religion" like Marxism. For a lapsed Confucianist, the path to Marxism was in many ways an easier one than that to the individualistic tenets of liberal democracy.

If the Confucian cultural heritage made Vietnam a fertile breeding ground for Marxism, did it make a Communist victory in Vietnam inevitable? That seems doubtful. For one thing, the majority of Vietnamese were not deeply imbued with Confucian ideology. Indeed, as party leaders soon came to recognize (and as Marx would have conceded long before), the Communist vision of a future classless utopia had only a limited appeal in a society composed primarily of illiterate peasants and urban petit bourgeois intellectuals. It was in deference to this fact that the party eventually learned to tailor its program to respond to issues of broad popular appeal, such as national independence, social justice, democratic freedoms, and land reform. References to communism were muted, and even after the seizure of power, the transformation to socialist ownership took place only after the party had consolidated its rule and given the mass of the population at least a rudimentary indoctrination in Marxist teachings.

Under such conditions, the Communists, while possessing some obvious cultural advantages, could succeed only if they displayed the capacity to manipulate the objective situation in Vietnam to their advantage. As Lenin had argued to a different generation, revolutions do not just happen, they must be waged and won. The success of communism in Vietnam, then, must be ascribed above all to Ho Chi Minh and his colleagues, who were able to mobilize a mass movement with the driving force to bring the party to power in Vietnam. In the contemporary world, there are no better students of Leninism than the Vietnamese.

NOTES

1. Douglas Pike, *History of Vietnamese Communism: 1925–1976* (Stanford, Calif.: Hoover Institution Press, 1978), p. 136, citing Lao Dong Party Directive 31 CT/TW, June 4, 1957, p. 7.

6

The Economy

Like most of its neighbors, Vietnam has been a predominantly agrarian society since its emergence from prehistory more than twenty centuries ago. For the Vietnamese, agriculture, almost by definition, implies the cultivation of wet rice. Indeed, recent archeological evidence suggests that the Vietnamese may have been one of the first peoples in Asia to master the cultivation of rice. By the time of the Chinese conquest in the late second century B.C., the Vietnamese had already become advanced practitioners of irrigation in agriculture.

The hydraulic character of Vietnamese civilization has had a significant impact on the nature of the Vietnamese economy. It has sharpened the self-image of the Vietnamese people as rice farmers living in lowland river valleys or along the seacoast, scorning the peoples living in the mountains along the horizon as barbarians lacking in proper culture. It has shaped the value system of its inhabitants and led them to emphasize the importance of cultivable land and agriculture in the overall scheme of human activities and to denigrate commerce and manufacturing as subordinate and even vulgar occupations. If the contentions of some historians are valid, the hydraulic character of Vietnamese civilization even helped to shape the political culture itself, encouraging the growth of a professionally competent but rigid and potentially oppressive bureaucratic system characterized by centralized controls and headed by a despotic monarchy.

Whatever the truth of such speculations, there is no doubt that traditional Vietnam was a classical example of a water-based agricultural society similar to some of the famous riparian civilizations in China, in India, and along the Tigris, the Euphrates, and the Nile in the Middle East. From time immemorial, the wealth—indeed the very survival—of Vietnamese society was based on agriculture.

This is not to say that premodern Vietnam was entirely lacking in manufacturing and commercial skills. Archeological evidence shows that the Vietnamese were familiar with the arts of woodwork, metalworking, lacquerware, and silk weaving and had engaged in regular commercial contacts with their neighbors since the time of the Lac Viet. Under Chinese rule and later, after the restoration of independence, trade and manufacturing continued to develop. Handicrafts attained a degree of sophistication comparable to that in China and other advanced societies in East Asia. Vietnamese embroidery, ceramics and porcelain, and metalwork were renowned throughout the region. The capital of Hanoi emerged as a major commercial and manufacturing center. Cottage industries began to appear in villages, and markets developed along the major highways. Salt and iron were exchanged with mountain peoples for forestry products, and ships built in Vietnamese ports plied the South China Sea.

Such developments, however, did not significantly alter the agricultural character of Vietnamese culture. Unlike neighboring Champa, Vietnam did not become a major factor in regional commerce. Nor was it touched by the Islamic invasion, which created a trading network stretching from the Spice Islands in the Indonesian archipelago to the shores of East Africa and the Middle East. Throughout the precolonial period, commerce was subordinate in importance to agriculture in Vietnam. As in North China, merchants were scorned as corrupt and low-class, and much of the commercial activity in Vietnam was handled by foreign residents, such as the Chinese, who began to arrive in increasing numbers after the fall of the Ming dynasty in the seventeenth century.

THE EFFECTS OF COLONIALISM

The advent of the West in the sixteenth and seventeenth centuries introduced Vietnam to the spreading world market but did not at first substantially affect the nature of Vietnamese society. Western countries set up small trading stations along the central coast, but Vietnam had few of the tropical products that had lured adventurers to the islands further south, and eventually Western economic interests found greater profits elsewhere. By the early eighteenth century, few traders remained.

In the nineteenth century, fundamental changes took place in the pattern of European economic activity throughout Asia. The increasing pace of the industrial revolution caused Western nations increasingly to view Asia as a source for industrial raw materials and a possible consumer market for manufactured goods produced in Paris, Manchester, and Rotterdam. The French conquest of Vietnam was related to this process, albeit initially only indirectly. At first, French advocates of colonial expansion in Southeast Asia viewed Vietnam more as a steppingstone to the mythical Chinese market than as an area of economic wealth of its own. Once the conquest was completed, however, colonial interests were not slow to see that, although Vietnam lacked the economic resources of some other colonies in the region, it was by no means totally bereft of commercial potential. The primary source of profit was the export of rubber and rice. Rubber, produced in plantations in the *terre rouge* area along the Cambodian frontier, became a major source of export earnings in the early twentieth century. Rice production was stimulated by the opening up of new lands in the coastal provinces of the lower Mekong. Marshlands in the Plain of Reeds were drained, and an irrigation network was constructed, making it possible to cultivate for the first time thousands of acres of previously unusable land. By the early years of the twentieth century, rice exports had begun to increase and exceeded 300,000 metric tons annually by the late 1920s.

The effects of colonial rule in urban areas were no less lasting. Stimulated by official policies and the import of European capital, a commercial and manufacturing sector began to emerge. For the most part, economic growth took place primarily in light industries such as sugar refining, food processing, assembly of bicycles and small appliances, and textiles and pharmaceutical manufacturing. There was a relatively unspectacular but steady growth of local production in the coal mines along the coast north of Haiphong. Transport and communications were vastly improved with the construction of the best road and rail network in Southeast Asia.

Defenders of French colonialism pointed to such developments as evidence that French rule had brought benefits to the peoples of Indochina: Vietnam had been introduced to the expanding international economic market and the first seeds of a new capitalist order had been planted. A commercial bourgeoisie and a small but growing industrial proletariat also appeared. Critics charged, however, that the benefits of such changes to the local population were minimal. Denying the alleged benefits of the *mission civilisatrice*, they pointed out that French policy did not really promote the growth of trade and industry in Vietnam. To the contrary, the aim of the colonial regime was to discourage the local production of goods that might compete with French manufactured goods exported, at low import duties, to the colonies. Such commercial activity as did exist tended to be dominated by Europeans, Indian moneylenders, or the ubiquitous overseas Chinese. Even the manufacture of *nuoc mam*, the popular Vietnamese fermented fish sauce, was monopolized by Chinese interests. According to some estimates, non-Vietnamese dominated up to 90 percent of all trade and manufacturing in the commercial center of Saigon-Cholon.

Whether or not French agricultural policies were of overall benefit to the local population is equally a matter of dispute. The draining of the marshlands in the Mekong River delta, the development of a cash crop economy, and the expansion of rice exports were all pointed to by defenders of the French colonial regime as proof that Paris was fulfilling its *mission civilisatrice* by building a modern agricultural economy in Indochina. Others assert that such superficial indications of progress are seriously misleading. The commercialization of land and the draining of the marshes, while undoubtedly expanding the amount of land under cultivation, did not raise the rural standard of living. Rapid population growth and rising exports tended to wipe out gains in rice production, and per capita food consumption may even have declined during the colonial period. Nor did colonial policy lead to the growth of a new class of private landholding farmers. Commercialization led to further land concentration and in the Mekong Delta, where new lands were opened to the highest bidder, to the development of a class of wealthy landlords, many of whom lived in Saigon. Land-hungry peasants flocking to the area from crowded parts of the country were reduced to working as tenants or landless laborers. Others sought employment in the crowded and unsanitary factories or on the rubber plantations along the Cambodian border, where they worked long hours under abysmal working conditions for paltry wages.

Any estimate of the balance sheet of the colonial experience in Vietnam is bound to be affected by the prejudices of the individual observer. The introduction of Western capitalist techniques into Vietnam and the construction of an advanced system of transport and communications undoubtedly represented the first step in the emergence of a modern balanced economy. The human costs, however, were high. The early stages of industrialization have been difficult in all countries. What was tragic about the situation was that, in Vietnam, the poor suffered for so little. The end result of the French colonial experience in Vietnam was not the creation of a society on the verge of rapid economic development, but a classic example of a dual economy with a small and predominantly foreign commercial sector in the cities surrounded by a mass of untrained and often poverty-stricken peasants in the villages.

THE ECONOMY OF SOUTH VIETNAM

The Geneva Conference of 1954 split Vietnam into two separate zones, North and South, each with a distinct economic structure reflecting the competing ideologies in the Cold War. In the North, the Communists began gradually to build a socialist economy; in the South, the regime of Ngo Dinh Diem followed a modified capitalist model. For Diem, the primary challenges were the lack of a resource and industrial base and the inequality of landholding. Most of the nation's mineral resources—gold, iron, tin, and zinc—were located in the North. While the South possessed in Saigon the most vibrant commercial center in the country, its contribution to the national economy was primarily agricultural produce.

Diem's attempt to surmount these challenges had only indifferent success. Because of the limited resource base, industrial development in the South took place primarily in the consumer goods sector. With assistance from the United States and a number of other Western countries, industrial zones were established on the outskirts of Saigon and in some of the larger cities of the delta and along the central coast. Sugar refineries, cement works, and plants for the manufacturing of textiles, pharmaceuticals, processed foods, and paper products began to appear. At best, however, the South's small manufacturing industry did not meet the needs of its expanding population, and the country became increasingly dependent upon imports. With exports limited, Saigon's balance of payments was highly unfavorable, and the economy was sustained only by rising assistance from the United States.

If South Vietnam had only limited potential for industrial development, the agricultural picture, on paper, was more optimistic. With the rich rice lands in the Mekong Delta and along the central coast, and the redlands area along the Cambodian border suitable for rubber plantations, more than one-sixth of the total land area of the South was under cultivation. The major problems were low productivity and inequality of land distribution. Under U.S. pressure, the Diem regime inaugurated a land reform program in 1956 that called for the breakup of large landholdings in the delta and the purchase of lands at low interest rates by the tenants. Implementation was hampered by landlord resistance and loopholes in the regulations, however, and after several years of operation only about 10 percent of the eligible tenant families in the South had received any land under the program. Only in the late 1960s, with the inauguration of President Thieu's "land to the tiller" program, did the government begin to realize substantial progress in achieving a greater degree of equality in landholdings. Under the program, tenants received title to their lands without charge, while the government compensated previous owners.

Efforts to expand rice production and the export of agricultural products ran into similar problems. Plagued by low productivity and the disruption caused by civil insurgency, rice production failed to achieve a satisfactory rate of growth. After 1965, the South ceased to be a net exporter of rice and for the remainder of the war was compelled to import food. Rubber, the South's other major source of export earnings, encountered similar problems, and as the borderlands became the scene of contention between ARVN and insurgency forces, rubber production declined from 78,000 metric tons in 1961 to only 20,000 metric tons in 1972.

By the late 1960s, the South Vietnamese economy had become almost totally dependent on U.S. assistance. Imports of consumer goods, encouraged to prevent galloping inflation, were financed in large part by the U.S.-sponsored Commercial Import Program. Several hundred thousand Vietnamese worked for U.S. agencies in South Vietnam or otherwise served the needs of the large foreign population. Food imports from the United States made up for chronic shortages of production in the countryside. An affluent urban middle class thrived amid a swelling urban population of poor workers, beggars, and refugees flooding into refugee camps in the suburbs.

BUILDING SOCIALISM IN THE NORTH

The Vietnamese Communists, returning to Hanoi in triumph in the autumn of 1954, faced economic problems of equally intimidating proportions. The urban economy, relatively primitive in any case, had been badly neglected during the Franco-Vietminh conflict. Much of the nation's technological elite had left Hanoi to serve in the revolutionary armed forces or had emigrated to the South after the Geneva Conference to live under the noncommunist regime in Saigon. In the countryside, agricultural production was hindered by the low level of mechanization and the lack of artificial fertilizer. The per capita production of rice in Vietnam was one of the lowest in Asia.

In the longer term, of course, the party's solution to such problems was the abolition of private property and the building of a communist society. For the immediate future, however, the primary concern of party leaders was to consolidate their support among the mass of the population and to put the economy on a reasonably stable footing. Radical policies leading to nationalization of industry and collectivization of agriculture would only result in the alienation of many Vietnamese who had supported the Vietminh movement in its struggle for independence. For that reason, the economic policies adopted by the regime in the years immediately following the Geneva Conference were essentially moderate. Although major utilities, banks, and some of the largest business enterprises were placed under state control, trade and manufacturing was left in private hands and the middle class was reassured that its profits would be guaranteed and its talents would be used by the new regime. In order to extend government control over the economy and to make preparations for a future advance to socialist ownership, the regime did take steps to regulate wages, prices, and the allocation of goods and encouraged private enterprises to form so-called joint private-state enterprises, in which private firms agreed to accept a degree of government involvement in decision making and ownership in return for state subsidies and easy access to raw materials.

So long as the agricultural sector remained primitive, however, no program to develop the manufacturing and industrial sector could hope to succeed. The excess labor in the rural villages—well over 80 percent of the entire population of North Vietnam lived on the farms—would have to be driven from the countryside into the cities in order to relieve the population pressure in the villages and to provide workers for the growing industrial sector. To party leaders, the ultimate solution to the problem was collectivization. In the Marxist view, social ownership in the countryside would permit more effective use of the land through the breaking up of small farms and the introduction of widespread mechanization. In order to win the support of land-hungry peasants, for whom socialist ownership had no inherent attraction, the regime preceded collectivization with a program of land reform. Arable lands belonging to wealthy landlords were confiscated and distributed to the poor and landless peasants. Middle peasants and rich peasants (loosely defined as farmers who owned more land than they could cultivate with their own labor) were not generally affected. The objective of the program was political as well as economic. If the primary economic goal of land reform was to encourage peasants to increase grain production, the political objective was to destroy the power of conservative elements at the village level and to create a new village leadership made up of formerly poor and landless peasants who would be grateful to the party and loyally carry out its policies.

In some respects, the land reform program was a striking success. More than 2 million acres (800,000 hectares) of land were distributed; and more than 2 million farm families, well over half the total number in the D.R.V., received at least some land under the program. The power of the traditional landed gentry was broken, and a new village leadership composed of poor and middle peasants emerged. Behind such indications of success, however, some serious problems had arisen. In some areas, government cadres had been too zealous in carrying out the program, creating resistance among reluctant villagers. In others, villagers took advantage of the program to avenge themselves on their enemies by accusing them of counterrevolutionary activities. In some instances, revolutionary cadres of poor peasant background attacked the families of loyal members of the Vietminh who had just been released from military service after Geneva. Government directives were not always helpful in instructing local cadres how to carry out the program. Each village was expected to classify some local residents as reactionary landlords and to divide up their land, even though in some cases there were few landlords and no excess land in the village.

In 1956, the party formally conceded that errors had been made in the implementation of the program and that a number of innocent Vietnamese had been wrongly classified as enemies of the people and deprived of their land. Party General Secretary Truong Chinh and several other high officials responsible for carrying out the program were removed from office, although Chinh retained his membership in the Politburo.

COLLECTIVIZATION IN THE COUNTRYSIDE

In 1958, party leaders decided to begin the process of collectivization. The decision could not have been an easy one. Since the days of Lenin, Marxist doctrine had held that socialization of the countryside could not take place until mechanization was sufficiently advanced to demonstrate to suspicious peasants the real benefits of collective farming. Under this policy of "mechanization before collectivization," the transformation to socialist ownership in the countryside was supposed to be delayed until the urban economy had reached a relatively high level of industrialization. In the Soviet Union, collectivization began with the establishment of machine tractor stations in rural districts after 1928.

The Chinese were the first to abandon this premise. In 1955, facing the frustrating reality that industrialization could not be achieved on the foundation of a backward agricultural sector, the Chinese leadership sought to break out of the dilemma by reversing the process and putting collectivization before mechanization. By this reasoning, Chinese peasants were "poor and blank" and lacked the innate bourgeois tendencies of their counterparts in Europe. They would thus be willing to follow the party's lead and move to socialist ownership before mechanization brought the promise of increased food production. If party strategists were correct, collectivization by itself would lead to production increases, thus releasing capital and labor to stimulate the industrial sector.

In 1958, the Vietnamese, noting the relative success of the Chinese program, decided to embark on a similar road to collectivization. Following the Chinese example, the program was carefully crafted to achieve the maximum of voluntary support. The first stage consisted of the establishment of seasonal labor exchange teams, wherein peasant families shared labor during the harvest season but retained ownership over land and tools and kept the profits. The second stage involved the formation of semisocialist cooperatives the size of rural hamlets in which the peasants pooled their tools and their land and received a proportion of the final harvest in proportion to their labor and the amount of land brought into the organization. Membership was voluntary, and the individual peasant family could withdraw with its land and its tools and draft animals at any time. The final stage was the fully socialist collective farm. It was larger than the cooperative, and those peasants who joined abandoned their title to all land, tools, and farm animals contributed to the organization. Payment was made on the basis of work, not the amount of land contributed by the individual family.

By the early 1960s, the program was substantially completed, and more than 80 percent of all farm families in lowland districts (areas inhabited by mountain minorities, in general, were exempted from the program) had been enrolled in either semisocialist or fully socialist collective organizations. As in China, there had been little open resistance among the peasants, in part because the government permitted the peasants to cultivate food for their own use (or for sale at the local markets) on small family plots consisting of no more than 5 percent of the total land of the collective. To the disappointment of the regime, however, collective ownership did not result in significant increases in grain production, in part because mechanization remained low, with less than 7 percent of the land plowed by tractor. Output increased gradually from pre-Geneva levels but did not achieve planned goals, and with the rate of population increase running at well over 2.2 percent per year, the D.R.V. was plagued with a continuing shortage of food throughout the 1960s, forcing the government to import it.

The move toward collectivization had been accompanied by the transition to long-term planning within the economy as a whole. In 1955, the National Planning Board had been established and entrusted with the responsibility of preparing plans for the future development of a fully socialist, technologically advanced society. In 1958, a Three-Year Plan was inaugurated to accompany the first stages of socialism in the countryside and to prepare for the promulgation of a Five-Year Plan scheduled to begin in 1961. The primary objective of the latter plan was to complete the socialist transformation of the economy while promoting rapid development of the industrial and agricultural sector and advancing from small-scale to large-scale production. In some respects, the plan was a success. By the end of the plan in 1965, the public sector had achieved a dominant role within the national economy. According to official statistics, more than 90 percent of the industrial and agricultural sector was under national or collective ownership. Only in such areas as transport and domestic trade were private businesses (often those of overseas Chinese) still active. Significant advances were also realized in some areas of industrial production, notably in the output of coal and cement and the production of electricity. Much of this progress had been achieved as the result of assistance from the Soviet Union, China, and other socialist countries. According to one source, between 1955 and the end of the Five-Year Plan, Hanoi's socialist allies provided a total of more than $1 billion in economic aid. Eighty percent had come from the U.S.S.R. Most of the remainder had come from the P.R.C., with whose assistance the D.R.V. was able to build fertilizer plants and two power stations and to begin a major steel complex at Thai Nguyen, 40 miles (64 kilometers) north of Hanoi.

Initially, the regime had planned to follow the First Five-Year Plan with a second, scheduled to begin in 1966. By 1965, however, the growing needs of the war in the South had intervened, and until the end of the struggle in 1975, economic development took second place to the war effort. With males now being conscripted into the armed services and precious economic resources monopolized by the armed forces, the second plan was scrapped and replaced by annual plans. The launching of full-scale bombing of the North by the Johnson administration in 1965 undoubtedly added to the problem. Intensive bombing raids decimated the D.R.V.'s small industrial sector and its transportation network. To minimize damage, the government ordered the dispersal of industrial plants wherever possible into rural areas, and its socialist allies increased the level of economic assistance. According to government figures, aid from the Soviet Union, China, and Eastern Europe totaled $4 billion between 1965 and the end of the war ten years later. Despite such efforts, however, the overall effects of the war on the economy of the North were severe. Agricultural production stagnated while industrial output in key areas declined significantly from the levels achieved at the end of the First Five-Year Plan.

THE NATIONAL ECONOMY SINCE 1975

With the end of the war in April 1975, the regime was finally able to turn its attention once again to the economic front and to the arduous process of recovering from the war. The problems were intimidating. Throughout the country, the damage from a generation of conflict would have to be repaired and the economy placed on a peacetime basis. More than 2 million young people serving in the armed forces would have to be demobilized and returned to peacetime occupations. In the South, the residue of the American era would have to be eradicated. In Saigon and other major cities, an estimated 3 million refugees huddled in camps to escape the ravages of war in the countryside. Many rural districts were virtually depopulated. In the cities, industrial and commercial activity was at a virtual standstill and unemployment was in the millions.

Beyond such immediate economic problems lay an issue of compelling long-term significance. How long should the new Vietnam remain divided into two separate economic systems, one capitalist, the other socialist? As in 1954, the Communists approached the problem with caution. In order to attract the widest possible spectrum of support in the South, the program of the NLF had been cast in moderate terms, stressing basic issues such as land reform, higher salaries, and better working conditions and avoiding references to the ultimate goal of a communist society. For the moment, the party leadership decided to continue that pattern in order to reassure the population in the South and to encourage a resumption of productive activities. The new revolutionary authorities directed that all businesses remain in operation and promised that profits would be guaranteed. Banks, utilities, and a few major firms were nationalized. The property of wealthy entrepreneurs was confiscated, and a few, accused of speculation or the hoarding of goods, were charged with crimes against the people. A handful were executed. The government's ultimate objective was to restore the South to its traditional position as breadbasket for the entire country, while the North would assume the lead in manufacturing. This goal could not be achieved, however, until the peasants were lured back to the villages. During the last years of the war, vast numbers of peasants had fled from their villages to the security of the cities. By the early 1970s, nearly half the entire population in the South was living in urban areas, while nearly one-third of the arable land in the country was reportedly lying idle.

The first priority, then, was to persuade the refugees living in the cities to return to their farms. The regime's answer to the problem was to create so-called New Economic Areas (NEAs). The NEAs were extensive plots of unused land set up in selected areas of the country and scheduled for reclamation and resettlement by the government. Sometimes they were established in previously occupied areas that had been abandoned by their owners. In other cases, they were in piedmont areas adjacent to or in the

Workers clearing the ground in a New Economic Area in South Vietnam in 1975.
(TASS from Sovfoto)

Central Highlands that had not been previously used but were considered
appropriate for farming. The excess population in the cities—refugees and
the unemployed—would be encouraged to settle voluntarily in such areas.
In return, the authorities promised to provide them with tools, seeds,
materials for housing, and such basic amenities as electricity, water, schools,
and transportation. The original plan called for the eventual settlement of
more than 3 million people in the NEAs. Most would come from the
burgeoning cities in the South, but some were to be resettled from the
crowded provinces in Central Vietnam and the Red River delta.

   In theory, the program was to be voluntary, and it is probable that
the regime attempted to avoid compulsion wherever possible. But as the
program got under way in the summer and fall of 1975, complaints soon
appeared in the Saigon press that force had been used in some cases.
Some charged that the program was simply a plan to rid the cities of the
overseas Chinese and other elements considered potentially hostile to the
new regime. Official figures claimed that the program had achieved
substantial success in relieving the problem of overcrowding in the cities,
but reports soon began to circulate that it was beginning to run into
serious difficulties. Refugees claimed that many of the NEAs had been
poorly prepared by government cadres and that many settlers were
abandoning the areas to return in secret to their former residences in the
cities. The government denied that the program had been a failure (one

official report stated that the attrition rate from the NEAs was no more than 3 percent) but conceded that it had not lived up to early expectations.

In areas already under cultivation, the government followed a cautiously moderate line. Farmers were assured that their lands would not be seized (after some hesitation, Hanoi had decided that because of the success of earlier programs launched by the G.V.N. or by revolutionary authorities in liberated areas, a land reform program such as had taken place after Geneva in the D.R.V. would not be necessary in the South) and were encouraged to increase their grain production for sale on the market. There were few references to the future collectivization of the countryside, although a few pilot cooperatives were set up in areas considered sympathetic to the revolution. The authorities did take initial steps toward controlling the price and distribution of grain, however, by setting up an agency for the purchase and sale of grain and by directing retailers to obtain licenses from the government to continue their operations.

In sum, the government attempted to deal with the economic crisis at the end of the war with a combination of haste and caution. Problems requiring immediate attention, such as urban unemployment and rural depopulation, were approached with a sense of urgency. But in order to promote the revival of the productive forces in the South, the authorities refrained from taking measures that might frighten the middle class or the landholding peasants and disrupt the fragile postwar stability. Within a year after the fall of Saigon, official sources were openly stating that, although political unification had been quickly realized and the long-term goal was the creation of a socialist economy throughout the entire country, for the time being the government would tolerate a mixed economy, half-socialist, half-capitalist. Indeed, for the foreseeable future, the national economy was to be divided into five separate categories: (1) government ownership, (2) collective ownership, (3) joint private-state ownership, (4) private capitalist ownership, and (5) individual ownership. The ultimate goal of building a socialist society had by no means been abandoned, but it was conceded that the new Vietnam faced severe economic problems that could not be resolved in a period of five to seven years.

THE SECOND FIVE-YEAR PLAN (1976–1980)

The party leadership's long-term intentions for the economy began to clarify in December 1976, when the Fourth National Party Congress was convened in Hanoi. One of the primary purposes of the Congress was to approve a new five-year plan to cover the years 1976 through 1980. The plan had originally been drawn up after the Paris Agreement to undertake economic construction in the North. When victory in the South was realized earlier than had been anticipated, party leaders at first considered scrapping the plan until the postwar situation had become clear. Ultimately, however, it was decided to retain the plan and to use it to promote the party's economic objectives in both zones of the country.

In the broadest sense, the objectives of the new plan were to promote the transformation of Vietnamese society in terms of the so-called three revolutions—in production relations, ideology and culture, and science and technology. The primary emphasis, it was openly stated, would be placed on the latter. In the view of party leaders, the major obstacle to economic development in Vietnam was the backward state of the national economy. Industry and commerce were technologically primitive and characterized by small-scale and labor-intensive techniques. The creation of large-scale industry and mechanized agriculture would be an issue of the highest priority. It was conceded, however, that such improvement could not take place within the scope of a single five-year plan but would require at least thirty years.

Predictably, heavy industry was to receive high priority. National output in coal, iron, machinery, and hydroelectric power was to be substantially increased and the transportation and communications networks improved. Agricultural goals were equally ambitious, calling for an annual increase of nearly 8 percent in food production through a combination of improved irrigation and fertilizer, higher crop yields, increase in cropland, and the planting of subsidiary crops. One interesting aspect of the plan was the program to create new agro-industrial centers at the district level as a means of relieving population density and diversifying the productive capacity throughout the country. Patterned after the Soviet *agrogorods* developed under Nikita Khrushchev, the agro-industrial center concept had originally been launched during the First Five-Year Plan in 1961 but had achieved only limited success because of the war. Now the program was to be revived and given maximum support. Centers capable of supporting up to 30,000 to 40,000 people and focusing on both industrial and agricultural development were to be established at the district level throughout the country. It was projected that during the course of the plan 4 million people would be resettled in such areas, mostly through the improvement of the NEAs. Ultimately, the regime planned to move more than 10 million people into the new centers—mostly from the crowded North into less populated areas in the South.

Another major objective of the plan was to initiate the process of socialist transformation in the South. Although party leaders had been careful to reassure the local population that the system of private property would not be destroyed in the near future, they apparently had decided by mid-1976 that a long postponement of the socialist revolution in the South would be inadvisable and would pose a severe obstacle to the regime's determination to seize control over the southern economy. The decision to hasten the process of socialist transformation in the South was clearly set forth in the Second Five-Year Plan, which stated that the creation of socialist ownership in the South would be "basically achieved" during the course of the plan.

THE CRISIS ON THE ECONOMIC FRONT

The efforts of the regime to assert its control over the national economy and to stimulate economic growth soon ran into serious difficulties. Part of the problem came from inadequate financing. Hanoi had hoped for substantial assistance in carrying out its ambitious economic program from abroad, not only from its traditional allies, such as the Soviet Union and China, but from Western European countries, international organizations, and even from the United States, which had promised $3 billion in reconstruction assistance as part of the Paris Agreement in 1973. Such optimism, it turned out, was seriously misplaced. Soviet economic assistance was lower than anticipated, averaging only about $1 billion annually through the end of the decade. Chinese aid was even more disappointing. In 1975, Peking informed the Vietnamese that, because of domestic priorities, assistance from China would continue only at current levels. By 1977, Chinese assistance had become a casualty of increasing tension between the two countries. Early the following year, China cancelled several of its ongoing projects in Vietnam. In June, presumably reacting to the Chinese move, Hanoi accepted Moscow's invitation to join the Soviet-sponsored Council for Mutual Economic Assistance (CEMA). Peking reacted by canceling all remaining projects and withdrawing all its technicians from Vietnam. Hanoi was moderately successful in obtaining promises of assistance from European countries—notably France and Sweden—but its expectation of reconstruction aid from the United States was dashed when the Carter administration refused to honor the commitment allegedly made by President Nixon.

Hopes for assistance from private sources were also doomed to disappointment. Despite a new and relatively liberal investment code, the regime was unable to attract substantial foreign capital from Western countries, a problem that was exacerbated after 1979 when the United States, in response to the Vietnamese invasion of Cambodia, prohibited trade relations between the United States and Vietnam. One of Hanoi's major sources for optimism was the possibility of substantial oil finds in Vietnamese territorial waters in the South China Sea, and during the mid-1970s, a number of Western oil companies leased tracts in the area to undertake exploratory drilling. By the end of the decade, however, such optimism had declined and a number of companies had allowed their claims to lapse.

If the lack of foreign assistance was one cause for the S.R.V.'s continuing economic problems, it was by no means the only one. As official press reports conceded, Vietnam was having difficulty absorbing foreign aid even when it was available. Transportation of goods was a serious problem. Sometimes shipments were held up at dockside for lack of equipment or stevedores. After leaving port, goods were sometimes delayed in reaching their ultimate destination by transportation bottlenecks. At one time, according to one report, one-third of all trucks in Vietnam were idle because of a lack of spare parts. Insufficient technological and managerial experience plagued government and industry. Press reports frequently criticized administrators and cadres for their incompetence and inability to abandon the wartime "guerrilla mentality" and admitted that many cadres were having a difficult time making the transition from a wartime to a peacetime society.

Within the private economy in the South, the regime's uneasy efforts to "advance on two legs," one capitalist, one socialist, were not markedly successful. Hoarding of goods and price speculation by private producers and merchants, many of them overseas Chinese, created a thriving black market and chaotic conditions in the availability and distribution of consumer goods. The public sector made modest progress, but unemployment remained high as the program to resettle refugees in the NEAs stagnated. In rural areas, agricultural progress was hindered by bureaucratic ineptitude, unrealistic regulations, and bad weather. To keep down food prices, the regime attempted to compel peasants to sell their grain to government purchasing agents at low official prices. Recalcitrant farmers reacted by hoarding, selling on the black market, or feeding their grain to their livestock. A series of climatic disasters—floods and typhoons along the central coast, unseasonable cold weather in the North—kept down grain harvests, which consistently failed to meet annual targets, and the regime was compelled to use its precious hard currency reserves to import grain from abroad, notably from the Soviet Union. By the late 1970s, even imports had failed to meet national needs and food rationing was instituted.

TRANSFORMATION TO SOCIALISM IN THE SOUTH

Whether or not the deteriorating state of the economy was instrumental in persuading the regime to speed up its schedule for beginning the process of constructing socialism in the South cannot be said with certainty. Speeches by top party leaders at the Fourth National Congress in December 1976 had asserted that the transformation to socialist ownership in South Vietnam would be completed "in the main" by the end of the 1976–1980 Five-Year Plan. If allusions in the official press to inner-party discord over domestic policy are correct, the decision to move rapidly to extend government controls over the southern economy must have been a controversial one. Whatever the case, in late 1977 the party leadership decided to begin the process of socialist transformation in the South early the following year. The first stage would involve the abolition of private trade and manufacturing. Most remaining private enterprise, of course, was in the South, but a small private sector, involving mainly overseas Chinese, remained in the larger cities in the North. Once this step had been completed, the second stage of collectivizing the countryside in the South could begin.

The regime made its move on March 23, 1978. All major industrial and commercial enterprises remaining in private hands were declared nationalized, and their goods were confiscated. Only small firms under family ownership were permitted to continue in private hands. In an effort to avoid the disruption and hoarding of goods that had occurred at the time of the 1975 campaign against wealthy speculators in Saigon, the announcement came without advance warning. "Youth squads" were sent out to private businesses during the preceding night to confiscate all goods on the premises and prevent the owners from attempting to evade the provisions of the new regulations. The government promised that compensation would be provided for all goods seized (albeit at prices established by the government) and offered incentives to encourage merchants to establish joint private-state enterprises, join collective organizations, or find alternative sources of employment. At the same time, new regulations limited the amount of money that could be retained for private use. All amounts above the legal limit were required to be placed in savings accounts. Such funds could be withdrawn only by application to the authorities. In May, a new united currency was issued and the old southern bank notes (the southern *dong*, separate from that in use in the North) were withdrawn from circulation.

The reaction within the business community to the new government regulations was intense and generally unfavorable. Press reports contended that the move had been a success, resulting in the abolition of some 30,000 private firms throughout the South, but discontent led to turmoil in the urban sector of the economy and—by midsummer—to a growing flood of refugees attempting to escape Vietnam to other countries in the region. Many contended that the regime had deliberately moved to destroy the overseas Chinese community in Vietnam. Such attitudes were also common among ethnic Chinese in the North, where rumors of anti-Chinese regulations and the nationalizing of private enterprises led to concern and a mass exodus of Chinese refugees across the border into China.

At first, the regime was apparently taken aback by the intensity of the reaction to the new regulations and insisted that they had not been issued, as was charged, in order to destroy the economic influence of the overseas Chinese community. That Hanoi did not initially intend to force the Chinese to leave Vietnam is suggested by the fact that, in the beginning, those attempting to flee across the Chinese border were apprehended and returned to Vietnam. Eventually, however, government leaders, perhaps convinced that the Chinese merchant population could not be effectively assimilated into a new, socialist Vietnam, appeared to accept the situation and encouraged the departure of those who wished to leave, while attempting to prevent them from taking their savings out of the country.

The move to collectivize the agricultural sector in the South began in early 1978 and accelerated during succeeding months. The program represented an enormous gamble, because widespread dissatisfaction among private landholding peasants in the South could have a catastrophic effect on grain production. In order to minimize the risk, the regime followed the technique originally borrowed from China and used during the earlier collectivization campaign in the North. The first stage, launched in the winter of 1977–1978, involved the formation of low-level work exchange teams, in which peasants established contracts for production goals with government purchasing agencies but retained ownership over their land and draft animals. In the meantime, pilot cooperatives were set up in areas where peasants appeared receptive, where there was much wasteland or reclaimed land, or where private landownership was not well established. Throughout the remainder of the decade, the enrollment of southern peasants into collective organizations continued on a gradual basis. In areas where sentiment was relatively favorable, few difficulties were encountered. In the Mekong Delta, however, where private farming was rather well established, and particularly in sect areas traditionally resistant to outside control, farmers resisted joining the new organizations. In theory, the decision to join was to be voluntary, but press reports conceded that in many instances compulsion had been used by overzealous cadres. For the most part, resistance to the program was apparently passive rather than violent and usually took the form of evasion or refusal to heed production quotas.

By late 1979, the impact of the government's effort to socialize the South was clear. The flight abroad of refugees had reached truly significant proportions. Whether to China on foot, or to neighboring countries in Southeast Asia by sea, several hundred thousand residents left Vietnam in 1978 and 1979. According to some estimates, two-thirds of the refugees were ethnic Chinese, but the percentage of native Vietnamese began to increase in the final months of the decade. In the meantime, the economic crisis deepened, shortages of consumer goods were common throughout the country (according to foreign travelers, goods were more plentiful in the South than in the North), and despite stringent efforts by the government authorities to stop illegal traffic, black market operations thrived. The agricultural sector was particularly hard hit. Not all the problems could be ascribed to human actions. Bad weather continued to plague the country, and grain harvests in 1978 and 1979 fell well short of their targets. Food rationing may have equalized the burden, but it did not prevent widespread hunger and malnutrition. Per capita consumption was reportedly substantially below subsistence levels, and visitors to Vietnam noted the physical evidence on the Vietnamese population, notably on the children.

In November 1979, the Sixth Plenum of the party's Central Committee, in tacit recognition of the seriousness of the crisis, moderated its efforts to force the population in the South into a socialist mold. The sale of goods at open markets was permitted and limited private commerce and manufacturing were again tolerated. To persuade farmers to increase food production, various incentives were instituted. The official purchase price of grain was raised, and farmers were encouraged to grow crops on private land for sale on the open market. Subsidies were provided to those who reclaimed unused lands. Some foreign observers have described the new course as the equivalent of the New Economic Policy in the Soviet Union, or the pragmatic policies followed in China since the death of Mao. It is too early to determine whether the new liberalization represents a major change in course for the regime. Without further evidence to the contrary, it can best be viewed as a tactical shift to resolve the contemporary economic crisis rather than a major shift in the long-term intentions of the party leadership.

As for the economic effects of the new policies, it is perhaps too early to attempt a definitive evaluation. Reports from foreign visitors and official sources within Vietnam confirm that, despite vigorous efforts by the regime to solve the burgeoning problems, the economic crisis has continued into the 1980s. In apparent recognition of this fact, the Soviet Union in the summer of 1981 announced an increase in its economic and military assistance to the S.R.V. Thousands of Vietnamese have been sent for training in the Soviet Union, and increased numbers of Soviet, East European, and even Cuban technicians have been posted to Vietnam to assist it in resolving its economic problems. At the same time, several thousand Vietnamese workers have been sent to the Soviet Union and other East European countries to work in factories and increase their technological abilities. At the Fifth Party Congress in the early spring of 1982, it was announced that the S.R.V. has embarked on a new Five-Year Plan to cover the years 1981 to 1985. Primary emphasis will be placed on increasing food production and the output of consumer goods, while the policy of granting incentives to increase productivity that had been inaugurated at the Sixth Plenum in 1979 is to be continued. At the same time, party leaders announced the regime's intention of completing the socialist transformation "in the main" by the mid-1980s.

For the moment, then, the regime continues to grope for a solution to the economic problems that have confronted it since the seizure of Saigon in 1975. The problem has international implications. Isolated from many potential Western sources of aid because of its military occupation of Cambodia, Hanoi has clearly become almost totally reliant on the Soviet Union and its allies. Party leaders appear reluctant to increase their economic and military dependence on Moscow, and their pleas to foreigners that they would prefer to keep their economic options open through increased contacts with Western nations are probably sincere. Unfortunately, such relations will be difficult to realize given Hanoi's current unwillingness to withdraw from Cambodia. For the moment, policies followed by Western nations toward Vietnam have had the paradoxical effect of driving the S.R.V. into an even more dependent relationship with Moscow, a situation that is in the interest neither of Vietnam nor of the Western world.

CONCLUSION

One of the cruel ironies of the Vietnamese revolution is that the Communists (and, in their name, the Vietnamese people) are paying a high price for their success. For in choosing to seize power in a precapitalist society not yet entirely freed from the yoke of feudalism, the Vietnamese Communists, like their comrades in China and Russia before them, are now faced with the problem of building socialism in an economy still characterized by small-scale and labor-intensive forms of production. Moreover, they lack the presence—assumed by Karl Marx in his prognostications about revolution—of a large and politically sophisticated urban working class urging on the vanguard party in its struggle to build a classless utopia.

The implications are momentous and, at the very least, intimidating. How can the S.R.V. achieve an abundance of goods and a high rate of industrial productivity—both the products of capitalist society—without the most crucial instrument of capitalism—the profit incentive? And how can it revolutionize production relations and create the "communist man" in a society still fundamentally agrarian and acquisitive in its instincts? As has been noted above, the party's answer is, to borrow a Maoist term, to advance on three legs, to attempt to realize all goals—the revolutions in production relations, in culture and ideology, and in technology—at the same time. Put in practical terms, it is attempting to encourage production while decreasing the human instinct for private profit. The results have been less than satisfactory, and the decisions reached at the Sixth Plenum in the fall of 1979 and at the Fifth Party Congress in 1982 are a reluctant concession to this fact. Which road will the party choose? Will it insist on ideological rigidity at the expense of production, or compromise its principles in order to achieve a higher level of economic growth? Or, like China, will it lurch from one policy to another, at the cost of growing dissonance within the party? It is too early to say with certainty. Past performance suggests that, in the face of severe challenge, party leaders are willing to experiment, "to take one step backward in order to advance two steps forward," in the pursuit of the long-term strategic goal. The party will make tactical concessions when necessary but will endure hardships before compromising on basic principles. It will strive, above all, to maintain unity within the party leadership. In a word, it will be tough but flexible, determined but realistic. Can such an approach succeed in the postwar period as it succeeded in time of war? Only time will tell.

7

Culture and Society

It has sometimes been observed that Vietnam, although physically located in Southeast Asia, is actually a part of the cultural world of East Asia, led by Vietnam's great neighbor, China. The argument is persuasive. Not only was Vietnam for one thousand years under direct Chinese rule, but even after regaining their independence in the tenth century, the Vietnamese turned to China as a model for their literature, their art, their architecture, many of their religious beliefs, even their written language. For nearly ten centuries, the Vietnamese almost seemed to style themselves as a carbon copy of China. In the words of one modern Vietnamese historian:

> Our nation has been influenced by China in all regards, with regard to politics, society, ethics, religion and customs. As far as literature is concerned, we studied Chinese characters, practiced Confucianism, and gradually assimilated the thought and art of China. The scholars in our country studied Chinese classics and histories, read Chinese poetry and prose, and also used Chinese characters when reciting and composing. Even in literary works written in Vietnamese, authors could not escape the influence of Chinese literature. Some of the literary forms were distinctly ours, but most were borrowed from China. Even the characters used to write Vietnamese—Nom characters—were made up of elements of Chinese characters.[1]

Few contemporary Vietnamese would deny that historically their country has been strongly influenced by China. Many would contend, however (and in this they are joined by many Vietnam specialists in the West), that the degree of Chinese influence over Vietnamese society has been exaggerated and that many of the primary components of Vietnamese culture have roots indigenous to Southeast Asia.

Where does the truth lie in this matter? As is so often the case, there are important elements of truth in both points of view. Vietnam, culturally and historically as well as geographically, lies at the crossroads between the Sinitic world of East Asia and the Indianized world of mainland

116

Southeast Asia. And, as the civilization of the United States can be described only as a result of the interaction between foreign cultures brought by immigrants and the indigenous environment, so Vietnamese culture represents, in broad terms, the product of a similar interaction between Sinitic institutions and values and the native environment in Southeast Asia. For scholars, this polarity between Chinese and Southeast Asian elements is one of the more intriguing and persistent themes in Vietnamese history. The impact can be seen not only in the traditional period, when bureaucrats and Confucian scholars took their guidance from their counterparts to the north, but in our day, when the Vietnamese Communist movement borrowed liberally from the Maoist doctrines of people's war and the Chinese strategy of building a socialist society.

Unfortunately, too little is known about the nature of Vietnamese society prior to the Chinese conquest in the second century B.C. to permit a definitive assessment of the cultural roots of Vietnamese civilization. As we have seen above, the limited evidence suggests that in prehistoric times the Vietnamese were one among several Bronze Age peoples living in an area that stretched from the Red River delta to the Yangtze River valley in China. It seems likely that even at that early date the peoples in the Red River delta shared some cultural traits with their neighbors to the north, while displaying other traits absorbed from the local environment. The southward expansion of Chinese civilization and the integration of the state of Au Lac into the Han empire undoubtedly facilitated the introduction of Chinese elements into Vietnamese society. Earlier chapters noted the impact of Chinese control in politics. Chinese influence was no less manifest in social institutions and mores, religion, and the creative arts. This process of Sinification was the result of a deliberate policy of assimilation applied by Chinese administrators acting at the behest of the imperial court in Peking. It is a measure of the extent of the impact of Chinese influence that, after independence, Vietnamese rulers continued to rely on these cultural models as a means of governing society. Chinese influence was strongest, however, among the elite class and at court. Under this Chinese cultural veneer, the Vietnamese village was relatively untouched by winds from the north. Thus emerged one of the distinguishing features of Vietnamese civilization down to modern times—even into the colonial and postcolonial eras—the dichotomy between an elite culture at court (or, in the modern period, among the affluent middle class in the Westernized cities) and a popular culture, based primarily on indigenous roots, in the villages. In the interpretation of contemporary historians in Hanoi, this dichotomy reflected the tension between feudal elements, slavishly imitating foreign culture, and the oppressed urban and rural masses, representing the genuine force of Vietnamese identity and patriotism.

PHILOSOPHY AND RELIGION

In Vietnam, as in most other societies in Southeast Asia, philosophical and religious beliefs existed at two levels—the "Great Tradition" religions, or philosophical systems, like Confucianism and Buddhism, and the "Little Tradition" belief in the existence of village spirits, or spirits in nature, such as wind, water, and mountains. Belief in the existence of spirits in natural objects or forces goes back to prehistoric times in all human societies, and it can safely be assumed that the early Vietnamese possessed such beliefs themselves. It was probably only during or after the Chinese conquest that the Vietnamese became acquainted with the Great Tradition systems of Confucianism and Buddhism. Confucianism, more a social and political philosophy than a religion, was probably introduced by Chinese administrators or scholar-missionaries in the wake of Chinese expansion into Southeast Asia. Buddhism was brought to Vietnam during the early stages of Chinese rule by missionaries traveling between China and India, where Buddhism had originated several hundred years before.

As in China, Buddhism and Confucianism coexisted with spirit worship in Vietnam. Each, in effect, fulfilled different social, religious, and emotional needs in Vietnamese society. Confucianism served above all to provide the state with a political philosophy and a system of ethics to maintain social order and to promote the material welfare of the mass of the population. Through its emphasis on rule by merit, Confucianism helped to create a sense of professionalism in the bureaucracy, the key to efficient and honest government in an authoritarian society. Through its emphasis on filial piety and the subordination of wife to husband, son to father, and younger brother to older brother, it made the family the key unit in society. Through its emphasis on hard work and service to the community, it furnished the positive "work ethic" so necessary in an agrarian hydraulic society.

If Confucianism served the interests of social order and the state, Buddhism reached out to the individual, to the emotions and the spirit. Confucianism focused on this world and advocated improvement of this life; Buddhism was otherworldly and taught rejection of the material world in favor of quiescence and an effort to escape the evils of everyday material existence. Confucianism provided a vehicle for order in this life; Buddhism provided solace for the pain and a release from the evil of existence through a rejection of desire. Confucianism became primarily a philosophy for the elite, whereas Buddhism appealed to rich and poor alike and in rural villages supplemented spirit worship in providing a hypothesis about the nature of metaphysical reality.

After the restoration of independence in the tenth century, Buddhism was temporarily dominant in Vietnam, even at court. Kings took bonzes (monks) as their advisers, and great monasteries, controlling vast tracts of land and thousands of serfs, dotted the countryside. Even in the civil service examinations, *locus classicus* of Confucian doctrine, Buddhist and Taoist texts were included as frequently as those of the great Chinese master. In the long run, however, Buddhism fell victim to its own limitations as a philosophy of state. With its emphasis on passivity, individual salvation, and renunciation of the material world, Buddhism could not effectively serve as the official religion of a dynamic and centralizing monarchy, and it gradually lost influence to Confucianism. By the rise of the Le dynasty in the fifteenth century, Confucian literati had achieved great influence at court, and Confucian texts were dominant in the civil service examination. Buddhism retained its influence as the dominant religion of the mass of the population, but it lost its position in court circles and Buddhists were periodically persecuted by Confucian monarchs.

The triumph of Confucianism as the official philosophy of the state had a perceptible effect on social institutions and mores in Vietnam. With its emphasis on government by men of talent and virtue, it undoubtedly helped to break down the dominance of the landed nobility and provided opportunities for individual advancement for poor but able young men. No doubt it also had its uses in maintaining social order, a sense of commitment to public service and loyalty to the larger community and the state. Confucianism thus possessed considerable virtue as the official philosophy of a densely populated hydraulic society.

On the other hand, it also contributed to an increasing formalism and rigidity in Vietnamese society. The relatively informal social mores that had once characterized Vietnamese social life were replaced by a more hierarchical and inflexible system of human relationships. This was particularly noteworthy in the role of women in society. Before the Chinese conquest, women in Vietnam had many of the rights of the male sex. They were permitted to inherit family property and had more legal rights within the family than their counterparts in China. Throughout history, many women, following the model of the Trung sisters, had distinguished themselves as intrepid warriors defending Vietnam from invasion from the north. With Confucianism dominant, however, women's rights in Vietnam were severely restricted. They were not permitted to participate in the civil service examinations or serve in the bureaucracy. Within the family, their rights were severely restricted. Under the Confucian *san kang* (three obediences), they were clearly subordinate to their husbands, who possessed all property rights and were permitted to take a second wife if the first failed to produce a son. A shadow of the past remained, however. Under the famous Hong Duc Code, passed during the reign of Le Thanh Tong (1460–1497), women, in accordance with ancient custom, were permitted to own property and to perform limited ritual functions within the family. These rights were abrogated, however, in the nineteenth century when the Nguyen dynasty returned to a strict interpretation of Confucian social practice.

EDUCATION IN CONFUCIAN VIETNAM

It was, above all, through the educational system that Confucian doctrine was injected into the bloodstream of Vietnamese society. Historical records suggest that the Confucian system of education was first introduced into Vietnam during the era of Chinese rule, but it was only after the restoration of independence that a comprehensive system based on the features used in China began to take shape. At first, the system was tailored to fit conditions in the new Vietnamese state. Under the Ly dynasty, a temple of literature was built in Hanoi to provide training in Confucian doctrine for candidates for high office. In 1075, the first examinations were held for entry into the bureaucracy. In accordance with contemporary practice, however, the competition was limited to members of the aristocracy, who alone were eligible for high official positions. Eventually, however, the competition was opened to commoners, who gradually became eligible for high posts in the bureaucracy. By the same token, the content of the examinations, as noted above, at first included Buddhist and Taoist texts as well as Confucian classics (what was commonly called the "Three Doctrines"). By the fifteenth century, however, Confucianism had become the official doctrine of the state and was dominant in the examinations.

In theory, the Confucian educational system possessed a number of attractive features when compared to those used elsewhere. The emphasis on merit provided an avenue of upward mobility for poor but bright young males and reduced the dominant role of the hereditary aristocracy in Vietnamese society. By stressing the importance of talent and virtue, training in the classical Confucian texts also probably helped to enhance the sense of professionalism and integrity in the civil service and to promote a sense of loyalty and dedication to the community and the state.

Confucian theory, of course, was not always carried out. While schools (or private tutors) probably existed in most Vietnamese villages, there was no system of universal education, and many families could not afford to enroll their children in schools. In some cases, male children from poor families might be sponsored by a well-to-do relative, but generally speaking the system obviously favored those families with wealth or a tradition of education and service in the bureaucracy. Nor was training in the Confucian classics necessarily successful in promoting talent and inculcating in the student a proper regard for high moral fiber and compassion for the weak. In practice, Confucian education often degenerated into formalism and a ritualistic concern for recitation of texts rather than a comprehension of and dedication to the content. If the Confucian gentlemen (in Chinese the *chün tzu*, rendered as *quan tu* in Vietnamese) in theory was wise, compassionate, and fair, in actuality he was often an arrogant pedant who paraded his learning and exhibited more contempt than compassion for his intellectual inferiors. Still, on balance the adoption of Confucian institutions probably represented a net advantage to the Vietnamese state.

Children acting in a play at a nursery school in Hanoi. (Photo courtesy of *Vietnam pictorial*)

THE CREATIVE ARTS

If Chinese influence permeated the religious beliefs and social institutions of Vietnamese society, it was no less visible in the creative arts.

In literature, art, architecture, and music, the influence of Chinese models on Vietnamese culture was readily apparent from the period of Chinese rule down to the French conquest in the nineteenth century. Beyond form, however, Vietnamese art often reflected local motifs. For example, although Vietnamese music followed Chinese in the use of the five-tone scale, it also absorbed influence from neighboring Champa in the popularity of Cham music and dances and the use of the Cham rice drum. Similarly, Vietnamese porcelain broadly resembled its Chinese counterpart but used a type of green glaze not used in China. The most direct influence, perhaps, was in the area of architecture. Unfortunately, little architecture survives from the premodern period. What does exist closely imitated Chinese counterparts. The most prominent example of precolonial architecture was the imperial city at Hue, constructed in the early nineteenth century by the Nguyen dynasty in blatant imitation of the Forbidden City in Peking.

It was in literature that the interaction between Chinese and native influence was ultimately most clearly displayed. Unfortunately, examples of early Vietnamese writing are fragmentary. Prior to independence, however, Chinese influence was undoubtedly paramount, both in form and content. Literary Chinese was the official language at court and was used in all official communications. Even after the restoration of independence, the dominance of Chinese ideographs continued for several centuries. The earliest extant forms of literature in Vietnam show a strong imprint of Chinese models. The most common forms of literary creativity were historical writings and Buddhist holy texts. The most famous historical work, unfortunately not extant, was the *Dai Viet Su Ky* [History of Dai Viet] by the twelfth-century scholar Le Van Huu.

Still, although Vietnamese literature in the first centuries after the restoration of independence reflected a strong degree of Chinese influence, during this period, according to the respected present-day Vietnamese scholar Nguyen Khac Vien, a truly "national literature" began to flower. During the Tran (1225–1400) and early Le (1428–1788) dynasties, several works on the history of the Vietnamese state appeared. Although the fragments still in existence show a high degree of Chinese influence—in the Chinese pattern, they were primarily a chronology of official events— they display as well a high degree of national consciousness. The officially sponsored *Dai Viet Su Ky Toan Thu* [Complete history of Dai Viet] by the fifteenth-century historian Ngo Si Lien traced Vietnamese history back to the semilegendary Hong Bang dynasty.

The first centuries of independence saw a similar development in the field of poetry. The pacesetter was the renowned scholar, statesman, and military strategist Nguyen Trai, whose poetry combined Confucian morality and patriotic themes as he helped to spark the defeat of Chinese invading forces and the rise of the Le dynasty.

The dominant forms of literary creativity during the early centuries of independence were those of classical China, but an indigenous form of literature was gradually beginning to emerge. Much of it was in the form of folk literature—oral poetry, love songs, and popular theater—and was passed down by memory from generation to generation. Not all of this nonclassical popular literature went unrecorded, however. It was apparently at this time that a new form of demotic script called *chu nom*, or southern script, was invented and gradually became a popular form of written communication in Vietnam. *Chu nom* was an adaptation of Chinese ideographs to the spoken Vietnamese language. The precise date of its invention remains unknown, but it was probably already in use by the Ly dynasty. The earliest extant text dates from the Tran dynasty.

At first, the new script was not generally accepted by Vietnamese scholars, who considered it uncultured and clumsy, but eventually its value as a national form of written expression and its superiority to literary Chinese as a vehicle to express human emotions became apparent, and it came into general usage. Occasionally it was used for administrative purposes, and some classical texts were translated into *chu nom*, but its primary function was in the writing of fiction. During the Tran and early Le dynasties, it was frequently used for poetry, but its major expansion took place during and after the seventeenth century, when it gave rise to the flowering of a unique national literature. With the rise of the novel form written in *nom*, Vietnamese literature began to explore such new themes as individual happiness, sexual love, social criticism, and satire. Much of the new writing had a strong social and political message, attacking such evils of Confucian semifeudal society as corrupt officials, greedy landlords, and pedantic scholars. It also raised daring themes of social liberation for traditionally oppressed groups like women and peasants. Significantly, some of the new writers were themselves women, who used their satirical abilities like a rapier to stab at the male-oriented Confucian society around them. Most famous of the works of the period was the novel written in rhythmic prose, *Kim Van Kieu*, by Nguyen Du. Kieu was the poignant story of young lovers caught in the net of traditional morality. Appealing to Vietnamese of all classes, *Kim Van Kieu* became the single most popular and revered work in Vietnamese literature and was learned by heart by generations of illiterate Vietnamese.

Side by side with the rise of the novel form came the flourishing of other forms of literary writing: of poetry, of rural plays and operas such as *cheo* (a type of popular theater), of *phu* (long texts in rhythmic prose of *nom*), of *ca dao* (a form of lyrical song without instrumental accompaniment), and of *ve* (stories told in rhymed form). Such new forms of literature not only explored new types of creative expression, many of them marking the transition from ordinary prose to poetry and from literature to music, but they also gave visible evidence of the struggle within Vietnamese culture to transcend the limitations of Sino-Vietnamese style and social ethics. To the student of Vietnamese literature, they mark the clear emergence of a popular literature independent of—and often in direct opposition to—the official court style introduced from China. After centuries of cultural subordination to China, creative writers were declaring their independence from Confucian tradition.

While the seventeenth and eighteenth century gave rise to a vast outpouring of new forms of literature, the older court literature did not entirely disappear. Historical works reflecting the classical Chinese model continued to appear throughout the period. Some of the most famous were the *Kham Dinh Viet Su Thong Giam Cuong Muc* [Imperial historical mirror of Dai Viet], an official history sponsored by the Nguyen dynasty, Le Quy Don's *Dai Viet Thong Su* [Complete history of Dai Viet], and Phan Huy Chu's encyclopedic biographies of major figures.

WIND FROM THE WEST

The introduction of Western culture, culminating in the imposition of colonial regimes throughout much of Southeast Asia in the nineteenth century, had a traumatic effect on traditional societies throughout the region. Nowhere was this truer than in Vietnam, where Confucian institutions and values often conflicted in basic respects with those of the West. Where Confucianism emphasized the subordination of the individual to the family and the community, Western belief focused on the concept of individual freedom as a key element in human society. Where Sino-Vietnamese tradition preached harmony with nature and lacked a coherent doctrine of progress, the West glorified the conquest of nature and openly sought change and the improvement of man's material surroundings. Where Confucian thought was hierarchical and preached the superiority of the male sex, Western belief contained strong egalitarian tendencies and, by the early twentieth century, progressive circles began to preach the equality of the sexes.

The imposition of French rule in the late nineteenth century, then, inevitably exerted a markedly disintegrating effect on traditional culture in Vietnam. To some degree, this was a direct consequence of colonial policy, which, in the hands of activist and modernizing administrators like Governors-General Paul Beau and Albert Sarraut, took dead aim at Confucian traditions and sought the transformation of Vietnamese society through the introduction of Western values and institutions. In other cases, Western influence penetrated by more indirect means, through the growing presence of French *colons* in the cities or as the result of missionary activity, leading to the growth of the Catholic community in Vietnam to more than 2 million in the late colonial period. Western influence was strongest in Cochin China. As a colony and the source of much of the economic wealth of the country, it was most exposed to direct French influence. Western influence was weakest in Annam, where the imperial court retained the formal trappings of its erstwhile authority and, because of the lack of economic wealth, there were few European residents.

Above all, it was through the educational system that Western culture began to penetrate the minds of the Vietnamese and erode the old ways. The first generation of Vietnamese to experience French rule had been raised and educated under the traditional system. For them, Western ideas were filtered through an intellectual framework formed in the precolonial era. Beginning with the new century, however, the colonial regime gradually dismantled the old educational system and replaced it with a new one based partially on the French model. The system of civil service examinations leading to a career in the bureaucracy was abolished, thus undermining the original purpose of the system of Confucian schools in villages and towns throughout the country. In its place arose a new Franco-Vietnamese educational system designed to provide the Vietnamese with exposure to Western culture. It operated on a two-track basis, with an advanced system based on French language and culture and culminating in the University of Hanoi, opened in 1908 for the Vietnamese elite, and a system of popular education at the elementary level, based on the Vietnamese language, for the masses. Except in Annam, instruction in written Chinese fell into desuetude and exposure to the Confucian classics was limited to ethics classes. For the first generation of Vietnamese raised in the twentieth century, the Sino-Vietnamese heritage was already more a receding memory than a reality.

A crucial factor in the process of promoting Western knowledge was the change from the use of Chinese characters (in literary Chinese or the *chu nom*) to the romanized script called *quoc ngu*. *Quoc ngu*, a romanized transliteration of spoken Vietnamese, had been invented by the Catholic missionary Alexander of Rhodes in the seventeenth century as a means of facilitating the propagation of Christianity. Its use was limited to the missionary enterprise until the early colonial era, when it began to be used by the French (and by Vietnamese collaborating in the colonial effort) in Cochin China in preference to the aesthetically pleasing but pedagogically difficult Chinese ideographs. At first, use of the new script was resisted by the conservative Confucian scholar-gentry class, who considered *quoc ngu* vulgar (one is reminded of the contemptuous observation of one Chinese scholar that Western scripts moved horizontally across the page like an earthworm rather than up and down, as a dignified script should) and a tool of the imperialists. Eventually, however, its utility became increasingly apparent, and in the first decade of the new century, progressive members of the scholar-gentry class, led by Phan Chu Trinh, began to promote its use through a new school in Hanoi, the Dong Kinh Nghia Thuc, which also encouraged Vietnamese to adopt other aspects of Western civilization. Within a few years, *quoc ngu* had been widely accepted as superior to Chinese ideographs as an effective means of written expression in Vietnam.

From the schools, Western influence radiated rapidly outward into other areas of society and exerted a corrosive impact on Vietnamese institutions, values, and culture. The urban middle class above all absorbed the new cultural currents rushing in from the West. Affluent Vietnamese in Saigon aped French eating habits and dress; entered Western professions such as engineering, medicine, and law; and lived in Western-style houses. To many, the Confucian heritage appeared but a shadow of its glorious past, inadequate to meet the challenge of the new century and identified, through the effete imperial monarchy in Hue, with the French colonial regime. A few became almost entirely alienated from their native culture, chose French citizenship, and spoke French as their primary language. Western influence was slower to reach the tradition-bound villages where conservative peasants, still sheltered from the full force of Westernization in the cities, generally continued to honor the old ways.

Inevitably, Western modes began to affect the arts. Artists, composers, and musicians abandoned traditional styles and began to imitate Western trends. Literature, too, soon felt the impact of Western influence. During the first two decades of the twentieth century, a new journalism, influenced by trends in France, began to appear. Much of it was written in French and directed at moderate Francophile elements residing in the cities. Some, like Nguyen Van Vinh's *Dong Duong Tap Chi* [Indochinese review], were written in *quoc ngu*. Vinh, an outspoken advocate of modern Western ways, used the columns of his journal to promote social and cultural reform and was a pioneer in promoting a new role for women in Vietnamese society. In a column devoted to women, Vinh criticized them for their old-fashioned habits and urged them to imitate their progressive coun-terparts in the West. By the 1920s, Vietnamese journalists had become more daring, and a number of small journals sprouted in the cities. Although few survived for more than a few issues, they reflected a growing political radicalism in the intellectual community and a willingness to criticize the failings of the colonial regime. Not all the new journalism was so aggressively modernist in tone. Some conservative writers, notably the scholar-journalist Pham Quynh, defended the continued relevance of Confucian community-oriented values and called for a careful synthesis of modern Western and traditional cultural elements as the most effective means of enabling the Vietnamese to meet the challenges of the twentieth century. In his journal, *Nam Phong* [Wind from the South], sponsored by the colonial regime, Pham Quynh published essays on Eastern and Western culture and translations of the French classics and attempted to encourage the growth of a new Vietnamese literature based on *quoc ngu* and on a fruitful collaboration of Asian and Western elements.

Western influence was as strong in fiction as it was in journalism. After World War I, a new generation of Vietnamese novelists influenced by literary trends in France began to appear. At first, the new form shunned sensitive political and social themes that might activate official displeasure, and writers sought refuge in escapism and literary romanticism. In the early 1930s, however, several younger writers banded together in a literary group called the Tu Luc Van Doan (Self-reliance Literary Group) and began to use the novel form to criticize the political and social inequities in colonial society. In novels and short stories, such progressive writers as Nhat Linh, Khai Hung, and Hoang Dao promoted social reforms and described sympathetically the conditions of the urban and rural poor. Most of these new writers stayed within the bounds of moderate reformism, but a few, such as Ngo Tat To, followed the path of social revolution and opposed "art for life" to the bourgeois "art for art's sake."

CULTURE AND IDEOLOGY

The decade of the 1940s saw the opening stages of the long civil war (or, depending on the point of view, struggle for national liberation) that would engage the emotions and energies of countless Vietnamese for the next generation. During that period the nation would become divided, culturally as well as politically, into two separate societies. In French-controlled areas, the influence of the capitalist West intensified. In areas controlled by the Vietminh, the Communists attempted to construct a new culture based on the ideal of the "new" or "communist man" and the classless society. This bifurcation of Vietnam was accentuated after the Geneva Conference of 1954 with the de facto division of Vietnam into North and South.

The contrast was striking. In South Vietnam, the mounting U.S. presence under Ngo Dinh Diem and later Nguyen Van Thieu led to the growing influence of American culture and an acceleration in the breakdown of traditional values and institutions. For two decades the social and cultural environment in South Vietnam reflected an uneasy amalgam of Vietnamese, French, and American themes. American influence penetrated South Vietnamese society through a variety of means. U.S. economic and technological assistance stimulated the rise of an affluent middle class increasingly influenced by social and cultural trends in the United States. The educational system was remodeled on the pattern of the U.S. system used, and although the ideal of universal elementary education was not achieved, the literacy rate increased to levels substantially higher than those of the colonial period. In the creative arts, a subtle intermingling of indigenous and Western currents took place. In literature the influence of U.S. individualist culture produced a rush of novels and short stories laced with satire, romanticism, and sexual love themes. Many dealt with issues raised by the war, but others were frankly escapist and somewhat reminiscent of the bittersweet era of the 1920s. Popular music, too, reflected influences from the West. Popular tunes mingled indigenous themes with the rock beat of the contemporary West, and aided by the presence of half a million U.S. servicemen, the cultural heroes of the 1960s and early 1970s in the West achieved similar popularity in South Vietnam.

While South Vietnam continued to draw its cultural models from the

Life on a canal between Saigon and its sister city of Cholon. (By Wilbur E. Garrett © 1965 National Geographic Society)

capitalist West, the North took its guidance from the Soviet Union. During the early stages of its struggle for power, the ICP had understandably devoted more attention to revolutionary strategy than to the future shape of a socialist society, although, as we have seen, radical intellectuals had begun to create a socialist literature in the 1930s. Then, in 1943, the party issued a new cultural program drafted by General Secretary Truong Chinh calling for a new society based on the themes of national independence, people's democracy, and socialism. The promulgation of the program had, however, an immediate objective as well—to win intellectuals over to the party's cause in the struggle for national liberation. During the long Franco-Vietminh struggle, the Communists attempted to put this support to good use, calling on intellectuals to serve in the revolutionary armed forces and convening conferences for writers and artists in the liberated areas. The primary focus of the party's cultural work was to link the world of culture to economic and political realities and to create a popular literature based on the ideal of the communist man. As Ho Chi Minh noted in a brief address to artists in 1951: "With regard to your *creative work*, you must understand, get in close touch with and go deeply into the people's life. Only by so doing will you be able to depict the heroism and determination of our soldiers and people and to contribute to the development and heightening of these qualities."[2]

With peace restored in 1954, the Communists prepared to embark formally on the construction of a socialist society in North Vietnam. The party considered the cultural and ideological revolution of crucial importance to the process and gave it equal prominence with the technological revolution and the revolution in production relations as the primary objectives of the regime. The key role in this cultural struggle would be played by the educational system, for it was the children, uncontaminated by the poisonous weeds of Western capitalist society, who would eventually become the pillars of the socialist state. In place of the French two-track system, which had exposed a minority to Western education and the masses to little or none, the new system sought to achieve mass literacy through universal education at the elementary level. After completing nine years of compulsory elementary education the student would either continue on to secondary or vocational school, and thus increase the ranks of the socialist intellectuals, or would enter the work force. Beyond the obvious objective of contributing to the transformation of North Vietnam into an advanced technological society, the primary goal of education was to indoctrinate the masses with the virtues of the socialist system. This would not be an easy task, as regime spokesmen conceded, for the vast majority of Vietnamese, whether peasants or urban petit bourgeoisie, had little understanding of socialism.

Supplementing the educational system as a means of increasing socialist awareness among the mass of the population were the creative arts. To achieve this purpose, literature, music, and the visual arts would be revised to expurgate the perfidious influence of Western bourgeois culture and to create a new focus, nationalist in form and socialist in content. The importance of the dual emphasis on patriotism and ideology, an obvious reflection of the dual objectives of socialist construction and national reunification, was strongly emphasized in official statements dealing with the revolution on the cultural front. Party spokesmen went to great lengths to assert that patriotism and Marxist internationalism were not irreconcilable, but indeed were compatible.

The creative arts under party rule were thus dedicated to two major objectives: to stimulate a sense of national identity and commitment through the encouragement of indigenous forms of art, music, and literature and to promote the growth of a socialist ethic through the creation of a new culture based on the principles of socialist realism. In order to promote national pride, traditional forms of art, music, and dance were revived and transformed to serve modern puposes. The *ca dao* and other traditional forms of literary and musical expression were transformed into a medium for serving the cause of social revolution and national reunification. In novels, plays, and poems, North Vietnamese writers portrayed the glorious struggle of their countrymen to achieve the goals of constructing a socialist culture in the North and of reunification with the South. Historians, sponsored by the official Institute of History, wrote biographies of great national heroes such as Nguyen Trai, Tran Hung Dao, Phan Dinh Phung, and Phan Chu Trinh. Veteran revolutionaries wrote memoirs of the August Revolution and the War of Resistance or of their encounters with the foremost national hero, President Ho Chi Minh. The D.R.V. did not, however, deliberately create a "cult of personality" around the figure of Uncle Ho, as Peking and Moscow had done with party leaders Mao Tse-tung and Joseph Stalin. Ho Chi Minh was portrayed in the media and the arts as the founder and leader of the Vietnamese revolution, but his patriotism, his dedication, and his matchless sense of personal ethics (in some ways more reminiscent of Confucius than of Lenin) were stressed more than his all-knowing sagacity. Ho the collegial leader, the symbol of patriotism and self-sacrifice, rather than the irreplaceable, almost mythical national leader, was given prominence.

The regime's attempt to build a new Vietnam, united and socialist, had mixed results during the first two decades after Geneva. Of the success of its efforts to promote a sense of national identity and to mobilize mass support for national liberation there can be little doubt. The campaign to wipe out illiteracy and establish a system of universal education at the elementary level was undoubtedly one of the most successful in Southeast Asia. The effort to eradicate Western influence—notably that of the Catholic church, the only well-organized religious force in North Vietnam and a potential source of resistance to the regime—was relatively successful, for the church was placed under severe restrictions without a formal break in relations with the Vatican.

Less successful, however, was the regime's effort to produce a new culture based on socialist ideals. Remolding the character of the family-oriented Vietnamese was a major task and undoubtedly more difficult than mere statistics would indicate. Although the vast bulk of the rural population was successfully enrolled in collectives, the stubborn resistance of the Vietnamese peasant to the collective mentality—like that of his counterpart in China and the Soviet Union—was difficult to break. More-over, traditional habits, prejudices, and rituals proved resistant to the blandishments of the cadres of the revolution. Press reports confirmed that feudal attitudes (often a euphemism for male chauvinism) continued to thwart the efforts of the regime to promote the birth of a new egalitarian society. Party leaders were faced with similar problems in the cities. During the War of Resistance, the Vietminh movement had won considerable support from intellectuals (although relatively few fled to the liberated areas to serve in the revolutionary forces). In 1956, the party, following the example of the Hundred Flowers campaign in China, encouraged intellectuals to speak out in favor of domestic programs. Some, however, were emboldened to criticize the party's domination over politics and culture and called for a liberalized political system and increased freedom for creative expression. Shocked by the boldness of its critics, the regime cracked down on the dissidents and closed their most prominent mouthpiece, *Nhan Van*.

The crackdown on the dissident movement silenced the critics of the regime, but it did little to solve the problems that had aroused dissent. One of the major sources of public criticism was the increasing arrogance and rigidity of the bureaucracy. Party leaders were not unaware of the scope of the problem, and periodically official statements complained that many government officials and cadres were guilty of such sins as bureaucratism, "commandism," petty corruption, rigidity, and contempt for the masses. In China, evidence that party and government elites were beginning to adopt some of the less attractive habits of traditional officialdom had led Mao Tse-tung and his radical followers to launch the Cultural Revolution in the hope of cleansing the party and government and preserving the revolution. In North Vietnam, party leaders chose a more traditional route and attempted to resolve the problem through periodic rectification campaigns designed to improve bureaucratic behavior and weed out incompetent or corrupt elements. Although such programs presumably had some success, they clearly did not resolve the problem. By the early 1970s, official concern over bureaucratic misbehavior had increased and stringent regulations were issued to rid the party and government bureaucracy of impure elements. To provide a standard of behavior for youths entering the ranks of officialdom, a new "Ho Chi Minh" class of exemplary youths was set up as a model of revolutionary ethics.

Victory in the South in 1975 added a new dimension to the cultural challenge that the party faced in its attempt to construct a socialist society in Vietnam. Although over the years many southerners had been recruited, by conviction, moral suasion, or social pressure, into the revolutionary movement, the population as a whole had not yet been convinced of the superiority of the socialist system, and many awaited the new revolutionary regime with considerable anxiety. Many South Vietnamese had been poisoned by the "noxious weeds" of American bourgeois culture, a fact occasionally admitted by inner-party documents about conditions in the South. Worse yet, some of those most affected by U.S. influence were the so-called gilded youth of the big cities, many of whom had adopted a culture characterized by rock music, drugs, prostitution, and the individualist ethic. Even some of the political or religious groups considered hostile to the Saigon regime, such as the Buddhist Associations and the sects, were imbued with parochial or petit bourgeois attitudes.

To remove the legacy of Western influence in South Vietnam and sow the seeds of a new socialist culture would thus be one of the most complex challenges faced by the party after victory in 1975. The problem was one of considerable delicacy. Economic and political realities dictated a relatively moderate and gradualist policy to avoid provoking hostility or resistance from the indigenous population in the South. On the other hand, a good case could be made for urgency. So long as Western influence had not been eliminated from South Vietnamese society, the party's program of integrating the South and the North and embarking on the construction of socialism throughout the entire country would be severely hampered.

The new revolutionary authorities moved cautiously but with deliberation. The top priority was to expurgate the remnants of the American era from Saigon and other urban areas in the South. As one of its first acts, the new revolutionary government attempted to close the bars and drive the prostitutes, beggars, drug pushers, and juvenile gangs off the streets. The regime instructed cadres not to be overzealous in carrying out the policy, however, and on a few occasions, cadres were reprimanded for harassing local youths for their long hair or Western clothing. Training centers were established to provide reeducation for addicts, delinquents, and streetwalkers and orphanages for the homeless. According to reports by foreign journalists, the residue of the American era had not been entirely removed, and the new Ho Chi Minh City was still Saigon in disguise. Signs of the old culture persisted everywhere. As a February 16, 1976, report in *Time* magazine put it: "Good food and excellent French wines were still available at the Hotel Caravelle, a favorite hangout of foreigners in the old days. Lissome Saigonese women wore hip-hugging jeans and colorful *ao-dais*; although the P.R.G. frowns on prostitution, streetwalkers and bar girls were still hawking their charms. American pop songs blared out from the jukeboxes of cafes and bars, and the old Thieves' Market on Bac Si Calumette Street was jammed with TV sets, cameras, and transistor radios taken from abandoned American PXs."

The new revolutionary authorities did their best to remove the remaining sources of U.S. influence. Within weeks of victory, all schools in the South were closed, and teachers were compelled to attend retraining sessions before being permitted to return to the classroom. When the schools were reopened, new textbooks with a Marxist orientation, hastily sent down from the North, replaced those that had been in use under the Saigon regime. A campaign to confiscate books, tapes, and records reflecting Western bourgeois decadence was launched, and newpapers that had published under the Saigon regime, except for the moderately critical *Tin Sang*, were ordered to close their doors.

The fears of party leaders that the population in the South would not be easily assimilated into the emerging socialist culture in the North were only too well founded. Habits developed over a period of two decades of U.S. influence were not to be erased even by a regime as determined and well disciplined as the one in Hanoi. Despite the stringent efforts of the authorities, the population in the South proved stubbornly resistant to the blandishments of the regime. More than five years after the conquest of Saigon, foreign visitors continued to report that Ho Chi Minh City was still reminiscent of the Saigon of a bygone era. An official report written in 1980 noted: "Some of the youths who are influenced by neocolonialism and the old social system have been infected with such bad habits as laziness, selfishness, parasitism, vagabondism, pursuing a good time, etc."[3] Another official bemoaned the continuing influence of Western music over young people in the South, complaining that such music entices listeners to "shirk obligations, detach themselves from reality, turn their backs on our people's life of labor and combat, regret the past and idolize imperialism."[4]

To make it worse, the easy-going lifestyle in the South was beginning to erode the spirit of revolutionary puritanism and self-sacrifice of northern soldiers and cadres serving in the South. For inexperienced and innocent northerners, the manifold temptations of southern culture must have been hard to resist. According to press accounts, cadres from the North—many housed in the old Hotel Continental, now renamed the Hotel of the People's Insurrection—were too often seduced by the glittering temptations of city life in Saigon. Bribery, embezzlement, and the shirking of obligations became increasingly common among officials stationed in the South and began to occur in the North as well. By the end of the decade, the regime had grown sufficiently concerned about the situation to launch a major campaign against "decadent" influences in Vietnamese culture. Literature, music, and art that were considered harmful to the struggle to build a socialist society were to be banned. Books and printed songs that portrayed such alleged Western bourgeois attitudes as individualism, selfishness, sexual license, and mysticism were confiscated and burned. In their place, stories and folk songs reflecting the genuine spirit of the people were to be revived and propagated and new creative works were to be produced that would meet the standards of socialist idealism and help to create the new man. To promote the birth of this new culture, conferences sponsored by the Ministry of Culture were to be convened at all administrative levels to acquaint cadres with official guidelines.

The authorities soon discovered, however, that such standards were not always easy to apply. For example, an article written by the minister of culture and published in *Nhan Dan* conceded that it was often difficult to make the proper classifications of musical works. Some "normal, soft, and unharmful music" had been banned or confiscated by government officials, while some "rock music" superficially reflecting socialist themes had been spared. Moreover, the official campaign to cleanse the nation of foreign influence and create a new national and socialist literature and art was beginning to encounter resistance from within. An article by Ha Xuan Truong in the March 1980 issue of *Tap Chi Cong San* [Communist review] noted that some "artistic creators" had become "confused" about official policies and were inclined to blame deficiencies on the general line of the party rather than on faulty implementation at the lower level. The author was particularly critical of an article by Hoang Ngoc Hien in the June 1979 issue of *Van Nghe* [Literature and art], which complained that, under the current line, more attention was being paid to "conformist realism" than to artistic truth. Truong conceded that a mechanical and shortsighted application of the principle "literature and art serve politics" was a danger to be avoided, but at the same time (undoubtedly reflecting official policy) he emphasized that "we must enable everyone to clearly realize that the fierce and extremely complicated political struggle in the world and in our country demand that now more than ever revolutionary writers and artists must firmly grasp the party's political struggle goals." If it was necessary to overcome the diseases of formalism and superficiality, it was even more important to affirm that socialist realism must transform and construct life.

Similar efforts have recently been undertaken to transform the educational system into a more effective vehicle for building the communist man. Conceding that the existing system was inadequate and that many youths lacked discipline and socialist awareness, Vice-Premier To Huu in an article in the September 5, 1979 issue of *Nhan Dan*, discussed a resolution of the party Central Committee to set up a model for a new national educational system. The new system, according to To Huu, must devote increased attention to ideology, politics, and revolutionary ethics. It must emphasize the unity of theory and practice, combine studies with practical labor, and integrate the school system into society at large. Only thus could a new generation of young Vietnamese emerge with "the qualities and abilities of the New Man."

How successful has the party leadership been in the creation of a new and more egalitarian society in Vietnam? At this point, judgment must be guarded. In some respects, Vietnam under Communist rule has made impressive advances. Education has rapidly expanded, and the literacy rate is one of the highest in Asia. Health and sanitation are markedly improved over the colonial period. Many of the social and financial inequities of the old regime have been eliminated, and the disparity between wealth and poverty has been significantly reduced. Progress has been made in racial and sexual equality as well. The hill peoples are being gradually but inexorably integrated into Vietnamese society, and according to official statistics, many have been persuaded to give up their nomadic way of life for settled farming. The degradation of women, so deeply entrenched in Confucian Vietnam, has been markedly reduced, and women play an active role in socialist Vietnam, not only in the professions but in politics as well. Unquestionably, the new freedom for women is in part a consequence of the long liberation struggle, when women contributed actively to the war effort, not only replacing men in factories and farms but in some cases serving in the armed forces as well (although relatively few took part in combat operations, many served in intelligence, in the village militia, or in artillery units). As in many socialist societies, women have become active participants in the struggle to take Vietnam to communism.

Yet Vietnam continues to face massive problems in its efforts to build an advanced egalitarian society. Although schooling at the basic level has become virtually universal, Vietnam still suffers from an agonizing shortage of trained personnel, and higher education is still inadequate to meet the burgeoning needs of a developing society. Undoubtedly the recent agreement to send thousands of young Vietnamese workers to the Soviet Union to receive training and work in factories is related to this problem. The current shortage of food in the S.R.V. has created serious problems of malnutrition, and some foreign visitors have reported that the food problem appears even worse in Vietnam than in Cambodia. Income disparity has been reduced, but critics charge with some justification that equality has been achieved, but at the level of poverty. Not only is rural income low, but even in the cities, inadequate salaries and a shortage of consumer goods have caused a serious decline in the urban standard of living.

Even in achieving racial and sexual equality, the regime has been encountering serious problems. Unrest among hill peoples, often provoked by high-handed efforts by the government to disturb their traditional way of life, is on the rise. And although the position of women in Vietnamese society has undoubtedly improved, there are still signs that the traditional attitude of male superiority has not been entirely eliminated. Women are increasingly prominent at the lower levels of party and government, but it is worthy of note that there are no women in the party Politburo and only a handful in the Central Committee.

In summary, the struggle to build a prosperous and technologically advanced society continues to face severe challenges. And while the socialist system adopted by the Communist party presents certain advances in this effort, notably in social discipline, mobilization of effort, and long-term planning, there are also heavy costs to pay in ideological rigidity and loss of individual incentive. What makes this problem even more complicated is the presence of more than 20 million southerners, many of whom are as yet unconvinced of the superiority of the socialist system. Truly, for the Communists, the problems of peacetime are as challenging as, and perhaps even more complex than, those of war.

THE EVOLUTION OF VIETNAMESE CULTURE IN CONTEMPORARY MARXIST PERSPECTIVE

As noted above, the primary goal of the party leadership in Hanoi is to create a new Vietnamese culture national in form and socialist in content. The dream of a reunified nation, secure in its borders, economically prosperous, technologically advanced, and based on the egalitarian Marxist vision of a classless society, has been at the core of the party's enduring struggle in the half-century since it was first founded in 1930. Until recently, the party's attempt to combine Marxist internationalism with the concept of a national culture appeared directed primarily at defending the idea that Marxism and patriotism were not incompatible, and little attention was devoted to defining what was meant by a "national culture." The party's interpretation of Vietnamese history was orthodox Marxist and tended to emphasize class struggle over national issues. Although Viet-namese historians made occasional allusions to the historical defense of the Vietnamese homeland against Chinese invaders, the primary villain in Vietnamese history was the reactionary feudal regime and its primary representation at the local level, the corrupt mandarins and venal landlords. In their approach to contemporary problems, party leaders made little effort to define a strictly Vietnamese form of socialism and appeared willing to borrow liberally from the Soviet Union and China. Hanoi's debt to China was particularly marked. Although it was possible to differentiate Vietnamese socialism from its Maoist counterpart (particularly, after 1958, when China began to take a radical turn), many of the major components of Vietnamese socialism were borrowed directly from Chinese experience. Socialist Vietnam, like its Confucian predecessor, had found much to imitate in its great neighbor, China.

The recent deterioration in relations with Peking has provided a new anti-Chinese flavor to Hanoi's interpretation of Vietnamese history and has sharpened its image of the Vietnamese national culture. In this new perspective, the course of Vietnamese history was viewed as the long struggle of the Vietnamese masses against two hostile and destructive forces, the feudal reactionaries at home and neighboring China to the north. The Chinese are clearly the primary villain of the piece. In the prehistoric era, the Vietnamese people had already created an advanced Bronze Age culture in the Red River valley. Left to its own devices, this embryonic Vietnamese state would have developed into a prosperous society with a strong national character centuries ago. But Chinese conquest led to the transformation of Vietnam into a feudal society under Chinese political and cultural domination. Vietnamese independence was restored in the tenth century but did not eradicate the legacy of centuries of Chinese cultural domination. The Vietnamese ruling class, in order to retain its power and preserve the feudal form of society, relied on Chinese institutions and Chinese political and social philosophy. Beset by the three evils of Buddhism, Taoism, and Confucianism, the masses were reduced to a position of degradation and slavery.

Eventually, however, the force of Vietnamese identity, expressed by the oppressed mass of the Vietnamese population, rose against Sino-Vietnamese feudal domination and began to create a unique national culture. Colonial rule, imposed by the French in the late nineteenth century, set back the process, but in the modern era the Vietnamese masses, led by the Communist party, completed the triumph over reactionary forces within and imperialist forces without and resumed the struggle to create a unique national culture.

This interpretation, although certainly not totally false, is arguably somewhat simplistic. Present evidence suggests that Vietnamese society had developed recognizably feudal and elitist characteristics before the Chinese conquest and might well have developed further in that direction

even if Vietnam had not fallen to Chinese conquest. Chinese rule undoubtedly encouraged the trend and, after independence, made it easier
for Vietnamese rulers to consolidate their authority. But China should not
bear the entire blame for the imposition of Confucianism on the Vietnamese
state. Vietnam was capable of adapting foreign institutions to native
conditions on its own initiative. Moreover, as contemporary scholars in
Hanoi concede, Confucian culture in Vietnam was not entirely feudalist
or reactionary in tone. On many occasions, the power of the Confucian
monarchy and the professional bureaucracy contributed to the greatness
of the state. Progressive rulers attempted to reverse land concentration by
dispossessing feudal magnates and distributing the land to impoverished
peasants. In a word, Confucianism contributed in no small measure to
the growth of the Vietnamese state. As for the charge of subservience to
China, the fact is that, in times of crisis, many Confucian-trained scholars
and bureaucrats, in the words of party ideologist Truong Chinh, were
"deeply imbued with a national spirit," and many of the great heroes of
Vietnamese tradition, including Tran Hung Dao, Nguyen Trai, and Phan
Dinh Phung, were Confucian by training and conviction. Confucianism
did not blunt the Vietnamese sense of nationhood but, on the contrary,
may have sharpened it.

Today Hanoi is making a concerted effort to differentiate Vietnamese
socialism from "reactionary" Maoism, which, in the official view, continues
to be practiced even under Mao's more pragmatic successors. Maoism is
identified primarily as a form of "revolutionary romanticism," which, while
avowedly radical, is in actuality a form of petit bourgeois idealism.
Vietnamese socialism, it is now stressed, is Leninist in its inspiration and
not Maoist. There is some truth in this contention; in many respects the
Vietnamese have borrowed more from Lenin than from Mao Tse-tung.
Certainly Hanoi has deliberately avoided the open conflict between radicals
and pragmatists that has characterized the recent stage of the Chinese
revolution. In foreign policy, it has maintained its link with the mainstream
of the Marxist-Leninist bloc, led by the Soviet Union, while labeling
Peking's anti-Soviet foreign policy "big-power chauvinist." But whether
avowed or not, the influence of Chinese forms remains strong in the S.R.V.
And Hanoi has yet to imprint its own brand of socialism with a peculiarly
Vietnamese stamp. The search for a specifically "national" culture goes
on.

NOTES

1. Duong Quang Ham, *Viet Nam Van Hoc Su Yeu* [An outline history of
Vietnamese literature], cited in Truong Chinh; "The Long Struggle to Defend Our
National Culture," *Tap Chi Cong San* [Communist review], March 1979, p. 62.

2. Cited in "To the Artists on the Occasion of the 1951 Painting Exhibition,"

in Ho Chi Minh, *Selected Writings* (Hanoi: Foreign Languages Press, 1977), pp. 133–134.

3. To Huu, "Carry Out the Educational Reform in order to Train a New Generation of Socialist Vietnamese," *Nhan Dan*, September 5, 1979, p. 3.

4. Vo Van Kiet, speech broadcast on Hanoi Radio, May 10, 1981.

8
Foreign Relations

With the entry in 1975 of North Vietnamese troops into the beleaguered city of Saigon, a generation of civil strife came to an end. Unification, however, did not bring peace, for in less than five years the new united Vietnam was again at war, this time with its neighbors Cambodia and China. By 1980, Laos and Cambodia had become Hanoi's client states and tension was high between Bangkok and Hanoi as each massed troops on the Thai-Cambodian border.

For some, such activity undoubtedly served as a vivid confirmation of the famous "domino theory," according to which the fall of one state to communism leads quickly to instability, revolution, and communist takeovers in neighboring areas. In fact, however, the tension that has erupted in Southeast Asia as a result of the Communist triumph in Vietnam is better viewed as a reappearance of historical trends that were temporarily obscured during a century of colonialism and Cold War struggle. This is not to say that Vietnamese foreign policy since the end of the war has not been motivated in part by ideological factors. Official pronouncements by high party and government officials have repeatedly stated that Vietnam considers itself a loyal member of the socialist camp dedicated to the triumph of Marxist-Leninist doctrine throughout the world, and there is no reason to doubt the sincerity of such pronouncements. The recent course of international politics makes clear, however, that commitment to the cause of world revolution is not the sole or even the primary determinant of foreign policy in communist states. In Moscow, in Peking, and in Hanoi, the primary concerns of policymakers in foreign policy are those of nationalism and national security. Nowhere is this more the case than in Vietnam. Since its origins in the French colonial period, the fate of the Communist movement in Vietnam has been intimately linked with the national destiny. It is no coincidence that the party's climb to power commenced with its recognition that its foremost objective was the cause of national independence and unification.

Concern for national survival is indeed one of the dominant features in the history of the Vietnamese people. Cross-cultural comparisons are frequently misleading in Southeast Asia, but it is probably safe to say that no people in the region has developed a more tenacious sense of national identity throughout its history than have the Vietnamese. This sense of separate existence and the willingness to fight to maintain it probably appeared in embryonic form in the years before the Chinese conquest and increased in intensity during the long struggle to restore and retain independence. Combined with this tradition of historical resistance to China was Vietnam's strong and growing attitude of political and cultural superiority in its relations with its neighbors in Southeast Asia. From the beginning of the "March to the South," which gathered momentum in the fifteenth century during the reign of Le Thanh Tong, the Vietnamese displayed increasing self-confidence in their relations with their neighbors to the south and west. With the conquest of Champa and the collapse of Angkor, the Vietnamese became, with the possible exception of the Thai, the most dynamic people in mainland Southeast Asia. In part this was a product of military prowess; in part, too, it may have resulted from a conviction of the superiority of Confucian institutions. Whatever the case, Vietnamese rulers were often tempted to apply the same tributary status to their neighbors that the Chinese empire habitually applied to them. In general, Southeast Asian monarchs rejected such presumption, but by the nineteenth century weak monarchs in Laos and Cambodia had been compelled to accept tribute status with Vietnam, thus providing the latter for the first time with a sense of security on its long and vulnerable western frontier.

PERSPECTIVES DURING THE WAR OF LIBERATION

The French conquest in the late nineteenth century temporarily arrested this process. Vietnam was weakened by the division of the country into three separate parts; Cambodia and Laos were given equal status and secure boundaries, thus perhaps saving them from political extinction, and China's weakness removed an immediate threat from the north. Under these new conditions, the issue of national survival continued to be of primary importance but the nature of the threat had changed. Historical concern over frontiers and over the threat from China was replaced by the danger of national and cultural extinction at the hands of the West. Vietnamese nationalist leaders turned to China for assistance against the French colonial regime (much as the Nguyen had turned to the imperial court in Peking for protection against the French a generation earlier). Leaders of the Indochinese Communist party, while doubtless harboring some lingering suspicions about the long-term motives of their Chinese comrades, relied on the CCP for advice and assistance against the French and later the United States.

At first, Vietnamese nationalist groups, in their preoccupation with the issue of national independence, understandably devoted little attention to the future Vietnamese relationship with Laos and Cambodia. This attitude was clearly illustrated in the behavior of the nascent Indochinese Communist party. At the time of the formation of the party in early 1930, the founders of the organization, on the assumption that social revolution would be long delayed in the more primitive societies of Laos and Cambodia, did not include these areas in their new organization whose original name was to be the Vietnamese Communist party. It was only later in the year, on the instructions of the Comintern, that the name was changed to the Indochinese Communist party, thus signaling that the revolutions in Vietnam, Cambodia, and Laos were linked and should be waged under unified direction. Comintern strategists at that time were convinced that communist movements in small countries in Asia could not seize power on their own and should band together in larger federations in regions where, as in Indochina, economic and political conditions were similar.

The ICP apparently devoted little effort to building up revolutionary movements in Cambodia and Laos until after World War II; before this, only a few isolated party cells had been formed in each country. Most cells were composed of ethnic Vietnamese living in provincial or district capitals. During the Franco-Vietminh conflict, however, party leaders soon discovered the strategic importance of Cambodia and Laos to the Vietnamese revolution, and by 1950 recruitment among the local population in both areas was on the rise. But growth brought problems: Secret inner-party documents show that party members of Cambodian and Laotian extraction were increasingly restive under the direction of a Communist party dominated by the Vietnamese and apparently agitated for party organizations under native leadership. In 1951, at the Second National Congress, which announced the formation of the new Vietnam Workers party to replace the nominally defunct ICP, Cambodian and Laotian members were granted their own "People's Revolutionary Parties" to make their revolutions in concert with the Vietnamese. The VWP formally disavowed any intention to form a so-called Indochinese Federation, which had been originally proposed in 1930. Explanations in Vietnamese sources for the decision to separate the three parties point to nationalist susceptibilities in Laos and Cambodia and to the apparently slower pace of revolution in these countries. But such documents made it clear that, although the VWP was conceding a separate existence to its Laotian and Cambodian comrades, it did not intend to relinquish overall direction of the Communist movement throughout Indochina. According to one secret document written at the time, it reserved the possibility that at some future date the three fraternal parties might be reunited in a single Vietnam-Lao-Khmer Federation.

The importance of Laos and Cambodia to the Vietnamese revolution was also demonstrated during the later stages of the war against the Saigon regime and the United States. Hanoi used both countries as a conduit for the infiltration into South Vietnam of men and material from the North and as a sanctuary and staging area for revolutionary forces.

The Vietnamese helped their Cambodian and Laotian comrades wage their own insurgency movements in concert with the struggle in Vietnam, but there is some evidence that Hanoi was careful to guarantee that the needs of the revolutionary struggle in South Vietnam took precedence over those in neighboring Cambodia and Laos. Soon after the common victory in all three countries in 1975, the Pol Pot government in Phnom Penh asserted with considerable bitterness that during the 1950s and 1960s the VWP leadership had prohibited the Khmer Rouge from launching armed struggle against the Sihanouk regime in order to avoid provoking Sihanouk into striking at Vietnamese sanctuaries along the border and cooperating with the United States to wipe them out. Captured documents confirm that Vietnamese strategists sought to prevent the insurgency in Cambodia from interfering with the course of the war effort in South Vietnam. Although Laotian Communists have registered no public complaint along these lines, it is likely that Hanoi took equal pains to ensure that the pace of insurgency in Laos did not cause difficulties for the primary battlefield in South Vietnam.

Irritation over Vietnamese strategy fed latent suspicions about long-term Vietnamese motives in Cambodia and led to rising tensions within the Cambodian revolutionary movement. In the early 1960s the Cambodian Communist movement split over the issue and a dissident faction under the Paris-trained radical Pol Pot seized power. The new leadership attempted to purge pro-Vietnamese elements from the party and, in defiance of Hanoi's directions, launched an armed struggle against the Sihanouk regime. After the fall of the Sihanouk government and the acceleration of Cambodian insurgency in the spring of 1970, Hanoi attempted to reassert its control over the Khmer Rouge by introducing into the movement several hundred Cambodian party members who had lived in North Vietnam since the Geneva Conference. Many of these new arrivals, however, were purged in turn by the suspicious Pol Pot leadership, and by the end of the war in 1975, relations between the two parties had seriously deteriorated.

MARCH TO THE WEST

After the Vietnamese victory, these latent tensions soon broke out into the open. The Pol Pot regime in Phnom Penh, demanding the return of territories lost to the Vietnamese during the latter's expansion into the Mekong Delta centuries earlier, launched armed incursions into South Vietnam and raided islands occupied by Vietnamese troops in the Gulf of Thailand. Hanoi offered negotiations to settle the territorial issue, but Cambodia, now renamed Democratic Kampuchea, claimed that the Vietnamese were attempting to achieve dominance over their neighbors through the formation of an Indochinese Federation and continued to attack along the common border. Hanoi, while denying any intention of dominating Cambodia and formally declaring that the concept of an Indochinese

Federation had been abandoned in 1951, did insist that the shared experience of the struggle for national liberation and the continuing danger from world imperialism created the need for an "intimate relationship" between Vietnam, Laos, and Cambodia.

By early 1978, party leaders in Hanoi had evidently lost faith in the possibility of a peaceful solution to the crisis and decided to resolve the issue by force. In the fall, rebel leaders operating in eastern Cambodia announced the formation of the new Kampuchean National United Front for National Salvation (KNUFNS), which, with Vietnamese assistance, would free the Cambodian people from the tyrannical Pol Pot regime. In late December, Vietnamese troops, joined by Khmer guerrillas recruited from among the thousands of refugees who had fled to Vietnam to escape the cruelties of the brutal Pol Pot regime, launched an invasion directly across the border. After a series of short but bitter battles, the Pol Pot regime was forced to abandon the capital and sought refuge in the Cardamom Mountains, where it attempted to continue national resistance. In Phnom Penh, a pro-Vietnamese regime under the unknown Cambodian leader Heng Samrin announced the overthrow of Democratic Kampuchea and the formation of a new Democratic People's Republic of Kampuchea (DPRK). The radical policies followed by the Pol Pot regime were reversed, and Vietnamese occupation forces, estimated at nearly 200,000, attempted to mop up remaining resistance activities in the mountains and in the jungles along the Thai border.

The Vietnamese invasion of Cambodia provided Vietnam with security on the western frontier, but at a high cost. Global reaction to the invasion was generally hostile, not only among those nations—such as the United States—that had been persistently antagonistic to the Communist regime in Hanoi, but also among neutrals and many Third World nations. The strength of world reaction against the Vietnamese occupation reached measurable levels when a large majority at the UN General Assembly condemned the invasion, demanded a Vietnamese withdrawal, and refused to grant recognition to the new Heng Samrin regime in Phnom Penh.

Condemnation by a substantial segment of the world could be tolerated, of course, if the interests of national security appeared to require it. Party leaders in Hanoi were too wise in the ways of the world to allow the evanescent force of world public opinion to deflect them from those measures they felt were required for the survival and basic interests of the Vietnamese nation. Yet there was a tangible and painful price to pay. For years North Vietnam had enjoyed a measure of support and sympathy around the world for its courageous and tenacious struggle against the powerful force of the United States. After 1975, this sympathy was transformed into practical gestures of assistance as several Western European countries agreed to provide economic assistance to the new united Vietnam. Similar aid was soon forthcoming from international agencies. Even the Carter administration showed a cautious willingness to consider trade relations and the granting of economic aid to Vietnam. Negotiations stalled, however, when Hanoi, citing a 1973 letter from President Nixon to Prime Minister Pham Van Dong that promised to provide $3.25 billion to Vietnam for postwar reconstruction "without any political conditions," insisted on a U.S. commitment to provide such aid as "war reparations" prior to the normalization of relations, a demand rejected by the Carter administration. By 1978, Vietnam had implied that it was willing to drop such conditions, but by then the growing crisis in Southeast Asia (and, according to some observers, the prospects of a normalization of relations with mainland China) had severely reduced Washington's interest in establishing diplomatic ties. The Carter administration broke off its trade talks with Hanoi and imposed an embargo on U.S. trade with the S.R.V. The Vietnamese invasion of Cambodia was a sharp setback to Vietnam's relations with a number of Western nations; several other nations canceled or cut back their assistance to Vietnam. Clearly, the economic price of guaranteeing security along the western border was high.

The invasion had equally disruptive effects on Vietnam's relations with its neighbors in the region. Since the end of the war, Hanoi had been engaged in sporadic and delicate efforts to improve its relations with the five nations of the Association of the Southeast Asian Nations (ASEAN)— Thailand, Indonesia, Malaysia, Singapore, and the Philippines. Soon after the fall of Saigon, rumors appeared that the new communist governments in Hanoi, Vientiane, and Phnom Penh might be invited to associate themselves with ASEAN and thus usher in a new period of peace and stability in Southeast Asia. At first Hanoi appeared suspicious of such overtures and publicly labeled ASEAN a "tool of the imperialists," Later it seemed to become more receptive to negotiations but posed the unacceptable condition that the ASEAN states renounce military ties with Western nations. Still, there were signs that relations between the communist and noncommunist states in the region were gradually improving, and some observers hoped that, as the tensions resulting from the long Indochina conflict subsided, Southeast Asia might indeed become a region of "peace, neutrality, and freedom" (to use the slogan of the program set forth by the ASEAN states), free from the tensions of the Cold War.

The Vietnamese invasion of Cambodia frightened the ASEAN states and revived their latent suspicions concerning Vietnamese imperialistic expansionism. Periodic meetings of the ASEAN foreign ministers resulted in joint calls for the withdrawal of Vietnamese occupation forces from Cambodia and the holding of national elections under international supervision. Despite their common distaste for the now deposed Pol Pot regime, the ASEAN states continued to recognize it as the legitimate government of Cambodia and pushed resolutions condemning Hanoi's behavior in the United Nations. Most hostile in its response was Thailand. The military government in Bangkok viewed the Vietnamese action as confirmation that Hanoi was determined to dominate both Cambodia and

Laos, thus destroying the historic buffer between Thailand and Vietnam and putting Vietnamese troops along the Thai border. In response, Bangkok led the ASEAN chorus of condemnation and provided fairly overt support for the anti–Phnom Penh activities of rebel groups along the frontier.

Hanoi reacted to ASEAN behavior with a combination of belligerence and conciliation. It offered to withdraw its forces from Cambodia, but only on condition that hostile forces supported by world imperialism stop supporting rebel activities led by the Pol Pot regime and that the ASEAN states recognize the legitimacy of the Hanoi-supported regime in Phnom Penh. It offered to withdraw its forces from the border and to sign a mutual nonaggression pact with Thailand on condition that the latter refrain from assisting the guerrilla units in Cambodia. Bangkok, however, would not budge from its demands for complete Vietnamese withdrawal and supervised elections in Cambodia. Hanoi asserted that the survival of the current government was nonnegotiable, claiming that national elections were the affair of the DPRK. To emphasize its demands, Hanoi launched punitive raids into Thai territory to clean out the Pol Pot guerrilla sanctuaries and threatened by implication to support insurgency activities in Thailand. It attempted to isolate Bangkok by taking a relatively conciliatory position in discussions with Thailand's more reluctant allies, Malaysia and Indonesia.

As the 1980s began, the situation had temporarily reached a stalemate. The ASEAN states, led by Thailand and supported to varying degrees by China, the United States, and other foreign powers, continued to refuse to recognize the fait accompli in Cambodia and reiterated their demand for Vietnamese withdrawal and national elections. To maintain pressure on Hanoi, they provided low-level assistance to rebel activities in Cambodia while they attempted to promote the formation of a united front of various political groups opposed to Vietnamese domination of the country. Playing key roles in this process were the moderate Cambodian politician Son Sann and the exiled leader Prince Sihanouk. To some, Sihanouk was the only figure who could bring together the disparate factions—Sihanoukists, supporters of Pol Pot, and ex-followers of Lon Nol—who shared antagonism to the current regime in Phnom Penh. To others, he was a quixotic and mercurial figure from the past, a frail support on which to build an effective policy to contain Vietnamese expansion in Southeast Asia. In any case, ASEAN leaders considered the unification of the various factions essential to maintaining support in the UN General Assembly, and a unity conference in Kuala Lumpur in June 1982 resulted in the formation of a coalition government of the three major anti–Phnom Penh forces. Yet the presence of the widely detested Khmer Rouge within the alliance continued to pose problems, and observers wondered whether meaningful cooperation between the groups could really take place.

For Hanoi, the disarray in the opposition camp provided a welcome opportunity to stabilize the situation in Cambodia and present the world with its fait accompli. To emphasize the permanent nature of the new situation and the closeness between the new government in Cambodia and the S.R.V., the two countries signed a mutual security treaty. A similar accord was reached with Laos, now under Communist rule and a close ally of the S.R.V., which retained several thousand troops in the country. In Cambodia, Vietnamese troops maintained order and launched sweep operations against rebel groups operating along the western border, while the regime of President Heng Samrin attempted to legitimize its rule and win popular support from the local population. Domestic policies were deliberately moderate. Urban residents who had been driven from their homes into the countryside during the brutal reign of Pol Pot were permitted to return to the cities. Normal economic activities were resumed as the government tolerated a degree of private enterprise; churches and temples were reopened and the mass of the population was reassured that they could resume their normal lives. In order to improve the image of legitimacy of the new government, the Phnom Penh regime announced that a constitution for the new DPRK would be drafted and national elections would be held. Economic life, badly disrupted during the Pol Pot era and the civil war that followed, was still perilous, but peace and grain from abroad had apparently reduced the danger of mass starvation among the local population. In the summer of 1982, in a patent attempt to win further international support for its position, Hanoi announced a partial withdrawal of its occupation forces in Cambodia. The Cambodian people's attitude toward their new rulers was difficult to discern, but many foreign visitors reported that, although few Cambodians appeared to welcome Vietnamese occupation, they preferred it to the horrors of the previous regime. For the moment, at least, Hanoi had brought peace to Cambodia.

RELATIONS WITH CHINA

Although Hanoi had achieved temporary stability on its western flank, the possibility that party leaders could divert their attention from military to peacetime concerns was still remote. For the end of the Vietnam War in 1975 and the events that followed it had led to a virtual breakdown in relations with China and, in 1979, to war.

The signs of incipient difficulties between Peking and Hanoi were visible before 1975 only to the most discerning eye. Virtually from the moment of Communist victory in mainland China in 1949, the P.R.C. had provided substantial amounts of military and economic assistance to North Vietnam in the latter's struggle to seize power and unify the country. Some foreign observers speculated (and Peking sources explicitly claimed) that the Vietminh victory at Dien Bien Phu had been engineered largely with Chinese advice and material assistance. Throughout the war Chinese leaders had vocally supported Hanoi and had promised to stand shoulder to shoulder with their Vietnamese comrades in fending off the vicious attacks of the Western imperialists. In turn, the D.R.V. had publicly declared its gratitude for the fraternal assistance provided by China. More important, Hanoi had adopted a position of rigorous neutrality in the increasingly bitter Sino-Soviet dispute, and Ho Chi Minh, in the evident belief that the split was disadvantageous to the Vietnamese revolution, frequently attempted to use his considerable diplomatic skills to bring the two sides together. When necessary, however, the Vietnamese attempted to play one off against the other. This was particularly evident in the early 1960s when Hanoi, irritated by Moscow's reluctance to approve a new policy of heightened struggle in the South, adopted a pro-Peking stance while criticizing Soviet "revisionism," the signing of the Nuclear Test-Ban Treaty with the United States, and Moscow's entire policy of peaceful coexistence with the West. According to Vietnamese sources, Peking then offered to increase its aid to the D.R.V., but only on condition that the latter refuse further assistance from the U.S.S.R. Hanoi was unwilling to risk an irrevocable break with Moscow, however, and rejected the offer. With the fall of Khrushchev and the rise of the new leadership of Brezhnev and Kosygin in the fall of 1964, the Soviet Union adopted a more tolerant attitude toward Hanoi's policies in the South and relations with Moscow improved. For the remainder of the war, Hanoi attempted with some success to retain amicable relations with both China and the Soviet Union.

Behind the facade of mutual esteem, however, trouble was brewing in Sino-Vietnamese relations. For their own reasons, Chinese leaders were increasingly irritated at Hanoi's aggressive policy in South Vietnam and periodically advised Hanoi to adopt a cautious strategy of guerrilla warfare until China was strong enough to provide massive assistance. In turn, the D.R.V. was angered by the Chinese effort to improve relations with the United States in the early 1970s and particularly resented Peking's invitation to President Nixon to visit China at a time when the United States had resumed its heavy bombing raids on North Vietnam during the Eastern Offensive.

Below the surface, even more durable issues loomed. According to a White Paper issued by the S.R.V. Ministry of Foreign Affairs in 1979, Vietnamese party leaders had harbored suspicions of China's long-term intentions in Southeast Asia as early as 1949, when Mao Tse-tung and his colleagues first rose to power in Peking. To the skeptical eye of the Vietnamese, the ultimate objective of Maoist foreign policy in Southeast Asia was to keep Vietnam divided and weak in order to facilitate Chinese domination of the entire region. For that reason, contended the White Paper, Chou En-lai had compelled the D.R.V. delegation to accept the partition of Vietnamese territory at the Geneva Conference in 1954. For the same reason he had joined with representatives of the imperialist powers in refusing to concede the legitimacy of the revolutionary movements in Laos and Cambodia, thus preventing their presence at the conference. According to Hanoi, similar motives were behind Chinese policy after

Geneva when, despite China's ostensible support for the liberation struggle in South Vietnam, the ultimate goal of Chinese policy was to keep Vietnam weak, divided, and under Peking's domination.

Whether or not such contentions are valid is not an issue that can be confirmed here. What is clear is that throughout the long conflict in Vietnam, Vietnamese party leaders harbored a deep distrust of China's motives, despite its "fraternal assistance" and frequent protestations of friendship. With the end of the war in 1975, such underlying tensions quickly rose to the surface. The first clear indication came in the form of clashes along Vietnam's northern border. That border had originally been formally delineated by agreements between France and the Manchu empire in the late nineteenth century and during the remainder of the colonial period had rarely been an issue in Sino-French relations. After the Communists seized power in North Vietnam in 1954, several minor disagreements over the location of the border had arisen at the local level. For the most part, the disputes concerned such issues as land use, precise demarcation of the boundary along rivers, and so on. The issue was referred to the central governments, and in 1958 the two countries agreed to postpone the settlement of border disputes until the end of the Vietnam War.

A second area of territorial disagreement was the delineation of territorial waters in the Gulf of Tonkin and the ownership of two sets of islands in the South China Sea, the Paracels and the Spratlys. Here the historical record was ambiguous. Earlier agreements between France and China on the territorial demarcation of the Tonkin Gulf had, in accordance with contemporary practice, gone no further than the three-mile limit. As for the ownership of the Paracels and the Spratlys, China and France, as well as the Philippines and Taiwan, had registered conflicting claims based on somewhat imprecise historical records, but because they lacked economic importance, the islands had been occupied only sporadically. In 1974, Chinese Communist troops, perhaps anticipating future problems with Hanoi, seized the major islands of the Paracels while driving off a small South Vietnamese occupation force. After 1975, rising tensions and the lure of offshore oil deposits in the Gulf of Tonkin and the South China Sea resurrected these issues and led both Hanoi and Peking to assert ownership over both sets of islands and present conflicting claims in the Tonkin Gulf. To underline its claims, the S.R.V. seized several small islands in the Spratly group; others were occupied by the Philippines and Taiwan.

With the Vietnam War at an end, these territorial disputes rapidly intensified. Armed clashes broke out among the populace at various points along the border. China and Vietnam traded claims and charges over the delineation of the Gulf and the ownership of the island groups in the South China Sea. When the Vietnamese crackdown in 1978 on private commerce resulted in the flight of thousands of Chinese nationals across the border into South China, Peking protested that Hanoi was persecuting ethnic Chinese living in Vietnam, thus breaking a 1955 agreement between the VWP and the CCP calling for gradual and voluntary integration of Chinese nationals into Vietnamese society. In May, Peking dispatched two ships to Vietnam to pick up thousands of overseas Chinese who were clamoring for permission to leave the S.R.V., but Hanoi claimed that the Chinese action represented interference in Vietnamese internal affairs and refused permission for the two ships to dock at Vietnamese ports. Chinese diplomatic officials were accused of stirring up trouble among the local Chinese population, and Peking's consular office in Ho Chi Minh City was shut down.

Such issues were a clear indication of growing strains in Sino-Vietnamese relations, but they were by no means the prime cause of the breakdown that led to war in 1979. Indeed, they were only a minor irritant compared to the broader strategic question raised by the Cambodian crisis and its impact on great power rivalries in the region. For Peking, Vietnamese occupation of Cambodia not only resulted in a decline of Chinese influence in the area; it also by extension raised the specter of Soviet influence over an area vital to Chinese national security.

The prospect that Cambodia might become a major focus of Sino-Vietnamese or great power rivalry had appeared reasonably remote at the close of the Vietnam War. Chinese relations with the new Pol Pot government were relatively amicable, but Peking had by no means appeared anxious to commit its prestige in the area to such a slender reed. The events of the late 1970s soon foreclosed China's options, however, and forced it to back the Pol Pot regime as its main client in Southeast Asia. By early 1978, Peking was providing increased military aid to Phnom Penh and warning that Vietnamese military action might trigger a response from China. As the crisis in Cambodia worsened and Sino-Vietnamese recriminations over Hanoi's treatment of its ethnic Chinese reached a boiling point in late spring, China reduced and then canceled its remaining aid projects in the S.R.V. Hanoi responded by accepting a Soviet invitation to join the Soviet-dominated Council of Mutual Economic Assistance, thus agreeing to tailor its economic planning to that of the U.S.S.R. and its allies. In November, following increased Chinese threats against Vietnam, Hanoi signed a treaty of friendship and cooperation with Moscow. Although the pact did not call for an automatic response in case of an attack on either party, it did call for mutual assistance and consultation.

To Chinese leaders, the Soviet-Vietnamese agreement was a final confirmation that Hanoi had become Moscow's puppet, a "small hegemonist" or an "Asian Cuba" that would serve the objectives of the Soviet Union in Southeast Asia. Vietnamese officials retorted angrily that the pact with Moscow did not infringe upon Vietnamese independence and had been signed only to demonstrate to China that the S.R.V. had powerful friends who would help it to defend itself against the arrogant and domineering Chinese. Whether or not Peking's charges that Hanoi had signed away its independence of action were justified (in light of Vietnamese past behavior, an unlikely occurrence), it had indeed been a fateful step, a final provocation that made reconciliation with China highly improbable, short of a major shift in global relationships. In that sense, it was a tragic development for both countries and for the prospects of a reduction of tensions in the area as a whole. Although we should not dismiss out of hand Hanoi's assertion that the S.R.V. had not signed away its capacity to adopt an independent foreign policy, there is little doubt that the pact severely restricted Vietnamese freedom of maneuver in foreign affairs at a time when such freedom was patently in Hanoi's interest. At the same time, Vietnamese reliance on Moscow represented the apparent fulfillment of Peking's worst fears—the introduction of Soviet power on China's sensitive southern doorstep. One consequence of the Soviet-Vietnamese agreement was increasing Soviet use of Vietnamese airfields and port facilities. Hanoi vigorously denied Peking's charges that the Vietnamese ports of Da Nang and Cam Ranh Bay (the latter a massive naval facility built by the United States during the Johnson administration) had been transformed into Soviet naval bases and retorted that Vietnam was doing no more than other Southeast Asian states were doing when they opened their port facilities to U.S. ships in the area. To Peking, such distinctions were hardly reassuring.

The seeds of hostility sown by the growing Sino-Vietnamese rivalry were not long in bearing bitter fruit. In February 1979, China launched an invasion across the border into Vietnam's northern province to "teach Hanoi a lesson." During a bloody three-week attack, Chinese forces penetrated several miles into Vietnamese territory in a variety of locations, destroying bridges, roads, and military and civilian installations. Moscow announced its willingness to come to the aid of its ally and heightened the military preparedness of its troops stationed along the Chinese border, but S.R.V. spokesmen proclaimed that it was capable of handling the invading forces without massive assistance from the Soviet Union. Events showed that Hanoi's brave words were more than bravado. Resistance from local Vietnamese military units was unexpectedly stiff, and although Peking may have achieved its minimum objectives of diverting some Vietnamese main force units from Cambodia to the Red River delta and demonstrating China's will to back up its threats, the invasion also showed the military weaknesses of the Chinese armed forces and, if government sources in Hanoi are to be believed, unified Vietnamese public opinion against the invaders. Indeed, one official source contended that party leaders had found it easier to mobilize public resistance to Vietnam's historic enemy to the north than to the United States during the previous conflict in South Vietnam.

Peking had maintained virtually from the outset that its aims were limited, and in mid-March Chinese forces withdrew across the frontier. Peace talks began soon after but broke down when it became clear that the issues that had led to the war had not been resolved. As the price of settlement, China demanded Vietnamese withdrawal from Cambodia, renunciation of its alliance with the U.S.S.R., an end to the persecution of Chinese nationals in the S.R.V., and recognition of P.R.C. territorial claims along the border and in the South China Sea. As Vietnam had not in fact been militarily defeated, such peace terms were clearly unreasonable. In fact, the war had changed little except to strengthen Vietnamese distrust of China and to persuade party leaders to devote increased attention to preparations for a possible resumption of hostilities.

For the one remaining great power with substantial interests in Southeast Asia, the deepening crisis in the region presented excruciating dilemmas. The Carter administration ardently desired a defusing of tensions in the area and normalization of relations with its old adversary in Hanoi. In 1977, it actively pursued diplomatic talks with Vietnamese representatives in an effort to surmount the legacy of bitterness and place mutual relations on a new footing. Hanoi's insistence on a U.S. commitment to fulfill Nixon's promise of construction aid, however, was politically difficult for the beleaguered administration, and when Hanoi proved intransigent, the normalization talks broke down. By 1978, the S.R.V., facing growing economic difficulties, showed signs of flexibility on the issue of reconstruction aid. By then, however, the growing crisis in Cambodia and increasing Vietnamese intimacy with the Soviet Union had raised doubts in Washington about Vietnamese intentions in Southeast Asia and negotiations were again aborted. The Vietnamese occupation of Cambodia in 1979 and the treaty with Moscow that preceded it destroyed the already fragile hopes for normalization and led the Carter administration to announce an embargo on trade with the S.R.V.

The failure of normalization efforts with Vietnam was uneasily reminiscent of the events that had followed the end of the civil war in China more than twenty years before. Then, the Truman administration had attempted briefly to refrain from involvement in the unfolding drama of the Chinese revolution, and although unwilling to grant the request of the new Communist government in Peking for diplomatic recognition, it did indicate its refusal to defend Taiwan, Chiang Kai-shek's seat of government, against attack from the mainland. But a combination of domestic political pressures and turbulence in East Asia defeated such intentions, and by the summer of 1950 Washington was embarked on a new policy of nonrecognition of and resistance to the new China. To the credit of the Carter administration, it had attempted to avoid a repetition of the tragic events of the early 1950s. Even the militant anti-Vietnamese stance after the invasion of Cambodia in 1979 was adopted with some reluctance, as if in recognition that such a step was repeating history. But Washington's freedom of action was hampered by the moral constraints of U.S. foreign policy and the realities of international politics. However distasteful the Pol Pot regime appeared to be, however provocative its actions on Vietnam's sensitive western border, in Washington the Vietnamese invasion and occupation of Cambodia represented too blatant a transgression of accepted international behavior to be condoned. The image of Vietnamese bellicosity and intransigence was accentuated by the domestic crisis that in preceding months had driven thousands of Vietnamese residents to seek refuge abroad. On a more practical plane, the U.S. desire to avoid a policy of total hostility with Vietnam clashed with the realities of U.S. policy in East Asia, which was based on support for the ASEAN states and rapprochement with China. Normalization of relations with Vietnam could only undermine the delicate efforts of the ASEAN states to maintain a solid front against what they viewed as Vietnamese expansionism and antagonize Chinese leaders at a time when Sino-American cooperation had become a keystone of U.S. foreign policy in Asia.

The tragic irony of the situation was that, by adopting a stance of unremitting hostility to Hanoi and by attempting to compel it to withdraw from Cambodia, Washington, Peking, and the ASEAN states were in effect driving Hanoi further into the arms of the Soviet Union, a condition that all parties (including, perhaps, the Vietnamese themselves) fervently wished to avoid. In adopting a hard-line policy toward the S.R.V., the Reagan administration appeared to believe that only constant pressure would compel Hanoi to withdraw from Cambodia and abandon its aggressive behavior in the region. For its part, Peking had evidently concluded that Hanoi could not be brought to reason until the current leadership under Le Duan had been replaced by a new faction more amenable to rapprochement with China.

Whether or not such policies will be effective in modifying Vietnamese behavior to conform to the interests of China, the United States, or the ASEAN countries is open to question. The current policy has succeeded in isolating Hanoi in world opinion and has exacerbated the already straitened economic conditions in the country. It would be risky to assume, however, that such pressures will force a change in Vietnamese policies. Although there have been scattered signs of disaffection within the party and government over current policy, there is no evidence of organized opposition to the current leadership. The Vietnamese party has a long history of unity, despite inner disagreements, against an external threat, and even Hoang Van Hoan, one of the current regime's harshest critics, who now lives in Peking, has conceded that at present Le Duan and his supporters have managed to suppress the emergence of serious opposition within the party and the government. In any event, it is likely that the current strategy of maintaining a stubborn posture in Cambodia has wide support within the leadership in view of the importance of the area to national security. Vietnamese leaders may well look to recent history as a guide. Patience, tenacity, and perseverance are the great strengths of the Vietnamese revolution. It is not improbable that the Vietnamese are confident that, whatever happens, they will be able to outwait their adversaries.

Hanoi's position, however, is not a comfortable one. It not only makes a rapprochement with Washington and Peking more difficult, but it also locks the S.R.V. into a reliance on the Soviet Union that Vietnamese leaders may well wish to avoid. Even now, there are indications of tension within the relationship, resulting not only from the inadequacy of Soviet economic aid to the S.R.V. but also over disparate objectives in Southeast Asia. Recent reports suggest that an element of rivalry has emerged between Moscow and Hanoi over Cambodia, and it is by no means out of the question that the present government in Phnom Penh, as a means of obtaining greater freedom from Vietnamese domination, could call upon assistance from the Soviet Union. The pattern of Soviet foreign policy suggests that Soviet leaders are not unwilling to take full advantage of such opportunities.

What, then, of the future? On the surface, conditions in Southeast Asia appear to be approaching a point of at least temporary stalemate. Vietnamese leaders, in their determination to secure their western flanks, may not be amenable to compromise on the issue of Cambodia. To appeals for a withdrawal of Vietnamese occupation forces, they reply that a pullback can take place only when the external threat to the Heng Samrin government disappears. To suggestions for national elections with participation by all factions involved in the civil struggle, they respond that socialism in Cambodia is an irrefutable fact not to be undone. Yet, other states with interests in the area will find it difficult to accept long-term Vietnamese domination over all of Indochina. A resurgent China will inevitably resent the presence of a hostile and belligerent Vietnam dominant over the bulk of the Southeast Asian peninsula. The ASEAN states, particularly Thailand, are fearful that an aggressive Vietnam, having secured its position in Indochina, will embark on new adventures, invoking the cause of world revolution.

How likely is it that Vietnam will attempt to spread revolution elsewhere in the region? On the record, the prospects are not clear. Hanoi has formally denied any intention of interfering in the internal affairs of its neighbors and recently offered to sign a treaty to that effect with Thailand. Given the magnitude of the problems currently facing the Vietnamese, an open invasion of Thailand, or even a serious effort to incite revolution against the military government in Bangkok, appears unlikely. Serious difficulties would ensue not only with China and the United States but quite possibly with the neutralist bloc and even with the Soviet Union, which can hardly be anxious to add to its obligation to Vietnam at a time when Soviet capacities have been severely strained by heavy commitments in Afghanistan and Poland. Moreover, Vietnamese support for an intensification of insurgent activity in Thailand would be hindered by the fact that the current leadership of the Communist party of Thailand is openly pro-Chinese and could be expected to be suspicious of any effort to increase Vietnamese influence in the area.

On the other hand, Hanoi has on numerous occasions stated its support for the cause of world revolution and openly declared that the victory of communism in Vietnam had opened the door to a new and final stage in the triumph of communism throughout the globe. Western intelligence reports indicate that this commitment has on some recent occasions been expressed in the form of low-level assistance to aspiring revolutionary movements in Africa and Central America. Whether Hanoi will be tempted to promote armed insurgency elsewhere in Southeast Asia, and specifically in Thailand, is apt to depend on several factors—the internal situation in Thailand, domestic conditions within Vietnam, the resolution of Hanoi's current obligations in Cambodia, and the state of its relations with China.

Can the United States influence the course of Vietnamese foreign policy, as some allege, and perhaps wean it from its dependence upon the Soviet Union? U.S. capacity to moderate Vietnamese behavior, at least for the moment, is probably quite limited. Although there seems little doubt that Hanoi would like to achieve a better working relationship with Washington in order to improve its economic position and to gain more room to maneuver in foreign affairs, there is little prospect that Vietnamese leaders would be willing to abandon their commitment to revolutionary principles or to accept a significant reduction in their close relationship with the Soviet Union as the price for doing so. Nor is it particularly likely that U.S. policies could induce them to become more amenable to compromise on the issue of Cambodia. To Vietnamese leaders, Cambodia is a matter of vital national concern, of crucial strategic importance in the defence of Vietnam against hostile forces in China and the West, and Hanoi is probably sincere in its insistence that the current situation in Cambodia is essentially nonnegotiable, whatever the cost.

U.S. policy toward Vietnam, then, may have to be focused, at least for the time being, on more long-term objectives: to help promote a settlement of the immensely complex Sino-Vietnamese dispute (without which an overall reduction in tensions in the area is unlikely to be realized), to help create conditions that will ultimately lead to a workable settlement of the Cambodian problem acceptable to all parties, and to reduce Hanoi's virtually total dependence on Moscow. In themselves, these objectives will be difficult to achieve, for the geopolitical and emotional factors that have created the current crisis are deep-seated, and the maneuverability of the U.S., deeply committed to its present policy of friendship with China, is severely restricted.

For the moment, then, it is probably unrealistic to hope that the current crisis in Southeast Asia can be resolved in the near future. The crux of the problem lies in the clash between the dynamic forces of revolutions in two countries, China and Vietnam, and their competing desire to achieve influence in Southeast Asia. That competition in turn is related to the larger global framework of the Sino-Soviet dispute and the

Cold War balance of power. Perhaps the best that can be hoped for in the immediate future is that a gradual reduction in tension in the region will take place as the forces unleashed by the end of the Vietnam War and the sharpening of the Sino-Vietnamese dispute subside. In the long run, a reduction in such tensions can only rebound to the benefit of Vietnam, of the United States, and of Vietnam's neighbors as well.

Annotated Bibliography

This brief bibliography is appended for the benefit of those readers who would like to undertake further exploration into various aspects of Vietnamese society. It is limited for the most part to titles in English, but I have included a few works in French dealing with Vietnamese literature, a subject that has received little treatment in English. This list is not comprehensive and fails to mention a number of noted books of considerable value to specialists. But it does include a useful selection of widely available works dealing in some detail with subjects that have been referred to elsewhere in this short volume.

VIETNAMESE HISTORY

The Precolonial Period

Buttinger, Joseph. *The Smaller Dragon*. New York: Praeger, 1958.
    A popular history of premodern Vietnam.
Coedes, George. *The Making of Southeast Asia*. Berkeley: University of California Press, 1966.
    A scholarly but readable survey of early Southeast Asian history by a renowned French cultural historian.
Hodgkin, Thomas. *Vietnam: The Revolutionary Path*. New York: St. Martin's Press, 1981.
    A detailed factual history of Vietnam from its origins to the August Revolution in 1945. Although the title suggests a concentration on the twentieth century, much of the book deals with the precolonial period.
Nguyen, Khac Vien (Ed.). *Traditional Vietnam: Some Historical Stages*. Vietnamese Studies No. 21. Hanoi: Foreign Languages Press, no date.
    A brief survey of traditional society by the Institute of Historical Studies in Hanoi.
Woodside, Alexander. *Vietnam and the Chinese Model*. Cambridge, Mass.: Harvard University Press, 1971.
    A detailed investigation of nineteenth-century Vietnamese society by a respected scholar. Particularly useful for its analysis of Confucian institutions in Vietnam.

156

Colonial Vietnam

Duiker, William J. *The Rise of Nationalism in Vietnam, 1900–1941*. Ithaca, N.Y.: Cornell University Press, 1976.
> An analysis of the evolution of the nationalist movement in Vietnam up to the beginning of Japanese occupation in the Pacific war.

Gurtov, Melvin. *The First Vietnam Crisis: Chinese Communist Strategy and United States Involvement*. New York: Columbia University Press, 1967.
> A thoughtful analysis of the road to Geneva and the U.S. attitude to the Franco-Vietminh War.

Hammer, Ellen J. *The Struggle for Indochina, 1940–1955*. Stanford, Calif.: Stanford University Press, 1955.
> A dated but still useful general study of the Franco-Vietminh War and its aftermath.

McAlister, John T. *Vietnam: The Origins of Revolution*. New York: Doubleday, 1971.
> An inquiry into the causes of Communist success in the early stages of the conflict with France. Concentrates on the rise of the Vietminh and the August Revolution of 1945.

McAlister, John T., and Mus, Paul. *The Vietnamese and Their Revolution*. New York: Harper & Row, 1970.
> An English-language synopsis of Paul Mus's renowned sociological treatise on the Franco-Vietminh conflict, *Sociologie d'une guerre*. Somewhat impressionistic but full of insights.

Marr, David G. *Vietnamese Anti-Colonialism, 1885–1925*. Berkeley: University of California Press, 1971.
> A ground-breaking study of the early stages of Vietnamese resistance to French rule. Particularly strong on social history.

————. *Vietnamese Tradition on Trial, 1920–1945*. Berkeley: University of California Press, 1981.
> An intensive study of the social and intellectual changes in colonial Vietnam. Written for the scholar but useful for the general reader.

The Vietnam War, 1954–1975

Duiker, William J. *The Communist Road to Power in Vietnam*. Boulder, Colo.: Westview Press, 1981.
> An analysis of the evolution of Communist strategy in Vietnam from the birth of the party in 1930 to the fall of Saigon.

Fitzgerald, Frances. *Fire in the Lake*. New York: Vintage, 1972.
> A prize-winning study of the U.S. failure in Vietnam. Essentially two separate books, an analysis of the reasons for Communist success in the South and a narrative of the political musical chairs in Saigon, it provided for many Americans the reasons why U.S. policy in Vietnam did not succeed.

Goodman, Allan G. *The Lost Peace*. Stanford, Calif.: Hoover Institution Press, 1978.
> Similar in thematic treatment to Gareth Porter's *A Peace Denied*, but somewhat less critical of U.S. policy.

Halberstam, David. *The Best and the Brightest*. New York: Random House, 1972.
> A brilliant analysis of the personalities involved in bringing the United States into the Vietnamese conflict.

————. *Making of a Quagmire*. New York: Random House, 1965.
> A famous journalistic account of the last years of the Diem regime. Influential

in raising questions among thoughtful Americans about the U.S. role in the war.

Harrison, James P. *The Endless War: Fifty Years of Struggle in Vietnam.* New York: Macmillan, 1981.

   A comprehensive and well-balanced account of the U.S. role in the Vietnam conflict from the formation of the Communist party to the fall of Saigon.

Kahin, George M., and Lewis, John W. *The United States in Vietnam.* New York: Delta, 1969.

   An introductory account of the U.S. involvement in the war by two respected American scholars. Somewhat impressionistic in its treatment of the origins of the war, but useful for its overview of the U.S. role. Strongly critical of U.S. policy.

Kattenburg, Paul M. *The Vietnam Trauma in American Foreign Policy, 1945–1975.* New Brunswick, N.J.: Transaction Books, 1980.

   A thoughtful interpretation of the U.S. role in Vietnam by a former State Department official. Perhaps the best available introduction to the war from the American side.

Lewy, Guenter. *America in Vietnam.* Oxford: Oxford University Press, 1978.

   An analysis of U.S. policies in Vietnam. Considered by critics to be an apologia for the U.S. role in the war, it presents U.S. policy as miscalculated but based on honorable motives.

Pike, Douglas. *Viet Cong.* Cambridge, Mass.: M.I.T. Press, 1966.

   A definitive study of the organization and techniques of the insurgent movement in South Vietnam. Difficult reading but well worth the effort.

Porter, Gareth. *A Peace Denied.* Bloomington: University of Indiana Press, 1975.

   A trenchant study of the long struggle for a negotiated settlement in Vietnam, written by one of the most respected critics of U.S. policy.

Race, Jeffrey. *War Comes to Long An.* Berkeley: University of California Press, 1972.

   A classic study of the rise of the revolutionary movement in one province of South Vietnam. Very useful for understanding the origins of the war.

Shaplen, Robert. *The Lost Revolution: The U.S. in Vietnam, 1946–1966.* New York: Harper & Row, 1966.

   A fast-paced and readable account of the early stages of the war by an experienced journalist.

Snepp, Frank. *A Decent Interval.* New York: Random House, 1977.

   A detailed treatment of the fall of Saigon in 1975 by a young CIA analyst who was on the spot. Harshly critical of the failure of U.S. policymakers to anticipate the final debacle.

Van Tien Dung. *Our Great Spring Victory.* New York: Monthly Review Press, 1977.

   An account of the final campaign in the South by the military commander who planned and led it.

Vo Nguyen Giap. *People's War, People's Army.* New York: Praeger, 1962.

   A classical study of people's war in Vietnam by the party's foremost strategist.

Woodside, Alexander B. *Community and Revolution in Vietnam.* Boston: Houghton Mifflin, 1976.

   A wide-ranging study of the Vietnamese people's search for community, from the colonial period to the final years of the war.

POLITICS AND GOVERNMENT

Goodman, Allan G. *Politics in War: The Bases of Political Community in South Vietnam.* Cambridge, Mass.: Harvard University Press, 1973.
    An analysis of the effort to build a democratic political system in South Vietnam by a respected American scholar.
Le Duan. *This Nation and Socialism Are One.* Chicago: Vanguard Press, 1976.
    A useful collection of General Secretary Le Duan's writings on the construction of socialism in Vietnam.
Nghiem Dang. *Vietnam: Politics and Public Administration.* Honolulu: East-West Center Press, 1966.
    A study of the growth of political institutions under the Saigon regime.
Nguyen Long. *After Saigon Fell: Daily Life Under the Vietnamese Communists.* Berkeley: University of California Press, 1981.
    A personal account of life in contemporary Vietnam by a disillusioned intellectual. The author, a U.S.-trained university professor, remained in South Vietnam after 1975 but left secretly four years later.
Pike, Douglas. *History of Vietnamese Communism: 1925–1976.* Stanford, Calif.: Hoover Institution Press, 1978.
    A short but useful introduction to the growth of the Communist party from its origins to the end of the war. Particularly strong on organization and party building.
Turley, William S. (Ed.). *Vietnamese Communism in Comparative Perspective.* Boulder, Colo.: Westview Press, 1980.
    A series of articles by U.S. and French scholars on Vietnamese communism. Particularly useful on the political system.

ECONOMICS

Chaliand, Gérard. *The Peasants of North Vietnam.* Harmondsworth: Penguin, 1969.
    A survey of agricultural conditions and policies in North Vietnam by a French scholar who visited North Vietnam during the height of the conflict.
Duiker, William J. *Vietnam Since the Fall of Saigon.* Athens: Ohio University Center for International Studies, 1981.
    A brief survey of political and economic trends in Vietnam since the fall of Saigon.
Murray, Martin J. *The Development of Capitalism in Colonial Indochina, 1870–1940.* Berkeley: University of California Press, 1980.
    An exhaustive study of the colonial economy in French Indochina. Deals with all phases of economic development.
Nguyen Khac Vien (Ed.). *Tradition and Revolution in Vietnam.* Berkeley, Calif.: Indochina Resource Center, 1974.
    A series of articles on various aspects of Vietnamese society. Contains an interesting description of collectivization in North Vietnam.
Nguyen Tien Hung. *Economic Development of Socialist Vietnam, 1955–1980.* New York: Praeger, 1977.
    A scholarly analysis of the construction of socialism in North Vietnam from 1954 to the end of the war in 1975. Includes a brief treatment of postwar economic policy.

Popkin, Samuel. *The Rational Peasant*. Berkeley: University of California Press, 1979.
> A provocative study of the effects of modernization on Vietnamese peasants during the colonial period.

CULTURE AND SOCIETY

Bui Xuan Bao. *Le roman vietnamien contemporain* [The contemporary Vietnamese novel]. Saigon: Nhan-van, no date.

DeFrancis, John. *Colonialism and Language Policy in Viet Nam*. The Hague: Mouton, 1977.
> A thorough analysis of language reform policy during the colonial era in Indochina. Concentrates on the development of *quoc ngu* as the national written language.

Durand, Maurice M., and Nguyen Tran Huan. *Introduction à la littérature viet-namienne*. [Introduction to Vietnamese literature]. Paris: Maisonneuve et Larose,1969.

General Education in the DRV. Vietnamese Studies No. 30. Hanoi: Foreign Languages Press, 1971.
> A survey of educational progress in the D.R.V., issued by the Hanoi regime.

Hickey, Gerald C. *Village in Vietnam*. New Haven, Conn.: Yale University Press, 1960.
> A ground-breaking study of life in rural Vietnam during the early years of the war. Offers a detailed picture of village life.

Huynh Sanh Thong. *The Heritage of Vietnamese Poetry*. New Haven, Conn.: Yale University Press, 1979.
> A collection of Vietnamese poetry from the traditional period down to the twentieth century.

Kunstadter, Peter (Ed.). *Southeast Asian Tribes, Minorities, and Nations*. 2 vols. Princeton, N.J.: Princeton University Press, 1967.
> Includes a chapter on the ethnic minorities in Vietnam.

Nguyen Khac Vien (Ed.). *Mountain Regions and National Minorities in the Democratic Republic of Vietnam*. Vietnamese Studies No. 15. Hanoi: Foreign Languages Press, 1968.

Provencher, Ronald. *Mainland Southeast Asia: An Anthropological Perspective*. Pacific Palisades, Calif.: Goodyear, 1975.
> A survey of the various peoples of mainland Southeast Asia. Includes one chapter on Vietnam.

Sully, Francois (Ed.). *We the Vietnamese: Voices from Vietnam*. New York: Praeger, 1971.
> A set of articles on various aspects of Vietnamese society for the general reader. Contains useful questions on resources, urban and rural life, religions, customs, and education. One of a series.

FOREIGN RELATIONS

Chen, King C. *China and Vietnam, 1938–1954*. Princeton, N.J.: Princeton University Press, 1969.

An exhaustive survey of the role played by the two Chinas—Nationalist and Communist—in the early stages of the Vietnam War.

Elliott, David W. P. *The Third Indochina Conflict.* Boulder, Colo.: Westview Press, 1981.
A trenchant analysis of the recent conflict involving Vietnam, China, and Cambodia. Contains articles by several respected specialists.

Race, Jeffrey, and Turley, William S. "The Third Indochina War." *Foreign Policy,* no. 38 (Spring 1980), pp. 92–115.
A thoughtful and provocative article on the contemporary crisis in Southeast Asia.

Smyser, W. R. *The Independent Vietnamese.* Athens: Ohio University Center for International Studies, 1980.
A sober and informative evaluation of Vietnamese policy toward its allies during the war.

U.S.-Vietnam Relations, 1945–1967. Washington, D.C.: Government Printing Office, 1971.
The "Pentagon Papers." Documents dealing with the U.S. role in the Vietnam War.

Zagoria, Donald. *Vietnam Triangle.* New York: Pegasus, 1967.
An analysis of the complicated relationship between Vietnam and its two socialist allies, China and the U.S.S.R. Dated, but still useful for an understanding of the period.

Abbreviations

ARVN	Army of the Republic of Vietnam
ASEAN	Association of the Southeast Asian Nations
CCP	Chinese Communist party
CEMA	Council for Mutual Economic Assistance
DMZ	demilitarized zone
DPRK	Democratic People's Republic of Kampuchea
D.R.V.	Democratic Republic of Vietnam
FULRO	Front Unifié pour la Lutte des Races Opprimées
G.V.N.	Government of Vietnam
ICC	International Control Commission
ICP	Indochinese Communist party
KNUFNS	Kampuchean National United Front for National Salvation
NEA	New Economic Area
NLF	National Front for the Liberation of South Vietnam
PAVN	People's Army of Vietnam
P.R.C.	People's Republic of China
P.R.G.	Provisional Revolutionary Government
PRP	People's Revolutionary party

SEATO	Southeast Asia Treaty Organization
S.R.V.	Socialist Republic of Vietnam
VCP	Vietnamese Communist party
VNQDD	Vietnamese Nationalist party
VWP	Vietnamese Workers' party

Index

Afghanistan, 153
Agriculture, 2–3, 5–7, 13–14, 16–17, 19, 32, 97–115 passim, 130
Agro-industrial centers, 109
Agrovilles, 55–56
Albuquerque, Alfonso de, 20
Alcohol monopoly, 32
Alexander of Rhodes, 21, 125
Angkor, 20, 40
Annam. *See* Central Vietnam
Annamite Mountains. *See* Central Mountains
Architecture, 16, 122
Aristocracy, 14–15, 17, 20, 73, 119–120
Armed Forces Council, 78
Army of the Republic of Vietnam (ARVN), 56, 59, 62, 64–65, 67, 69–70
ARVN. *See* Army of the Republic of Vietnam
Art, 16, 122, 126, 129
ASEAN. *See* Association for the Southeast Asian Nations
Associated State of Vietnam, 43–46, 77
Association for the Southeast Asian Nations (ASEAN), 144–145, 152
Au Ca, 15
August Revolution, 39–40, 83, 86, 130
Au Lac, 14–15, 117
Austroloid-Negroid, 4, 14

Ban Me Thuot, Battle of, 68
Bao Dai, 39, 43, 50
Bao Dai government. *See* Associated State of Vietnam
"Bao Dai solution," 43–44, 77
Bay of Pigs, 55
Beau, Paul, 30, 124
Ben Hai River, 46

Bien Hoa, 20, 37
Binh Dinh Province, 20, 22
Bolshevik Revolution, 76
Border disputes, 142–143, 148
Bourgeoisie, 34–37, 75–76, 101, 126–127, 129
Brezhnev, Leonid, 94, 147
Bronze Age, 13–15, 117, 136
Buddhism, 3, 6, 9–10, 118–120, 136
Buddhist advisers, 19, 73
Buddhist associations, 55, 57, 88, 131
Bureaucracy, 3, 15–16, 18–19, 28, 34, 73–74, 91–94, 97, 116, 118, 125, 131
Burma, 24, 26

Ca Dao, 122
Ca Mau Peninsula, 1
Cambodia, 2, 6, 20, 25, 28, 31, 47, 49, 65–66, 68, 89–90, 95, 98–110, 114, 139–147, 149–154
Canada, 46
Can Lao (Personalist Labor party), 51
Can Tho, 31
Cao Dai, 10–11, 35, 38–40, 50, 88, 131
Cash crops, 2, 31, 99
Catholics, 8–10, 21, 24, 50–51, 57, 88, 124, 130
CCP. *See* Chinese Communist party
CEMA. *See* Council for Mutual Economic Assistance
Central Highlands (Tay Nguyen), 1–2, 6–9, 45, 51, 53, 59, 68, 91, 107
Central Mountains (Truong Son), 2
Central Vietnam (Annam), 1, 4, 6–7, 19, 28, 30, 32–34, 39–40, 43, 74–75, 107, 124–125
Ceramics, 17, 98, 122
Cham, 6–7, 19
Champa, 6, 18–20, 98, 122, 140

Chao T'o. *See* Trieu Da
Chiang Kai-shek, 38, 43, 151
Ch'ien Lung, 22
China, 4, 13–14, 25, 58, 140
  assimilation of Vietnam, 14–15, 18, 117
  conquest of Vietnam, 15–18, 97, 137
  influence on Vietnam, 15–16, 18, 27,
    72–74, 84, 89, 104, 116–124
  relations with Vietnam, 22, 26, 40,
    136–137
"China incident," 38
Ch'in dynasty, 14–15
Chinese Communist party (CCP), 43–44,
  81, 89, 140, 148–149
Chinese people, 4, 6, 16
Cholon, 5, 99
Christianity, 3, 8–10, 21
  persecution of Christians, 21, 23–24
Chu nom (Southern script), 117, 123, 125
Chu Van Tan, 8, 89
Civil service examinations, 73, 118–120,
  125
Climate, 2, 4
Coal mining, 4, 31–32, 34, 39, 109
Cochin China, 25–26, 28, 30, 32, 35,
  37–41, 74, 124–125
Coffee, 2, 31
Collectives, 102–115 passim, 130
Collectivization, 11, 39
Co Loa, 14, 16
Colonial Council, 30
Colons, 30, 124
Combat villages, 90
Comintern (Communist International), 37,
  88
Commerce, 4–5, 7, 9, 17, 19, 21–25,
  28–34, 97–115 passim
Commercial Import Program, 101
Committee of the South, 40
Commune lands, 19, 22, 37
Communications, 31, 98–99, 109–110
Confucianism, 3, 9–10, 16, 50, 79–80, 96,
  117–120, 123, 134, 136
  decline of, 27, 34–35, 74–75, 124, 126
  in politics, 19, 72–74, 118
  strengths and weaknesses of, 73–74,
    118–119, 123
  in traditional Vietnam, 16, 19, 21, 23,
    27, 117–124
Congregations (*bang*), 5
Council for Mutual Economic Assistance
  (CEMA), 110, 149
Cuba, 55, 114
Cultivated land, 1–2

Dai Viet (Greater Viet), 16, 18–19

Dai Viet Su Ky (History of Greater Viet),
  122
Dai Viet Su Ky Toan Thu (Complete History of Greater Viet), 122
Dalat, 42
Da Nang, 1, 21, 23–24, 31, 68
D'Argenlieu, Thiérry, 42
de Lattre de Tassigny, 45
Demilitarized zone (DMZ), 46, 62
Democracy, 29–30, 32, 35, 61, 71–72, 74,
  82, 95
Democratic Kampuchea, 142
Democratic party, 82
Democratic People's Republic of Kampuchea (DPRK), 143, 146
Democratic Republic of Vietnam (D.R.V.)
  armed forces, 39, 43–44, 53, 88–90
  attitude to Geneva Accords, 48, 53–54
  constitution, 83
  cultural policies, 127–135
  economic policies, 40, 101–115 passim
  educational policies, 129, 132, 134–135
  founding of, 39
  invasion of Cambodia, 143
  land reform, 40, 55, 101–115 passim
  minority policy, 8–10, 55, 104, 131
  national elections of 1946, 40
  policy in South Vietnam, 40, 52–56,
    58, 61–62, 90–91, 106–109
  political institutions, 40, 81–88
  political parties in, 82, 84
  in Sino-Soviet dispute, 93, 147,
    154–155
  suspicion of China, 146–147
Devaraja concept, 72
Dien Bien Phu, Battle of, 46, 53, 62, 146
Do, Mount, 13
Domestication of animals, 13
Dong Duong Tap Chi (Indochinese Re-
  view), 126
Dong Kinh Nghia Thuc (Hanoi Free
  School), 125
Dong Son culture, 13, 15
DPRK. *See* Democratic People's Republic
  of Kampuchea
Drama, 9, 123
D.R.V. *See* Democratic Republic of Viet-
  nam
Dulles, John Foster, 47, 49
Duong Van (Big) Minh, 57–58, 69, 88
Dupré, Jean-Marie, 25
Dupuis, Jean, 25
Dutch East India Company, 20

Easter Offensive, 66–67, 147
Education, 16, 30–31, 35, 120–121,

124–125, 127, 130, 132, 134–135
Eisenhower, Dwight David, 51
Elysee Agreement, 43
England, 20, 24, 26
Ethics, 73, 118–119, 130
Ethnic groups, 4–12

Faifo. *See* Hoi An
Famine, 18, 146
FCP. *See* French Communist party
Feudalism, 17, 19, 136–137
Fishing, 2, 4, 6
Fontainebleau Conference, 42
Food, 1, 31, 104, 106, 113–114
Ford, Gerald, 68
Foreign trade, 4–5, 17, 19, 23, 32–33,
    98–101, 110
Four Points, 64
France
    colonial system in Indochina, 5, 28–33,
        74–77, 98–100, 124–127
    conquest of Vietnam, 24–26, 73, 98
    Franco-Vietminh War, 43–46
    initial interest in Vietnam, 20–23,
        28–29
    minority policy, 5–7
    negotiations with Vietminh, 41–42,
        45–48
    repression of nationalism, 35–37
    return to Vietnam in 1945, 40–41
Franco-Vietminh War, 42–46, 84, 86, 102,
    128, 130
Free French, 39
French Communist party (FCP), 37
French Union, 41
Fukien, 5
FULRO. *See* United Front for the Struggle
    of Oppressed Races

Garnier, Francis, 25
Geneva Accords, 47–48, 68
Geneva Agreements. *See* Geneva Accords
Geneva Conference, 5, 9, 45–49, 51–53,
    55, 81, 100, 102, 127, 142, 147–148
Genouilly, Charles Rigault de, 24
Germany, 38
Gia Long (Nguyen Anh), 22–23
Government of Vietnam (G.V.N.), 48–50,
    95
    armed forces, 56–57, 64–65, 88
    constitution, 57, 61, 78
    establishment of, 49
    fall of, 68–70
    land reform, 52, 61, 101, 108
    minority policy, 7, 9, 11, 52–53
    pacification, 55, 59, 64

political institutions, 51, 61, 78–81
    weakness of, 60–61, 80–81
Gracey, Douglas, 40
Grandière, Benoit de la, 25
"Greater East Asia Co-prosperity Sphere,"
    38
Guerrilla mentality, 92
Guerrilla war, 19, 34, 39–43, 54, 56, 61
Gulf of Thailand, 11, 22
G.V.N. *See* Government of Vietnam

Hai Ba Trung. *See* Trung sisters
Haiphong, 4, 31, 99
Handicrafts, 4, 17, 97–98
Han dynasty, 15, 117
Hanoi, 4, 14, 22–23, 25–26, 31
    University of, 125
Ha Tien, 22
Ha Tinh Province, 37
Heavy industry, 31, 109
Heng Samrin, 143, 146
Hill peoples (montagnards), 3–4, 6–8, 17,
    91
Hinduism, 3
Historical writing, 122–124, 130
Hoa Binh Province, 7, 13
Hoa Hao, 10–11, 35, 40, 50, 88, 131
Hoang Dao, 127
Hoang Van Hoan, 93, 157
Ho Chi Minh (Nguyen Ai Quoc), 36–45,
    50, 77, 82–83, 85–86, 94, 96, 128,
    130
Ho Chi Minh City. *See* Saigon
Ho Chi Minh class, 131
Ho Chi Minh trail, 62
Hoi An (Faifo), 21
Hong Bang dynasty, 14, 122
Hong Duc Code, 19, 73, 119
Honolulu Conference, 61
Ho Quy Ly, 18
Ho-Sainteny Agreement, 41–42
Hue, 17, 20, 23–25, 37, 57, 63, 68, 122
Humphrey, Hubert, 64
Hundred Flowers Campaign, 83, 130
Hunting, 2, 13
Huynh Phu So, 11
Hydraulic society, 19, 97, 118–119

ICC. *See* International Central Commis-
    sion
ICP. *See* Indochinese Communist party
India, 19, 23, 46, 97, 116–118
Indians, 33, 99
Indochinese Communist party (ICP),
    38–39, 42, 76, 128, 140–141
    founding of, 37

membership, 76–77
Second National Congress, 81, 86
Indochinese Federation, 142–143
Indochinese Union, 25, 28, 30
Indonesia, 144–145
Indonesian peoples, 4
Intellectuals, 27, 30, 34–36, 53, 83, 96, 126, 129
  and Marxism, 76–77, 83, 96, 130–131
International Control Commission (ICC), 46–47
Irrigation, 31–32, 109
Islam, 3, 19

Japan, 10
  conquest of Vietnam, 38
  interest in Vietnam, 37–38
  surrender in 1945, 39–40
Jarai, 6–7
Java Man, 13
Jesuits, 21
Johnson, Lyndon Baines, 58–59
  decision to negotiate, 64
  escalation of war, 58–59
Journalism, 34, 126

Kampuchea. See Cambodia
Kampuchean National United Front for National Salvation (KNUFNS), 143
Kennedy, John Fitzgerald, 55–56, 58
Khai Hung, 127
Kham Dinh Viet Su Thong Giam Cuong Muc (Imperial Historical Mirror of Greater Viet), 124
Khe Sanh, Battle of, 62
Khmer, 6
Khmer Rouge, 47, 142, 145
Khrushchev, Nikita Sergeevich, 53, 109, 147
Kim Van Kieu (Tale of Kieu), 123
Kipling, Rudyard, 29
Kissinger, Henry, 67
Korea, 56, 58
Kunming, 31
Kwangtung, 51

Labor exchange teams, 104, 115
Lac Long Quan, 15
Lac Viet, 14
Land area, 1–2, 20, 31
Land ownership
  in DRV, 102–105
  under French, 32, 99–100
  in GVN, 52–53, 61, 109–110
  in traditional Vietnam, 146–147

Land reform. See Democratic Republic of Vietnam, Government of Vietnam
Lang Son Province, 13
Languages, 3–4, 125–126
Laos, 2, 25–26, 28, 45, 47, 49, 53, 58, 62, 95, 139–143, 146–147
League for the Independence of Vietnam. See Vietminh
Le Duan, 85, 93, 152
Le Duc Tho, 67
Le dynasty, 19–20, 22–23, 25, 27, 74, 122–123
Legal system, 19, 73, 126
Le Loi, 18–19
Le Quang Ba, 8, 89
Le Quy Don, 124
Le Thanh Tong, 19, 73, 119, 140
Light industry, 31, 99
Literacy, 125, 130, 134
Literature, 122–123, 126–127, 129
Lon Nol, 65–66, 145
Lowland peoples, 3–4, 6–8
Ly dynasty, 16–20, 120, 123
Ly Thai To, 16
Ly Thanh Ton, 16

Macao, 21
Mahayana, 6
Malacca, 20
Malayo-Polynesian, 6, 19
Manchu dynasty, 4, 33
Mandate of Heaven, 72
Manufacturing, 4–5, 17, 31, 33–34, 97–115 passim
Mao Tse-tung, 89, 117, 130–131, 137, 147
March to the South, 6, 19–20, 140
Marx, Karl, 36–39, 76, 115
Marxism, 76–77, 81, 102–103, 135, 139
  appeal in Vietnam, 76, 95–96
Mass line, 88
Ma Yüan, 15
Medicine, 126
Mekong delta, 1–2, 4, 6, 11, 19–20, 31–32, 52, 59, 91, 99–100, 113, 142
Mekong River, 1–3
Mendès-France, Pierre, 46
Meo, 6–7
Mesolithic era, 8
Military Revolutionary Council, 57–58
Ming dynasty, 4, 18–19, 98
Minh Mang, 23
Minority groups, 2, 4–12, 53, 55, 91, 97, 104
Mission civilisatrice, 29–30, 34, 74, 79
Mongoloid peoples, 4, 14

Mongols, 18
Mon-Khmer, 4
Montagnards. *See* Hill peoples
Mountains, 1–4
Muong, 7
Music, 16, 122–123, 126–127, 129, 131
My Tho, 31

Nam Dinh, 31
Nam Phong (Wind from the South), 126
Nam Viet, 15–16
National Assembly, 81, 83, 90
National Council of Reconciliation and
    Concord (NCRC), 67
National Fatherland Front, 90
National Front for the Liberation of
    South Vietnam (NLF, or National
    Liberation Front), 55, 67, 90, 94
Nationalism, 16, 18, 26, 33–34, 36, 51,
    117, 135–137, 139–140
Nationalists, 40
Nationalization of industry, 39–40, 102,
    105, 111–113
National Salvation Associations, 88
NCRC. *See* National Council of Reconcili-
    ation and Concord
Neolithic civilization, 4, 13–14
Netherlands, the, 20
New Economic Areas (NEAs), 5,
    106–109, 111
Nghe An Province, 36–37
Nghe An Soviets, 37
Nghe Tinh Revolt, 37
Ngo Dinh Diem, 50, 77, 88, 95, 100, 127
    attitude toward Geneva Conference, 48,
        54
    forms government in South, 50–51
    lack of popular support, 52–53, 56–57
    land reform policy, 52
    minority policy, 5, 7, 9, 11
    overthrown, 57
    persecution of communists, 52, 54–55
Ngo Dinh Nhu, 51–52, 57
Ngo Quyen, 16
Ngo Si Lien, 122
Ngo Tat To, 127
Nguyen Ai Quoc. *See* Ho Chi Minh
Nguyen Anh. *See* Gia Long
Nguyen Cao Ky, 60–61, 71, 79, 88
Nguyen Chi Thanh, 85, 89
Nguyen Du, 123
Nguyen Duy Trinh, 83, 93–94
Nguyen dynasty, 23, 25–26, 33, 119, 122,
    124
Nguyen family, 20, 22–23
Nguyen Hai Than, 40

Nguyen Huê. *See* Quang Trung
Nguyen Huu Tho, 94
Nguyen Khac Vien, 122
Nguyen Trai, 19, 122, 130
Nguyen Van Thieu, 60, 64, 67–69, 71,
    80, 88, 95, 127
    elected president, 61, 79
    reelected, 80
    resigns, 69
Nguyen Van Vinh, 126
Nhan Van [Humanities], 83, 130–131
Nhat Linh, 127
Nha Trang, 6
Nixon, Richard Milhous, 64, 66, 68, 110,
    147, 151
NLF. *See* National Front for the Libera-
    tion of South Vietnam
North Vietnam (Tonkin), 4, 9, 20, 23,
    26–28, 30, 32, 38–40, 74, 111–113,
    148–149
Northwest, 7
Novels, 126–127, 129
Nung, 6–7

Oil, 110
Opium, 32
Overseas Chinese, 4–6, 33, 53, 92, 98–99,
    107

Paracel Islands, 148
Paris Agreement, 68–70, 108
Pass of the Clouds, 1
Pathet Lao, 47
PAVN. *See* People's Army of Vietnam
Peasant rebellions, 20, 22, 27, 33, 36–37,
    103
Peasantry, 17, 19, 27–32, 36, 102–106,
    129–130
Peking Man, 13
People's Army of Vietnam (PAVN), 64,
    66–70, 91
    casualties, 61–62
    final offensive, 68–70
    infiltration into South, 58
    role in the South, 58, 61–62
People's Liberation Armed Forces (PLAF),
    55, 63–64
People's Liberation Army. *See* People's
    Army of Vietnam
People's Republic of China (P.R.C.), 5, 8,
    44, 103–104, 114–115, 130
    aid to the D.R.V., 44, 46, 53, 61, 93,
        105, 110, 147–148
    relations with Vietnam, 8, 58, 61,
        89–90, 139, 144–155
People's Revolutionary party (PRP), 90

Pham Hung, 85, 94
Pham Quynh, 75, 126
Pham Van Dong, 83, 85, 93, 144
Phan Chu Trinh, 75, 125, 130
Phan Dinh Phung, 34, 130
Phan Huy Chu, 124
Phan Rang, 6
Philippines, 144, 148
Phnom Penh, 20
Phu Quoc Island, 22
Pigneau de Behaine, 22–23
Pike, Douglas, 84
Plain of Reeds, 43, 99
Poetry, 123, 129
Poland, 46, 153
Pol Pot, 142, 145
Population, 2–4, 12
Portugal, 20–21
Potsdam Conference, 40
Poulo Condore (Con Son) Island, 23, 25
P.R.C. *See* People's Republic of China
P.R.G. *See* Provisional Revolutionary
    Government
Proletariat, 29, 32, 36, 76, 101
Provisional Revolutionary Government
    (P.R.G.), 67–68
PRP. *See* People's Revolutionary party

Quang Nam Province, 22, 75
Quang Ngai Province, 22
Quang Trung (Nguyen Hue), 22, 74
Qui Nhon, 31
Quoc ngu (national language), 21,
    125–126

Rach Gia, 11
Radical Socialist party, 82
Rainfall, 1–2
Red River, 3, 25
Red River delta, 1–2, 4, 6, 8, 13–19,
    26–27, 44–45, 107, 117, 136, 150
Reeducation camps, 91
Refugees, 5–7, 9–10, 57, 106–107
Religion, 3, 8–11, 21, 118–119
Residents superieurs, 28
Resources, natural, 21, 30, 38, 100
Revolutionary Youth League (RYL), 37,
    76
Reynaud, Paul, 31
Rhadé, 6–7
Rhodes, Alexander of. *See* Alexander of
    Rhodes
Rice, 1–4, 14, 17, 31–32, 97–115 passim
Rivière, Henri, 26
Rubber, 2, 32, 37, 101
Rural Development Centers, 7, 9, 51

RYL. *See* Revolutionary Youth
    League

Saigon (Ho Chi Minh City), 1–2, 10, 22,
    24–25, 31, 36, 38, 51–53, 63–64,
    68–70, 90–91, 99–100, 106, 126,
    132–133, 149
    Treaty of, 25, 33
Sainteny, Jean, 41
Salween River, 3
Sarraut, Albert, 30, 124
Scholar-gentry, 119–120
SEATO. *See* Southeast Asia Treaty Orga-
    nization
Self-reliance Literary Group (Tu Luc van
    Doan), 126–127
Shih Huang Ti, 14
Siem Reap, 20
Sihanouk, Norodom, 65–66, 145
Singapore, 144
Sino-Tibetan language, 4, 6
Slash and burn (swidden) agriculture, 3,
    7
Slavery, 14, 17
Socialist Republic of Vietnam (S.R.V.)
    constitution, 94
    dissent in, 91–92
    economic policy, 91
    established, 91
    minority policy, 91, 148–149
    political institutions, 91
    white paper, 147
Society of Foreign Missions (Societé des
    Missions Etrangères), 9, 21
Southeast Asia Treaty Organization
    (SEATO), 49–50
South Vietnam. *See* Government of Viet-
    nam
Spratly Islands, 148
S.R.V. *See* Socialist Republic of Vietnam
Stalin, Joseph, 130
Strategic hamlets, 56–57
Sugar, 31, 100
Sung dynasty, 16–17
Sweden, 110

Taiwan, 148, 151
T'ang dynasty, 16
Tan Son Nhut Airport, 69
Taoism, 10, 14, 119–120, 136
Tay Au (Hsi Ou), 14
Tay Nguyen. *See* Central Highlands
Tay Ninh Province, 10, 68–69
Tay Son Rebellion, 22
Tea, 2, 32
Terre Rouge (Redlands), 31, 98

Tet Offensive, 62–66
Textile industry, 12, 31, 100
Thai, 6–7
Thailand, 20, 22, 25, 140, 144–145, 153
Thanh Hoa Province, 13, 18–19
Theravada, 6
Tho (Tay), 6–7
To Huu, 134
Ton Duc Thang, 36, 94
Tonkin. *See* North Vietnam
Tonkin Gulf, 148
Tonkin Gulf Resolution, 58
Tonle Sap, 20
Tran dynasty, 18–19, 122–123
Tran Hung Dao, 18, 130
Tran Quoc Hoan, 94
Trieu Da (Chao T'o), 15
Trinh family, 20, 22
Truman administration, 44
Trung sisters, 15, 119
Truong Chinh, 85, 93–94, 103, 128
Truong Son. *See* Central Mountains
Tu Duc, 26, 33
Tu luc van doan. *See* Self-reliance Literary Group

Unemployment, 106–107
Union of Soviet Socialist Republics
    (U.S.S.R.), 8, 38, 46, 93–94, 103, 114,
    128, 130, 135, 149, 152
    aid to DRV, 42–44, 53, 61, 105,
        110–111, 114, 149–150, 153
    relations with Vietnam, 53, 58
    treaty with Vietnam, 149
United Front for the Struggle of Op-
    pressed Races (FULRO), 7–8, 91
United Nations, 144
United States of America, 38, 110, 117,
    140–143, 145, 147, 150
    aid to France, 44–45
    aid to G.V.N., 49–70 passim, 78–81,
        100–101, 127
    attitude toward Geneva Conference,
        46–48
    attitude toward Vietnam, 38, 41–42, 44,
        70–71, 143–144, 151, 153–154
    introduction of combat troops in Viet-
        nam, 56
    negotiations with Hanoi, 64–70

Van Lang, 14–15
Van Tien Dung, 89, 94
VCP. *See* Vietnamese Communist party
Vichy French, 38

Viet Bac, 7–8, 43–44
Viet Cong. *See* People's Liberation Armed
    Forces
Vietminh (League for the Independence
    of Vietnam), 39–40, 42–45, 81, 88,
    90, 127, 130
Vietnamese Communist party (VCP)
    factionalism, 93–94, 153
    Fifth Congress, 92–93
    formed, 90
    leadership, 93–95
    membership, 92
    role in SRV, 92–94
    Sixth Plenum, 113–115
Vietnamese language, 4
Vietnamese Liberation Army. *See* People's
    Army of Vietnam
Vietnamese Nationalist party. *See*
    VNQDD
Vietnamese people, 2–4, 7, 11–12, 16
Vietnamese Worker's party (VWP), 10,
    82, 90, 141
    factionalism, 85–86, 93
    membership, 87
    organization, 84–87
    role in DRV, 84–88
Vietnamization, 65, 67
Vinh, 31, 37
VNQDD (Vietnamese Nationalist party),
    38
Vo Nguyen Giap, 44–45, 83, 85, 89,
    93–94
VWP. *See* Vietnamese Worker's party

Western influence on Vietnam, 20–32, 35,
    74–81, 98–103, 124–129, 131–132
Westmoreland, William C., 59–60, 62–64,
    66
"White man's burden," 29
Women, role in Vietnamese society, 89,
    119, 124, 126, 130, 134–135
Woodworking, 17, 97
Written language, 3, 15–16, 21, 122–123,
    125

Xuan Loc, Battle of, 69

Yangtze River, 14, 16, 117
Yao (Zao), 6–7
Young Pioneers, 87
Yüan dynasty, 18
Yüeh (Viet) peoples, 14
Yung Lo, 18

Zao. *See* Yao